Artemas Bowers Muzzey

Prime Movers of the Revolution Known by the Writer

Being reminiscences and memorials of men of the revolution and their families

Artemas Bowers Muzzey

Prime Movers of the Revolution Known by the Writer
Being reminiscences and memorials of men of the revolution and their families

ISBN/EAN: 9783337386511

Printed in Europe, USA, Canada, Australia, Japan

Cover: Foto ©ninafisch / pixelio.de

More available books at **www.hansebooks.com**

Prime Movers of the Revolution

KNOWN BY THE WRITER

Being Reminiscences and Memorials

OF

MEN OF THE REVOLUTION

AND THEIR FAMILIES

By A. B. MUZZEY, D.D.

FULLY ILLUSTRATED

BOSTON
D. LOTHROP COMPANY
WASHINGTON STREET
OPPOSITE BROMFIELD

PREFACE.

THE purpose of this book is twofold. First, to give recollections of men of the Revolution, and members of their families, with whom the writer has had more or less personal acquaintance. This explains the omission of others equally prominent, and otherwise entitled to the same notice. Occasional exceptions to the course indicated will be seen, especially in the case of men very distinguished in our Revolutionary history. Secondly, the aim of the book is to give records of these men in their public positions, and in their family relations both to those born before themselves and to those living subsequently to their death.

I have thought it consistent with the plan and method laid down, to introduce occasionally traditions and incidents not in the direct line of the men noticed, yet important as illustrating customs and events which did much to shape or illustrate their particular characters. This statement may meet objections, otherwise pertinent, of an apparent lack, at some points, of coherence and relativity between the several parts of the book. It also relieves the writer from the charge of occasional repetitions, unavoidable in his plan. It explains, too, the need he felt, in some instances, of bringing before the reader narratives and quotations not entirely fresh, but still helpful to his purpose, and which can hardly be too often repeated in American history.

In a work like this — abounding in details, and resting, as all history does, more or less on probabilities — slight errors are almost unavoidable. A book of mingled reminiscences and records cannot always name its authorities. I have, generally, avoided footnotes, — often not read at all, and seldom wholly agreeable to the reader.

One chapter has been in print before, but it seems important to the completion of this volume. It contains a few statements embraced in previous chapters, which could not, however, I found, be separated from their connections.

Many thanks are due to those who have encouraged and aided the author in his work. To name all those who have kindly supplied me with books essential to the completion of this volume would require a large space. And to add to this list the many who have given me assistance by conversation and by personal services is quite beyond my ability. I do not forget the call on my gratitude of those upon whom I had no special claims. Nor am I insensible of obligations to those to whom, although previously strangers, I am indebted for valuable suggestions and information.

I have been led by personal acquaintance and connections to confine my notices of men and their families largely to my immediate vicinity. This has occasioned a fear of local prejudices, and of injustice to those in other sections of the country. Our debt to them is very great. Lest it should be underestimated in this book, I have added a special chapter on the Patriots of the Middle and Southern States, and hope it may show at least an attempt to do strict justice both to the military and civil services of those States in the noble work of resolving upon and achieving our national independence.

The work has extended much beyond the original plan of the author. If, in its wide range of characters, any part of it shall give the reader a small portion of the interest felt by the writer in the long line of illustrious men brought before him, in this cursory review of their high purposes and generous sacrifices, his reward will be ample.

A. B. MUZZEY.

CAMBRIDGE, November, 1882.

PREFACE TO SECOND EDITION.

THE call for a new edition of this book affords an opportunity to correct a few errors in the first edition. The author has thought best, also, to give it a new title. These, with the alterations in its external appearance, will, it is hoped, add to its attractiveness, and make it more worthy of the friendly reception and exceptionally favorable notices it has already received.

CAMBRIDGE, May, 1891.

CONTENTS.

CHAPTER I.

INTRODUCTION.

	PAGE
IMPORTANCE of the Revolutionary period	1
Needs of the historian	1
Facts, the basis of history	2
Materials for history largely biographical	2
Scope of biographies	3
Influence of individuals	4
Discipline in the French War	4
Work of yeomen at Lexington, April 19, 1775	4
Heroes in the ranks	5
Desire for their annals	5
Interest in Revolutionary families	5
Political education in the family	6
Power of heredity	6
Loss of good words, such as *homestead*	7
Resemblance of parent and child	8
Webster on family obligations	8
Remark of John Quincy Adams	9
Influence of the families of the "Mayflower"	9
Those of the Otises, Adamses, and Winthrops	9
German, French, and English families	10
Dangers of indifference to our ancestry	10
Lafayette on the connection between family and country	11
Mutual help of the towns, and the Provincial and the Continental Congresses	12
Menaces from the British throne and Parliament	13
Strong men from good homes the need of the hour	13
A hero to command essential, and a "military family"	14
Importance of the Society of the Cincinnati foreseen by Washington at its foundation	15
Relation between America and the mother country	16
Our British ancestors	16
Alienation between Great Britain and the United States waning to-day	17
"Era of good feeling" after the war of 1812	17
Harmonizing influences	17
Lecture of Edward Everett	18
South and North unite after the Civil War	18
Interest of Queen Victoria in the sickness of Garfield	18
Love of home and of country one with love of *kin, kindred, kind*	18
Patriotism the parent of philanthropy	19
English victories for the right; Hampden, Pym, Sydney	20
Elder and younger members of the British family alike governed by high principles	20
Change of feeling between the New and the Old World welcome	20

CHAPTER II.

OTIS FAMILY.

Harrison Gray Otis and Josiah Quincy speak in Faneuil Hall	21	Family of Samuel and Bethia (Otis) Moseley in the Revolution	24
The lineage of Mr. Otis	22	Colonel James Otis prominent and popular	26
Rev. Samuel Moseley	23		

	PAGE		PAGE
Harrison Gray Otis, when a boy, saw the British Regulars on their way to Lexington	28	Invited to preside at 200th anniversary of Harvard College; prevented by bereavement; his intended address	38
Was at the Latin School under Master Lovell	28	Toast of Mr. Otis	38
Recollected to old age the excitement at the burning of Charlestown by the British	29	William Foster, son of Harrison Gray Otis; gifts descended from the father	39
Began professional life as a minister	29	His striking illustration in the State Legislature	40
Left the ministry for the law	30	His marriage with Miss Emily Marshall, the Boston beauty	40
Complimented by Bishop Cheverus	30	Personal resemblances between parent and child	41
Counsel in a theatre case; eulogized by Samuel Adams	30	James Otis, the patriot, the orator	42
In 1811, president of the senate; Joseph Story, speaker of the House; and Elbridge Gerry, governor	31	His course in college as a student, and in professional life	43
Unsurpassed eloquence of Otis	31	His filial respect	43
His eulogy on the death of Hamilton	31	His marriage	44
In Congress, easily first among equals	32	Connection with General Lincoln's family	44
Member of the Hartford Convention; its pure purposes	33	His speech on the Writs of Assistance	45
In 1818 in the United States Senate	34	Spirited letter to Mauduit in London	45
Candidate for governor against Eustis; anecdote	35	Threatened with arrest for his paper on the rights of the colonies	45
Otis and Quincy, anecdotes	35	Wounded by a British ruffian	46
Burning of the Catholic Convent at Charlestown: "The old man eloquent" speaks	36	Repeal of the Stamp Act celebrated in a song	46
		Otis retires from business insane	46
		Is killed by a thunderbolt	47
Argues a case in court	37	His publications	47

CHAPTER III.

ADAMS FAMILY.

Personal recollections of John Quincy Adams	48	Remark of Mr. Adams on a sermon of the author, Mr. Adams not sectarian	53
Anecdote of John Adams	49
"The most dangerous man to British domination in America"	49	The church-going habits of John Adams and his son	54
Anecdote of his absorption in the American cause	49	Anecdote showing religious disposition of J. Q. Adams	54
"Four pillars essential to a republic"	50	My meeting Mr. P. P. F. Degrand at Mr. Adams's table	54
Anecdotes of English ignorance of America	50	Anecdote, "Mrs. Pierce goes to Brattle Street"	55
Oration of Rev. George Whitney, July 4, the day of the death of Adams and Jefferson	51	Character of Mr. Adams; "He knew not the fear of man"	55
Sentiment of Adams	52	His interest in slave emancipation	56
Oration of Webster commemorating Adams and Jefferson	52	Anecdote of Fichte	56
Habits of John Quincy Adams	52	Moral resolution of Mr. Adams	57
		His youth full of promise	57
My interview with Mr. Adams at the ordination of my classmate Whitney	53	Letter to his father in the tenth year of his age	58
		Private secretary of Francis Dana, at the age of fifteen	58

CONTENTS.

	PAGE
Remarkable qualities of his mother	58
Courtship of the elder Adams	59
Suitors of Rev. Mr. Smith's two daughters	59
Coolness of the father toward Mr. Adams	60
Two sermons on the marriage of the daughters	61
John Quincy Adams inaugurated President at the age of fifty-eight	62
Too impartial to be re-elected	63
Faithfulness, his motto	63
My impression on seeing him in his seat in Congress	63
What he had seen in his long life	63
Honors at his burial	64
An illustration of the continuous spirit of the best Revolutionary families	64
Remark of J. Q. Adams on the name given him at his baptism	65
Outlines of the family lineage	65
Marriage of John Adams with Miss Abigail Smith	66
Marriage of John Quincy Adams with Miss Louisa Catherine Johnson	66
Sketch of the life of his son, Charles Francis Adams	67
Samuel Adams, "the personification of the American Revolution"	68
The Revolution planned in his meetings, at the Green Dragon Tavern, with a few kindred spirits	68
Testimony of John Adams regarding Samuel Adams	68
Language ascribed by Webster to John Adams, actually used by Samuel Adams	69
Portrait of Samuel Adams, by Copley	69
Staked everything dearest to him upon the issues of the Revolution	69
Samuel Adams and John Hancock at Lexington for safety, 18th of April, 1775	70
"What a glorious morning for America"	70
Account of Mr. Adams's personal expenditures, now first published	70
Mr. Adams "no man of business;" this shown in his boyhood	71
Receipt for eight years' medical attendance	71
Charges for funeral expenses	72
Tax-bill of the year 1803, with comments	72
Bill rendered after the death of Mrs. Adams	73
Anecdote of Doctor Samuel Danforth	74
Legacies of rings to friends	74
Mr. Adams strangely misunderstood in England	74
Anecdotes of the customs of his day	75
Bill of Mr. Adams for three months' "shaving and dressing"	76

CHAPTER IV.

QUINCY FAMILY.

	PAGE
Personal acquaintance with Hon. Josiah Quincy	77
A long line of prominent men	77
Edmund and Judith Quincy come from England to escape persecution; settle at Mt. Wollaston	77
John Hancock marries Dorothy, daughter of Edmund Quincy	78
Of his two grandsons, Edmund and Josiah, the latter lived at Mount Wollaston, subsequently renamed for him	79
Tomb of Edmund Quincy, and record of his burial	79
Neglect of ancient cemeteries	80
Daniel, son of Edmund, had a son John Quincy, for whom John Quincy Adams was named	80
Leonard Hoar's will, giving a "black serge gown to my sister Quincey"	80
Josiah Quincy, Jr., the patriot, died April 26, 1775	81
His son Josiah describes the old meeting-house in Andover	82
Kindness to him of Rev. Mr. French	82
The author's first personal acquaintance with Hon. Josiah Quincy	82
Placed by him on college committees	83
Customs of the committees at that time	83
Anecdote relative to Rev. Dr. Stebbins	84
Mr. Quincy's residence at Cambridge	84
Dignity and attractiveness of Mrs. Quincy	84
Mrs. John Adams, a right arm of strength to her husband	85

CONTENTS.

	PAGE		PAGE
Washington's wife and mother	85	President Walker's tribute	92
Quincy's lapse of memory	86	Quincy's estimate of Joseph Dennie	
College presidency	87	and J. Q. Adams	93
Anecdote of Otis and Quincy	88	Antislavery sentiments	94
Adams in Quincy's oration	89	Member of Congress, and mayor	
His Boston Centennial Address	90	of Boston	95
Oratorical resemblance of his great-		Publications and statue	96
grandson	90	Josiah a common family name	97
Lexington speech, 1835	91	Miss Eliza S. Quincy's note	98
Apt quotation from Hancock and		War of the Rebellion	99
Adams	92	Edmund Quincy	99

CHAPTER V.

LINCOLN FAMILY.

Author's personal interest	101	Family characteristics	107
Countess of Lincoln	102	Gen. Benjamin Lincoln's life and	
President Lincoln's remark	103	services	107
Origin of the Lincolns in the same		His facetious spirit	108
English county	103	Activity after the Revolution	109
Thomas the Husbandman	104	The Shays Rebellion	110
Genealogy	105	Washington's esteem	111
Rev. Calvin Lincoln of Hingham	106	Anecdote; Knox's friendship	112
Rachel Lincoln Boutelle	106	Lincoln homestead	113

CHAPTER VI.

PARKER FAMILY.

Family claims and origin	114	Wedding-day resolutions	122
Settlement at Cambridge Farms	115	Pulpit exchange with the author	123
Captain John Parker in the Rev-		Mental and moral traits	124
olution	116	Wish once expressed in the old	
His bravery and discretion	117	cemetery	125
Presentation of memorial muskets	118	Monumental stones	126
Lifelong acquaintance with Theo-		His prophecy and death	127
dore Parker	119	Everett's Eulogy on Jonas Parker	128
Visit to the Parker homestead	120	Thaddeus Parker	128
Famous South Boston Sermon	121	Ebenezer Parker	129

CHAPTER VII.

MUNROE FAMILY.

Their bravery in the Revolution	130	His life in Lexington	133
Irish and Scotch origin	130	Ancestry in the Reformation	134
European and American war		Immigration of Wm. Munroe	134
record	131	Clannish habits	135
Colonel William Munroe	132	Captain Edmund Munroe	135

CHAPTER VIII.

Brown Family.

	PAGE		PAGE
"Scotland" in Lexington	138	Rolls of the minute-men	140
Francis Brown's military services	138	Sergeant Brown's adventure on	
James Brown's memories of the battle	139	April 19, 1775	141
		Character and death	142

CHAPTER IX.

Kirkland Family.

Kirkland lineage	143	Birth and education of John Thornton Kirkland	151
Samuel Kirkland	144		
Mission to the Indians	145	Patriotism; choice of profession; training under Dr. West	152
Revolutionary services	146		
Skeneando, an Oneida chief	147	Interest in history, politics, and the Indians	153
Return to Stockbridge	148		
Onandago, an Indian chief	149	Presidency of Harvard College	154
Visit to one of Kirkland's old schools	150	Rev. Samuel Kirkland Lothrop, D.D.; lineage and ministry	155

CHAPTER X.

Ellery Family.

Channing and his grandfather	157	Meeting with the Adamses	163
Wm. Ellery's education and law practice	158	Patriotism, abhorrence of war, and other characteristics	164
Declaration of Independence	159	Unsectarianism and strong political feelings	165
Letter on Amusements	160		
Theatrical entertainments	161	Transmitted hatred of Bonaparte	166
Horseback journeys; Hancock's style of travelling	162	Letter written in old age	167
		Death at ninety-three	168

CHAPTER XI.

William Ellery Channing.

Centennial commemoration	169	"Immortality;" differing treatment in two sermons	179
Pulpit services and personal appearance	169	Thanksgiving at a funeral	179
Power of mind over body	170	Impression on a child	180
Conflicting elements; health; indebtedness to his mother	171	Fast Sermon in 1812	180
		"Perils of the Union"	180
Liberality; Lovejoy meeting	172	Curse of war	181
Independence of criticism	173	Similarity of his opinions to his grandfather Ellery's	182
Father Taylor's remark	174		
Channing's doubts	174	Influence of his works and their translations	183
Dr. Charles Follen	175		
Slavery prophecy	176	Genius and goodness	183
Modesty; letter to Miss Aikin	177	Author's visit to Lenox, where Channing spent some of his last days	184
Coughing in church	177		
Consideration for other preachers; conversation	178	A monument merited	185

CHAPTER XII.

Society of the Cincinnati.

	PAGE
Its formation	186
Interest of Lafayette	186
Washington's letter to Count De Rochambeau	187
Establishment in France	188
Author meets French and German guests, 1881	188
Congress in Carpenter's Hall	189
Tenacity of Washington's friendship, and Tory injustice to him	190
Benjamin Church's treason	190
Relics of him in Cambridge	191
Pictures of Washington and Burgoyne	191
Their proclamations contrasted	192
Unfaithfulness of other generals; Washington calumniated	193
English ignorance about the Revolution	194
Loyalists; Colonel Vassal and Cambridge mobs	194
Tribute to Lady Washington	194
Insolence to "Mr. Washington"	195
Resolution of Virginian ladies	196
British writer in Charleston	196
Margaret Corbine's recompense	197
Surgeon Thacher visits General Washington	197
British hatred, and our dreary prospects	198
Aubury on privations of prisoners	198
Major Andre's doom; British evacuation, Washington's Farewell; peace	199
Washington's progress through New England in 1789	200
Whittier's poem	201
Revolutionary and civil career of Henry Knox	202
Washington's confidence in him	203
Naval record of Henry Knox Thacher	203
Baron Von Steuben	204
Letter of Washington	205
Career and habits of John Brooks	206
His war record	207
Washington's touching regard; civil honors	208
Personal description	209
Author's acquaintance with Dr. Joseph Fiske	209
Destitution of soldiers	210
Acquaintance with Captain Benj. Gould; his military prowess	211
Lafayette at Newburyport; Daniel Foster	211
Benjamin Apthorp Gould (father and son) and Hannah Gould	212
Astronomical services of Professor Gould	213
Moseley family in the Revolution	213
Ebenezer Moseley, missionary and soldier	213
Hon. Ebenezer Moseley; offices and life	214
Edward Strong Moseley; honors and financial positions	214
Family suffering in the Revolution	214
Newburyport as an illustration	215
Washington's visit	215
A remembered kiss	216
Military and civil record of Timothy Pickering	216
John Pickering, the linguist	217
John Pickering, Jr.	218
Louis Baury in the Revolution	219
Frederick Baury in War of 1812	219
Rev. Alfred Baury, appearance and preaching	219
John Hastings in the Revolution	220
Personal intimacy with Edmund T. Hastings	220
Edmund T. Hastings, Jr.	221
Africa Hamlin's talents and war service; a peculiar family	221
Asia Hamlin	222
Job Sumner in the Revolution	222
Charles P. Sumner; offices and culture	223
Charles Sumner; education and eloquence	223
Senatorship and assault	224
Personal visit; national honors	225
Gov. William Eustis; medical, military, and civil services	225
Literary honors	226
Poverty	227
Isaac Parker; personal recollections	227
John Popkin in the Revolution	228
Prof. John S. Popkin	229
Anecdotes	230
Constant Freeman; naval services	231
Personal acquaintance with Chas. Henry Davis	231
Naval career in Civil War	232
Acquaintance with Dr. John C. Warren	233
Public services and humor	234
Publications	235
Daniel Webster; recollections of his oratory	235
Famous will case	236
Dinner at Porter's	237
Remembrance of Webster and Wirt in court	238

CONTENTS. xiii

	PAGE		PAGE
Webster's magnetic influence	239	Gen. David Cobb	240
Nicholas Fish in the Revolution	239	Revolutionary career and subsequent valuable services; his portrait	
Hamilton Fish; national offices	239		
Public honors, and his personal impression	240		241
		Civic career of Samuel C. Cobb	242

CHAPTER XIII.

REVOLUTIONARY MEN IN THE WAR OF 1812.

War record of Henry Dearborn	243	The cold summer of 1816	251
Subsequent offices	244	Alarming portents	252
Characteristics	245	Romantic career of Abram Johnson	253
Services in War of 1812	246		
General Miller at Fort Erie	247	"End of the world;" veterans of 1812	254
An uncle's privateering trophies	247		
Lexington boys; personal and family memories of 1812	247	Recollections of Henry A. S. Dearborn; training and services	255
National songs	248	Authorship, industry, and honors	256
Perry's great victory	249	William Hull in the Revolution	256
What grandfather called the war	250	National honors	257
The great gale of 1815	250	Court-martial in War of 1812	258

CHAPTER XIV.

OLIVER HAZARD PERRY.

Christopher Raymond Perry	260	The Commodore's family	266
Oliver Hazard Perry	260	Recollection of a celebration on the scene of the battle	266
Naval exploits	261		
Battle on Lake Erie	262	Vase and statue	266
Perry's note of victory	263	Testimonials, and early death	267
Amusing song	264	Matthew Calbraith Perry; Japanese expedition	268
Snuff-box	265		

CHAPTER XV.

PERSONAL APPEARANCE OF REVOLUTIONARY OFFICERS.

Identity of looks and character	269	Engraving of John Lillie	278
Washington's face and figure	270	Marked face of Henry Lee	279
Trumbull's portrait	271	Physiognomy in general	280
Description of the opening of Congress	271	Personal impressions of our great civilians	281
A boy's effort to see Washington	272	Clay, Calhoun, Benton	281
The President's dress	273	Recollections of Edward Everett's thoroughness	281
His speech	274		
Portraits of Lafayette and Knox	275	Autographs of the Cincinnati, including those of leading Patriots	282
Lafayette revisits America in 1824	276		
Baron Von Steuben's portrait	276	De Grasse, Putnam, and others	283
Brooks, Marion, Eustis	277	Andros, Stark, and others	284

CHAPTER XVI.

ANDREW JACKSON.

	PAGE
Patriotic ancestors and early military spirit	285
New Orleans victory; Jefferson's principles; rallying-cry	286
Interview with Old Hickory	287
Harvard degree	288
National indebtedness to Jackson	289
His ambition	290
Boston excitement over the banking question	291

CHAPTER XVII.

THE ANTISLAVERY MOVEMENT.

	PAGE
The Union involved in slavery	292
Curious receipt for a boy	292
Significant advertisement	293
Henry Ware's interest	293
Cambridge Antislavery Society	294
Its record	295
List of members	296
Ideas of Follen and Garrison; sympathy with the former	297
Slavery in District of Columbia	298
Color prejudice; boyish interest in negro neighbors	299

CHAPTER XVIII.

BOUTELLE FAMILY.

	PAGE
Timothy Boutelle, the author's grandfather, in the war	300
Services in the Shays Rebellion	301
Visit to Leominster homestead	302
Sabbath customs, old and new	303
"The Cage"	304
Children of Timothy and Rachel	305
Timothy Boutelle's college class	305
Public services; military relics; a spontoon	306
"Melting of the caul"	306
War record of Dr. Caleb Boutelle; Charles Otis, and James Thacher, Boutelle	307

CHAPTER XIX.

LAFAYETTE.

	PAGE
Family and marriage	308
Devotion to America; testimonies to his excellence	309
Recollections of him in 1824	310
Dr. Bowditch's enthusiasm	311
Phi Beta Kappa anniversary	311
Everett's oration	312
A brilliant dinner	313
Personal introduction at the Lexington celebration	314
Fourteen survivors of the battle of Lexington	315
Lafayette's former imprisonment	315
Author's last sight of the hero	316
The Rev. Joseph Thaxter's half-century	316
Bunker Hill corner stone; Webster in his prime; Masonic services	317
Completion of the monument	318
Rejoicings during Lafayette's journeys; Newburyport; Washington's chamber	318
Address of the Hon. Ebenezer Moseley	319
A kiss at the levee	320
Old comrades	320
Tomb of Washington	321
Lafayette's influence in this country	322
Visited by Charles Pinckney; Rochefoucauld's remark; resemblance of Washington and Lafayette	323
The latter's courage in the French Revolution	324
Social hours of the two heroes	325
Marquis de Chastellux	326

CONTENTS. xv

	PAGE		PAGE
Visit to American camp	327	Romance of Lafayette's American career; letter to his wife	332
Lafayette despised for his youth	328		
Charge of weakness	329	Return to France; death	333
Surrender of Cornwallis	330	Everett's eulogy	334
Meeting with a veteran	331	Thanksgiving Day at the tomb of Lafayette	335
Reign of Terror	331		

CHAPTER XX.

EMERSON THE PATRIOT.

Ralph Waldo Emerson's ancestry and patriotism	337	Marriage service for the author	342
		Father Taylor's question	343
Chaplain William Emerson	338	Remembrance of lectures	344
Frederika Bremer and Emerson's mother	338	Conversation with the Rev. Dr. Francis	345
Battle Hymn	339	John Brown indignation meeting	346
Emerson's father	340	Edward Bliss Emerson	347
Personal recollections of Emerson's younger days	341	Longfellow's funeral	347
		Emerson's burial	348

CHAPTER XXI.

THE SOLDIER OF THE REVOLUTION.

Rank and file	349	A witness of the battle of Bunker Hill	354
Contrast of the two armies	350		
Sufferings at Valley Forge	350	Moses Hale and Captain Wilder of Winchendon	355
Neglect by public officers	351		
Treason at home	351	Town-offices	356
General faithfulness	352	Church and State	357
Ralph Farnham the centenarian, a representative Revolutionary soldier, seen by the author at the age of ninety-five	353	Artemas Hale, character and habits	358
		Masonic address on his 95th birthday	359

CHAPTER XXII.

THE BATTLE OF LEXINGTON: PERSONAL RECOLLECTIONS OF MEN ENGAGED IN IT.

The battle narrative heard in childhood	360	British evidence	367
		Hancock and Adams at Mr. Clark's	367
Importance of the first step	361		
The author's grandfather in John Parker's company	361	Paul Revere	368
		Spot of Samuel Adams's immortal utterance	369
A Menotomy veteran of eighty nearly killed	362		
		Description by the author's grandfather	369
Blood-stained room, and other traces of war in the author's ancestral home	363	Everett's oration	369
		Powder-horn	370
Prudence of Captain Parker	364	Percy's reinforcements	370
Reports of eye-witnesses	364	Pulpit and cannon-ball	370
Killed and wounded; Jonathan Harrington and Jonas Parker	365	Heroism of Jedediah Munroe and Francis Brown	371
The schoolhouse on the battlefield	366	Personal memories of survivors	371
Accounts of lookers-on	366	Dr. Joseph Fiske	371
Buckman house	367	Certificate from Washington	372

CONTENTS.

	PAGE
Author's youthful sympathy with Colonel Munroe's narrative	372
Town honors	373
Author's remembrance of Daniel Harrington's smithy and its relics	373
Bell-tongue	373
Mrs. Harrington, a daughter of Col. Robert Munroe	374
Lieut. William Tidd's account of the Regulars	375
His appearance in old age	375
Family and war services of Isaac Hastings	375
Family and incidents of his life	376
Acquaintance with the author	377
Depositions concerning the battle of Lexington	378
Conflicting British accounts	379
Connection of the Loring family with the battle; church plate buried; statement of losses	380
Anecdote of Polly Loring	381
Details of British ravages	382
Author's recollection of Benjamin Wellington	382
Revolutionary record and town services of Wellington and the Masons	383
Joseph Estabrook as a soldier and preacher	384
Women of the Revolution	385
Amos Locke's house and services	386
Personal recollections of Joel Viles	386
Family relations with John Parkhurst and Joshua Reed	387
Ebenezer Simonds and family	388
The last survivor	388
Many Harringtons and Munroes in two wars	389
Jonathan Harrington's mother	390
A babe's inheritance	390
Average age of the survivors; remarkable coincidence	391
Anniversary Sermon	391
Characters and estates of the Patriots	392
American *peasantry* and Lord Percy	392
Patriotic lessons	393
Peace restored	394

CHAPTER XXIII.

MEN OF THE SOUTHERN AND MIDDLE STATES IN THE REVOLUTION.

The Revolution not the work of New England alone	395
The Virginian leader	396
Southern earnestness and adventures	397
Florida, the Carolinas, and Middle States	398
Yorktown	399
Revolutionary halls in Boston and Philadelphia	399
Patrick Henry, Thomas Jefferson	400
Advanced patriotism of the Lees of Virginia	401
Thomas Nelson and John Laurens	401
Rutledge of South Carolina, and General Marion	402
General Sumter	403
His civil and military services	404
Francis Kinlock Huger	405
New Jersey as a battle-ground	405
The Keystone State	406
Anthony Wayne	407
Thomas Mifflin	408
General Muhlenberg, the gown and the sword	409
Tench Tilghman and Mordecai Gist of Maryland	410
General Screvener	410
Lyman Hall's mission to Massachusetts	411
Button Guinnett of Georgia	411
New York a pivotal colony	411
The Livingstons and Gen. James Clinton	412
Military, literary, and financial career of Alexander Hamilton	413
Ticonderoga	414
Washington's Farewell	414
British evacuation	415
Centennial of 1883	415

LIST OF ILLUSTRATIONS.

	PAGE
WASHINGTON	15
GARFIELD	20
MASTER LOVELL, AND THE OLD LATIN SCHOOL	35
ADAMS OPPOSING THE STAMP ACT FROM THE OLD STATE HOUSE	48
OLD SOUTH CHURCH	76
JOHN HANCOCK	78
QUADRANGLE, HARVARD COLLEGE	83
PLAN OF THE TOWN OF BOSTON, 1775	90
FIRST MEETING-HOUSE IN SALEM	129
HANCOCK HOUSE, BOSTON	137
THE OLD AND THE NEW	153
DOROTHY HANCOCK'S RECEPTION	156
BUNKER HILL MONUMENT	168
BATTLE OF BUNKER HILL	208
LIBERTY TREE, BOSTON	242
THE WASHINGTON ELM	259
THE HOLMES HOUSE IN CAMBRIDGE	268

LIST OF ILLUSTRATIONS.

	PAGE
THE STOCKS	299
LAFAYETTE	308
MOUNT VERNON	336
JAMES RUSSELL LOWELL	348
AMOS MUZZEY, in Capt. Parker's Company, April 19, 1775	360
BATTLE OF LEXINGTON	364
MINUTE MAN, 1775	377
DIAGRAM OF LEXINGTON ROADS	387
LEXINGTON MONUMENT	388
THE ENGLISH RIGHT OF SEARCH	394
WASHINGTON CROSSING THE DELAWARE	405
DIAGRAM OF CONCORD VILLAGE	416

REMINISCENCES AND MEMORIALS.

CHAPTER I.

INTRODUCTION.

THE period covered by the following pages is one whose importance, whether regarded in its inception, its progress, or its consequences, is hardly transcended by any in human history. It brings before us a people, — although now, after a century, fifty millions in number, only three millions at the outset, — who, by their spirit, their purposes, and their conduct, at that crisis, challenge competition with any other on record. The character and results of their work interest to-day the whole civilized world. But ably as they have been portrayed by men of learning, genius, and indefatigable labor, large portions of the field they have surveyed are still uncultivated, and contain treasures for present and future research. History is looking anxiously for new minds to enter upon and do justice to this unlimited subject.

But, first of all, the historian needs fresh materials for his work. The centennial era, through which we are now passing, is bringing to light ever accumulating fragments and details, of inestimable value to the accurate and thorough writer in this department. It is a time when wise men are reaching out in every direction for help in the production of broad, philosophical, and trustworthy history.

But the question arises: what is the basis of history, — true, reliable, enduring history? Only one thing, — facts. Over and over we have had theories, hypotheses, speculations, conclusions, based on nothing more solid than unreliable imaginings. Not to discredit the imagination, in its legitimate and healthy exercise, or deny, or even doubt, that it gives essential aid to the historian, we are still to guard resolutely against the illusions into which it leads him who gives it a loose rein in the field of history. We are to know, as far as possible, while we read a book in this department, whether the author has gathered copious materials from every authentic source, out of which to reach his conclusions, or has advanced opinions resting on but slight foundations. History deals in general views and conclusions. If these have not been attained through a broad, liberal, and impartial array of facts, the more confident the tone of the writer, the less we trust him.

What are the materials out of which history, to be trustworthy, must build its fabric? They consist largely of biography. If the writer has stored his mind with a full knowledge of the men whose deeds he has undertaken to record, whether in their individual capacity or as associated with others, and on every point, whether large or small, then we accept his work. The river cannot be pure, sweet, and healthful if its tributaries are impure, tainted, and unhealthful.

This being so, no work is more important in this connection than good biographies. They are the life blood of a nation's history. He who can furnish us a volume giving an accurate description of the men who shaped the destinies of a people, especially at a decisive point in their fortunes, renders us an invaluable service.

But the scope of these materials must be very large. We all acknowledge our obligations for good biographies of such men as Julius Cæsar, Peter the Great, Charlemagne, Alfred, Napoleon. These, and the like names, we are apt to think, embrace the whole history of the countries and the times in which they lived and ruled. We look upon them as embodying, each in his own age, the whole fortunes of Rome, Russia, Germany, England, France; and in many such instances, we are right. It is not too much to say that, at one period, Cæsar was Rome, Peter the Great was Russia, Napoleon was France. But we need caution here; for although, in barbarous periods, the despot bore unlimited sway over his people, with the inception and progress of civilization this condition often changes. The time comes at last when, not in despotisms or monarchies alone, but in governments of the people, single men, and those not in high office, possess a personal weight and carry an influence, scarcely inferior in its power and sway to that of the ruler of the most benighted people.

In all enlightened ages we find the general truth illustrated that it is the individual, not the official alone, who carries influence with him, and does what most affects the destiny of his country. There is a training in circumstances that we are apt to underestimate. Some of the men who had been engaged in the old French War,— not remarkable as seen at their homes in boyhood or youth,— when they had passed through that war, by their experience in it, and from previous British discipline, fought bravely the battles of the Revolution; and by their efficiency, helped largely to carry through successfully the hazardous undertaking of emancipation from the British yoke.

The War for Independence, which began at Lexington the morning of April 19, 1775, called out a little band of yeomen, obscure men the day previous, yet thereafter, as it proved, standing in that "imminent deadly breach," they were the germ of a nation's birth. Their number was small, but their spirit was large; their influence became the very bone and sinew of the great men who, on other fields, wrought out the liberty of these United States.

It was often seen that men in the ranks did brave things which no official title could have made more glorious. Many a man in this way, became, at some critical moment, a hero. We do not care to know where he had been, or how he had hitherto been esteemed; it is enough that, out of unpropitious days, and amid stern fortunes, straits, poverty, or neglect, he carved a destiny worthy a high place in his country's record. Such men are nature's nobility, and we want to hear and know all we can of them. If they were born in obscurity, we would do something to bring them to the light. Every such life is interesting,— not the mighty and renowned alone, but the humblest who did what he could for his native land in the hour of her need. We say to the biographer, write out all you can tell us, of your own observation or what you have heard from the lips of others, about these persons. Give us some account of their origin and ancestry. We think the stock from which they came must have had strength and value in it.

This request is natural. I think the desire is human, to become better acquainted with the annals of those who deserve well of their country. If we know nothing, at present, of their families, we wish to know a little, at least; and if we know something, we shall be glad to hear or read more. And, even though we have read or been told the story of their lineage, we should enjoy going over it again. All who bear their name ought to become to us "familiar as household words."

There is good reason for this interest in the families of our Revolutionary men. An influence descends, here as everywhere, more or less potent for generations. The son, it appears, had his prototype in his father or mother, or in a grandfather, or quite as often in a grandmother, so full of patriotism, so disinterested, so large-minded and large-hearted; there is where the person before us derived the germs of those noble qualities which the war brought out. There are certain names in our history which, when we hear of one bearing them, lead us to cast a loving and reverential, retrospective glance into the fair fame won by their line. They are stars of a bright constellation in the nation's history.

It is to be noted that, in the colonial period, often the family education was about all the children received on political subjects. Historians of the Revolution are surprised at the degree to which the broadest principles of government were understood by the mass of the people at that time. But the secret of it was in the common conversations of the fireside. The father had not read books, but he had thought on the great questions of the day, and the boy at the table, and sitting by the bright New England fire on long evenings, all eye and ear, had caught the inspiration, and was trained to feel, and resolve, when he became a man, to act for his country.

It is true there are sometimes degenerate sons in the best families, as there are illustrious men of whose eminence we find no traces in their ancestry; but this is not the normal course in domestic annals. Leaving out the often decisive sway of circumstances, — "environment," to use a word now popular, — we are more and more finding evidence of the power of heredity. Its subtle influence is sometimes detected where we least anticipate it. A patient and persistent massing of details, pressing into the secret records of the family, going not only through written documents, but the traditions of the past, interrogating, beyond kindred, the long line of neighbors and even transient acquaintances, brings to light at last traces of this great man in whose face, intent on reaching his every inmost trait, we are now gazing.

Amid the restless and changeful character of the modern American fireside, we are fast losing many of those healthful influences which gathered around and went out from the dwellings of our ancestors. Our habitations are no longer, as a whole, "the homelike nests" of those early days, "which had been warmed by the presence of father, grandfather, and great-grandfather, — every scratch on whose timbers was known and revered, — the very sanctuaries of family life." The good old words, *abiding-place, homestead,* and the like, are fast becoming obsolete. A very old house is now a wonder, its rarity attracting special attention. We may almost count on our fingers the houses in New England which have the ancestral lustre of those occupied in successive generations by such families as those of Otis, Adams, and Quincy. There was an education in such houses, and a place often became an eloquent memorial. The family traits thus descended, more or less distinctly, for generations.

We look for a physical resemblance between child and parent. So confident are we of finding this, that if a son does not bear the image of his father, we are sure he must look like his mother. It is not mere imagination which makes so many say, "That boy is the very image of his father," while another says, "No, he looks most like his mother." The truth is, most children resemble both parents more or less clearly. The physiognomist reads human faces between their lines, and can detect resemblances where the unpractised eye finds none.

The causes of these resemblances are not physical alone, or pre-natal alone. Daniel Webster says with truth: "There is a singular disregard of ancestry. There is a moral and philosophical respect for our ancestors which elevates the character and improves the heart. I hardly know what should bear with stronger obligation on a liberal and enlightened mind, than a consciousness of an alliance with excellence which is departed; and a consciousness, too, that in acts and conduct, and even in the sentiments and thoughts, it may be actively operating on the happiness of those that come after it." If the heritage of a grand national ancestry is, as we know, a motive with

many to worthy deeds, what should be that of
our domestic lineage in past generations? It
argues a strange insensibility in any one to care
nothing, in this regard, for his predecessors. He
who deliberately casts a blot on his family es-
cutcheon sinks perceptibly in our estimation.
Who, on the other hand, can doubt that the younger Pitt was constantly sustained in his masterly
course by the example and inspiration of his illustrious father? It adds to our veneration for that
exalted statesman in our own land, John Quincy
Adams, to see him put on record in his Diary,
that "from the moment he knew that he bore
the name of Quincy, given him by his mother,
he felt, on through his life, a call to act up to
the demands of that honored name."

No people ever owed more than we do to the
influence of good families. Begin with those who
came to Plymouth in the "Mayflower," — Brewster, Standish, Carver; to name the whole noble
catalogue is needless. Continue on, and down in
the annals of our colonies we find the Otises,
Adamses, Munroes, and how many others. Follow through the Revolution. Time fails us to
enumerate our obligations to the great company,
both in civil and military lines, of families either
directly or indirectly related to each other. Take
the Winthrops through eight generations, down to
the distinguished scholar, historian, and statesman
we rejoice to have today as our contemporary,
and we see and feel that we can scarcely portray

the value of such lineage, and the full influence, domestic and national, of our American ancestry.

So it has been in all nations who have occupied the foreground of history. What has not Germany received through her ever appreciated illustrious families? In that land the unit of society has been, — with few interruptions, throughout its various states and departments, — the family, sacredly guarded and piously transmitted. France, back to her barbarous period, has attached high value to the domestic bonds of her rulers. The long line of the Bourbon family, not in the fourteenth representative alone, but in others of deserved fame, has verified the worth of this special relation. Our mother country never loses sight of her obligations to the varied and shining list of Old England's Tudors, Yorks, Plantagenets, Stuarts.

That her American colonies should attach a commanding importance to the distinguished families in their history is legitimate and just. The memory of great men is the richest inheritance of their country. We should be false to our traditions, to the past, to the undisclosed future, if we allowed the domestic relations of our great and good men to sink into neglect. Indifference to our American ancestors, to the bonds that united those sages and heroes in their special home relations; to care little who were the progenitors of our Revolutionary men, or who are now standing in their line; never to mark and commend those who are worthy sons of those worthy sires, — this were to show ourselves recreant to the rightful claims of those progenitors upon us, and false to our trust as inheritors of the independence and liberty which we owe so largely to their patience in poverty, their toil to the bitter end, and their uncounted sufferings and endurance — how often, to mortal agony!

But there are wider relations of which this volume would speak. Lafayette, as broad-minded as he was warm-hearted, saw clearly the interdependence of all our social relations. He gave, both in theory and practice, its just weight to every claim the world has upon us. He had no narrow conceptions of his own personal rights, but he still merged his individual fortunes, at every point, in his love and care for others. It was truly said by one intimate with him under his own roof, as a friend and helper, "He preferred his family to himself, his country to his family, and mankind at large to his country." No man had more than he, in his early life, to attach him to home, — a bosom companion remarkable for her virtues, graces, and culture, all the comforts that wealth could procure, and the promise of promotion and honors to satisfy his ambition; but he left all these at less than the age of twenty, and, from his love of liberty, threw himself into the doubtful struggle of a people not bound personally to himself by any native ties, but thirsting for national independence. No born citizen of America could have sacrificed more than this foreigner and stranger did until the final battle was fought which sealed the freedom of America. Returning home, — after unprecedented sacrifices on the soil of Europe, and labors for the civil and religious freedom of his own country, with a naturally vigorous constitution worn down and exhausted by his eventful career, — he died, a Citizen of the World, honored and lamented wherever his merits had been known.

The spirit and example of Lafayette, second only in their lustre, power, and influence to those of Washington himself, did much to bring out, call into action, and sustain the long list of men, a portion of whom this book attempts to describe. Their lives were in this way taken up into the life of the new nation. We cannot understand its institutions, or comprehend their purpose, until we have penetrated into the motives and actions of those men who, in this spirit, laid the foundations of our government.

We read the record of the various movements of the people, their awakening and uprising in every direction. We see them gathering, associating, combining, in large or small bodies. The First Provincial Congress meets at Salem, Mass., September, 1774; and, while it is in session, the Continental Congress at Philadelphia is also in session. And the latter draws encouragement and support from the former. Nor is this all. The assemblies of the Provinces are animated by the patriotic course of the towns. They are, in all directions, meeting, and passing resolutions full

INTRODUCTION. 13

of wisdom, of determination, and a wide-spreading influence.

But to stop here would give us a most imperfect knowledge of the true springs of power, the heralds of increasing strength, and assurances of final success, which marked this eventful period. Not only was there a constant menace from the British throne, the personal authority of its representatives, the threats of a horde of officials to withstand, and every form of intimidation by new acts of Parliament, more and more oppressive to the American Colonies, to encounter, but the people themselves were by no means wholly united in their resistance to this array of obstacles to their freedom and independence.

What was needed to encounter this host of difficulties? Strong men to rise up out of families, distinguished, or perhaps as yet obscure, and express the growing indignation of a people conscious of their rights, and wanting only a sense of ability and means to assert them. Indispensable were a James Otis, "to breathe the breath of life" into the as yet feeble colonies; a Josiah Quincy, to write with a diamond-pointed pen those quickening words which he alone could write in the dawn of the movement; a Samuel Adams, with Spartan firmness and Roman wisdom, to do all, and having done all, to stand; a John Adams, to step forth and, in the face of all timid and reluctant spirits, who would delay action and hope for a peaceable redress of the wrongs and grievances of the hour, to say in effect, "Sink or swim, live or die, survive or perish, I give my hand and my heart to this Declaration of Independence." It needed a man, when the first moment had come for force and arms to work out our cause, one trained from his boyhood by a wise and devoted mother, who could take the head of our army, and — as judicious as he was energetic, as cautious as he was courageous, as self-controlled as he was powerful, as persistent as he was bold, — to take up the work, and to gain and keep the confidence of the people.

And more than this, our commander must not only be a hero himself, but know human nature through and through — to select the right man for every new post and position, for his own staff (his "military family"), and for the command of the various lines of the service. Each State must be united, and satisfied with those within its limits who should be selected, able to secure that union in which alone is strength, and that harmony of spirit and purpose without which this fearful and most hazardous attempt for freedom and independence would disastrously fail.

The hour brought the man; he, who alone had the gifts vital to our cause, was found. For eight long and dreary years the contest was waged; the hearts of an impoverished and war-worn people, were now a little encouraged, and now by some defeat cast down, and well nigh in despair; at length a victory clear, hailed at home and confessed abroad, crowned our arms.

GEORGE WASHINGTON.

We owe this result largely to the steady hand at the helm which guided our vessel on; but much also to the extraordinary adaptation of his subordinates to their several offices, and — notwithstanding those occasional jealousies, unavoidable in military as in civil relations — to the prevailing union of spirit and harmony in action of the officers in the army of the Revolution. This most observable and effective harmony of the men in command, through that trying period, received its brightest illustration in the immediate formation of that association established on the close of the war, which has existed down to the present day, the SOCIETY OF THE CINCINNATI, to be a military family, in its transmitted virtues of patriotism and high personal worth.

In a work on Revolutionary men and their families, the Cincinnati Society, made up as it is of the lineal and collateral descendants of Revolutionary officers, ought, we can see, to hold a prominent place. An institution was needed which should receive the sanction of Washington, of which he should be the first president, and to which the officers of the Revolution should give their approval; which should be favored by Lafayette, and of which, through his influence, a branch should be at once formed in France, — our noble ally in the war, without whose aid the British Lion might have never relaxed his hold upon us. This society was encouraged by our German allies, and Baron von Steuben and others of his country were members of it. Their descendants came, as representatives of the Society of the Cincinnati, to unite with us in our recent commemoration of the battle of Yorktown. For these and other reasons this institution deserves a much larger place than has hitherto been accorded to it in the historic and biographical memorials of the Revolution.

Let it not be imagined that, in the notices of men of the Revolution which follow, I would lose sight of that great field which lies far beyond our own special country, and encloses its claims. We ought never to forget that humanity is larger than any national limits. We separated ourselves, it is true, from the governmental control of England. But she was still our mother country, and it was as it is in the family when a son reaches his majority. America left her old home, and became free, not, in the deepest and truest sense, because of war and violence, — but this country became free because it was of age. The time had arrived when the change was in the course of nature.

We are to remember that very many of the oldest families of this country trace their ancestry back to Great Britain. In my boyhood I recollect my grandfather pointed out to me, in the old house where we lived, marks in the stairs of the attic, made by the prod of his grandfather's cane, as he went up to oversee his men at work on his large farm. Here was a bond going back six generations. The seventh took us to a British ancestor, who left Scotland, came to this country, and was made a Freeman in 1634. So are the two countries shown to be of kin by a comparatively short computation. Two parents, four grandparents, eight great-grandparents, sixteen great-great-grand parents, carry us ere long into a large population of our own kindred and name. Our temporary national separations, like family feuds, are usually healed in a no protracted period of time, and we return to the normal harmony of the domestic circle.

Thus the apparently wide alienation between Great Britain and the United States of America was destined in a single century to nearly disappear. After the Revolution had passed, there were disturbing elements still left, which led to the War of 1812; but when that closed, the peace that followed was welcome on both sides of the ocean; and "an era of good feeling" soon brought Federalist and Democrat together. The Northern and Southern States afterward came into collision, but Washington became at length once more a head-centre to our Republic. Edward Everett delivered a lecture on that great man, and was greeted by enthusiastic audiences North and South. True, no power could avert that civil conflict which sprung from the raging fires of slavery. The War of the Rebellion soon came; and when the old lady of ninety-six, whose hand in her youth had moulded bullets in the Revolutionary War, knit a pair of stockings, and accompanied the gift to our soldiers with the determined motto, "Let these toes always point toward the rebels," she represented the hostile spirit which animated every Free State of the country. But, the war over, in less than a score of years the South joins the North in celebrating the birthday of Washington, and now the family strife is fast fading out of sight.

Most touching was the harmonizing effect of the disastrous event which took from us our honored and loved Garfield, as it was seen in the domestic relations. The afflicted wife yearned toward her down-stricken husband, and the aged mother mourned for her suffering son, and through weary weeks and months the pains of his long agony moved, not only our own millions of stricken hearts with a personal sympathy, but the good Victoria, herself still mourning the loss of her own dearest and best, sent constant messages from a spirit anxious through all the sickness, and bowed in the common grief at the death, of our beloved President.

So have we learned the great lesson of the inappreciable strength of our domestic bonds, and that the love of country and the love of home are branches of the same earth-sheltering tree. *Kin, kindred, kind,* they all belong to a common vocabulary. The rills that start on the mountain side, symbols of the modest homes that grow heroes and patriots, flow into the rivers that gladden the nation, and mingle at last in one great ocean of humanity.

INTRODUCTION.

The life that was nourished at the calm fireside is given in its manliest years, to the service of its country; and, in the lapse of time the same men who stood up so bravely for their native land, become, by their generous deeds at home, examples and inspirers to the nations abroad. The War of the Revolution is thus every year accomplishing for the wide world a good, once not conceived possible, in stirring patriots on foreign soils to work out their civil redemption, and thus scatters the seeds of national liberty broadcast over the whole civilized globe. The domestic piety that nourished patriotism thus becomes the parent of philanthropy. He whose heart throbbed for his own hearthstone and his native land in her struggle for freedom and independence, through her day of small things, may become a light to some aspiring friend of freedom elsewhere, and nerve him to a courage and conflict with oppression and injustice, until he too shall see the light of liberty dawn on his own country.

We rejoice to think that our fathers came of a race whose lessons and examples awoke in them that spirit which had prompted their own sacrifice, and led, as it had in England, to noble results. They had behind them the record of English resistance to the oppressor, and of English victories for the right. They remembered what .the barons of England did to secure Magna Charta; how Hampden fought the demands of tyranny, and Pym led the way in the Revolution of their mother country; how Cromwell defended the people when assaulted by royalty; how Sydney, the soldier and martyr, laid his head on the block "with the fortitude of a stoic." And thus at length the elder of the British family instructed and inspired the younger to quit themselves like men, and throw off the yoke even when laid on their necks by their own parental government.

Thanks that all this is past,— that to-day we can meet in mutual respect and consideration to commemorate what was so bitter to England during our Revolution. The change of temper between the New and the Old World of the forefathers, is most welcome. We live in a pacific and conciliatory age; and may the time past, the period covered by this book, suffice both nations for any alienations and deep unfriendliness, or any acts contrary to the temper that becomes the great brotherhood of mankind.

JAMES A. GARFIELD.

CHAPTER II.

OTIS FAMILY.

HARRISON GRAY OTIS was, in the year 1828, a candidate for the mayoralty of Boston. The election being on Monday, as was the custom a caucus was held on the Sunday evening previous. Hon. Josiah Quincy was the opposing candidate. Two men of such ability drew a crowded audience. I regarded it as a feast to listen to both of them on the same occasion. Mr. Otis speaks first. His personal appearance is most striking : a large frame, tall, and well proportioned, with a bearing dignified and courteous, a true "gentleman of the old school,"— his complexion florid, with bright eyes, and a pleasing and gracious expression, he prepossesses general favor as he rises from his seat. This effect is enhanced by a voice mellow, flexible, and admirably modulated. His gesticulation is graceful, his whole manner persuasive. He is, in fine, of the Ciceronian School, that of the consummate orator.

As he unfolds the policy he shall pursue, if elected, it is evident he strikes the right key for success. He is applauded at frequent intervals, and resumes his seat amid deafening cheers. It is a trying moment for Mr. Quincy; there are few men who could follow such an effort entirely at their ease. Mr. Quincy, — a manly and noble figure, and with the prestige of that power he had exhibited in every station, from the humblest in civil life up to a seat in Congress, where he had been not only honored by his constituents, but "lauded by lauded men,"— on almost any other occasion would at once have borne the palm over the ablest competitor. But, with a constitutional hesitancy of speech, he feels, it is manifest, an unusual embarrassment. Mr. Otis, seeing clearly what he is attempting to utter, rises, and in a few flowing periods, gives an eloquent expression to the thought of his rival. The effect is electric. His noble magnanimity brings out cheer upon cheer; and it is followed by a speech from Mr. Quincy, comprehensive, logical, worthy of the man and of the occasion.

The lineage of Mr. Otis is so remarkable as to deserve notice. He descended in the sixth generation from John Otis, born in Barnstable, Devonshire County, England, in 1581, who came with his wife and children to Hingham in this country in 1635. He took the Freeman's oath in 1636, and was called Yeoman. His wife, Margaret, died June 28, 1653. He then removed to Weymouth, and married a second wife, Elizabeth Streame, a widow. He died in Weymouth May 31, 1657, aged seventy-six, leaving a widow who was living in 1663. John, son of John, born in England, 1620, married Mary, daughter of Nicholas Jacob, in 1652, and died January 16, 1683. He lived first in Hingham; then at Scituate in 1661; went to Barnstable in 1678, and took the Otis Farm; and finally returned to Scituate, and died there January 16, 1683.

John Otis, called "Colonel John," son of John, son of John, born in 1657 in Hingham, settled in Barnstable. He possessed extraordinary abilities, great wit, was affable, and had rare sagacity and prudence. He was Representative twenty years, commanded a regiment of militia eighteen years, was Judge of Probate thirteen years, Chief Justice of the Court of Common Pleas, and one of his Majesty's Council, 1706-27. He married Mercy Bacon, July 18, 1683, and died September 23, 1727, aged seventy. Joseph, brother of the above, was Judge of the Court of Common Pleas, 1703-14, and Representative from Scituate, 1700-13. He was a "public-spirited man, of ready wit and a sound understanding, and held in great esteem." His eldest daughter, Bethia, married first, Rev. William Billings; second, Rev. Samuel Moseley. She was born November 20, 1703, and died May 29, 1750, aged forty-seven. The "New England Historical Register" says: "She descended from an illustrious ancestry, became successively the wife of two ministers, and, what is more, was one of the subscribers for 'Prince's Chronology.'" Her second husband,

Rev. Samuel Moseley, was born August 15, 1708. He graduated at Harvard College, 1729, studied for the ministry, and was chaplain to Governor Belcher, at Castle William. In 1734 he was pastor at Windham, Connecticut; he was forty-eight years in the active ministry, and died July 26, 1791, aged eighty-three. "He was an accomplished gentleman and scholar, intrepid in whatever he thought his duty, both with regard to practice and opinion, but open to conviction, and frank in confessing his mistakes. Nine years a paralytic, his reason was undisturbed, and he continued patient, resigned, and full of faith to the last."

Among the children of Samuel and Bethia (Otis) Moseley was Samuel, born April 27, 1739. He was at the battle of Bunker Hill, Corporal of Captain Knowlton's Company, and the tradition is that he was killed and buried on the ground. Anna, daughter of Rev. Samuel and Bethia (Otis) Moseley, born May 23, 1746, died March 6, 1815. She married Deacon Daniel Dunham of Lebanon, Connecticut. They had twelve children, of whom Colonel Josiah, the eldest, graduated at Dartmouth College in 1789, and was appointed in 1793, by General Washington, a captain in the regular army. He left the army in 1808; and was Secretary of State in Vermont, and aid to the Governor, with the rank of colonel. In 1821 he established a female academy at Lexington, Kentucky, which had a wide reputation. He married Susan Hedge, sister of Professor Hedge of Harvard College.

He was born April 7, 1769, and died May 10, 1844.

Nathaniel Otis, born 1690, brother of John, born in 1687, was a prominent man, who settled in Sandwich. He was Register of Probate several years, and died in December, 1739. He married Abigail Russel, daughter of Rev. Jonathan Russel, who was ordained at Barnstable in 1683. President Stiles says: " She was every way a woman of superior excellence, of exceedingly good natural abilities, possessed of natural dignity and respectability, of considerable reading, and extensive observation." She died March 30, 1744. Their children were Abigail, born August 19, 1712; Nathaniel, born April 16, 1716, and died early; Martha, born December 11, 1719, married Edward Freeman of Sandwich, whose son was Nathaniel Freeman of Revolutionary fame; Solomon, born 1696, third son of Colonel John, graduated at Harvard College in 1717; was Register of Deeds, County Treasurer, Justice of Peace, &c., and died January 2, 1778. He had eight children, four of whom died early.

Colonel James, son of James, son of John, son of John, son of John, born 1702, married Mary Allyne in Connecticut. " She was a woman of very superior character." Their children were: (1) James, son of James, son of John, son of John, son of John, born February 5, 1725, — the Patriot, graduated at Harvard College, 1743. (2) Joseph, born March 6, 1723, — a General. (3) Mercy, born September 14, 1728; the Historian, in 1805, of the "American Revolution," in three volumes. She also wrote a volume of poems, and a poetical satire, "The Group," in 1775. She married General James Warren, and died at Plymouth in 1814, aged eighty-six. (4) Mary, born September 9, 1730, who married John Gray. (5) Hannah, born July 31, 1732, died unmarried. (6) Nathaniel, born July 9, 1734, died young. (7) Martha, born October 9, 1736, died young. (8) Abigail, born June 30, 1738, died young. (9) Samuel Allyne, born November 24, 1740, graduated at Harvard College in 1759, and became a merchant. (10) Sarah, born April 11, 1742, died unmarried. (11) Nathaniel, born April 5, 1743, died April 30, 1763. (12) A daughter, who died in infancy.

Colonel James Otis was a prominent and very popular man, as is shown by the address sent to him by the "Body of the People," met at Barnstable, September 20, 1744, to consider "the late oppressive acts of Parliament," he being then "one of his Majesty's Constitutional Council" of that Province. They "pray" that he will attend "the Great and General Court" at its next session, and proceed to say: "that you will continue those endeavors to obtain a redress of the grievances so justly complained of by the people, which have long distinguished you as an able defender of our Constitution and Liberties."

The "Body" voted that their committee present their address in person to his Honor, James Otis, and that "we will walk in procession to see it presented to our country's great benefactor and friend." Accordingly "the whole body marched in procession, with the committee at their head, attended by music, to the house where Mr. Otis was residing, — in solid body in rank and file," — and were courteously received by him, and he afterward replied as follows:

"GENTLEMEN, — Your very complaisant address to me as a Constitutional Councillor of this Province, desiring me to attend my duty at Salem on the 5th of October, I am obliged for; and for putting me in mind of my duty; and I am determined to attend at Salem at that time, in case my health permits.
'I am your very humble servant,
'JAMES OTIS.'
BARNSTABLE, September 26, 1774."

This reply of Colonel Otis "the whole Body" heard with their heads uncovered, and then gave three cheers in token of their satisfaction, and their high approbation of his answer, as well as esteem and veneration for his person and character. This done, they returned in procession to the courthouse.

Joseph Otis, second son of Colonel James, was appointed Collector of Customs by President Washington, was prominent as a Patriot in the Revolution, many years Clerk of the Court of Common Pleas, and a member of the State Legislature. He was a successful merchant, and a General.

After a long and honored life, he died September 23, 1810, aged eighty-two years.

Samuel Allyne Otis, born November 24, 1740, married first, Elizabeth, only daughter of Harrison Gray, Receiver General of Massachusetts Province; and second, Mary, widow of Edward Gray, Esq., and daughter of Isaac Smith. He held several important offices, was elected Member of Congress, 1788, and, after the adoption of the Constitution, was chosen Secretary of the United States Senate, and, for twenty-five years, was never absent from his place. He died at Washington, April 22, 1814, aged seventy-three years.

Harrison Gray Otis, son of Samuel Allyne Otis, was born in Boston, October 8, 1765, on the estate adjoining the present Revere House. He remembered standing, April 19, 1775, at the window, to see some of the British Regulars who were to march to Lexington. On leaving his father's house afterward, to go to the Latin School, he found the sides of what is now Tremont Street lined by the brigade commanded by Lord Percy, afterwards the Duke of Northumberland. The troops were drawn up from Scollay's Square to a point beyond School Street, and he was not allowed to pass into School Street; so, going round by that square, he reached the Latin School in time to hear Master Lovell give the order, "Deponete Libros." There were no lessons that day; and Lord Percy marched out to cover the retreat of the King's Troops, and met them about half a mile below Lexington meetinghouse, on their return from Concord.

Before this, Otis had attended a school in Hanover Street, kept by "Master Griffith." Every Wednesday afternoon the boys who had behaved well expected to receive a prize; and it was this, — shellbarks thrown out of the window, for which the boys scrambled.

He was nearly ten years old at the opening of the Revolution. His immediate ancestors resided in Barnstable, and he lived there when a boy, during the Siege of Boston. He recollected well hearing of the excitement when the news of the burning of Charlestown by the British reached Barnstable; every one seemed ready to rush to the cannon's mouth in defence of the country.

Mr. Otis, at the dedication of the Otis School, Lancaster Street, March 13, 1845, related many curious anecdotes of his early experience. He entered the Latin School in 1773. "What," he asked, "did the scholars then learn? A few Latin roots to squeeze them into college, and mere ciphering."

From the Latin School he entered Harvard College, where he graduated in 1785, having received the highest honors in a class in which were William Prescott and Artemas Ward. He began professional life, it is said, as a minister of the gospel. Having preached in a country parish, not far from Boston, a certain Sunday, he was asked, as he himself gives the story, by the deacon of the church, what he should pay him for his services. "What you think they are worth," was the reply. The good deacon gave him a pistareen, — twenty cents. "Upon that," says Mr. Otis, "I thought it expedient to take some other profession than the ministry." He determined on the law, and, having studied with Judge John Lowell, his decision proved wise; for, after being admitted to the bar in 1786, he became eminent as an advocate, and was distinguished in civil and political life. At a public meeting, on the subject of Jay's Treaty, he made a speech, at which time Bishop Cheverus was among those who thronged around him, after its close, with congratulations. "Future generations," said he to a bystander, "will rise up and call that young man blessed."

Mr. Otis was too young to take part in the Revolution; but he bore arms in repressing the Shays Insurrection, 1786–87, which required the military services of every able-bodied citizen.

In November, 1791, a town-meeting, in Faneuil Hall, instructed the Boston Representatives to obtain, if possible, the repeal of the act prohibiting theatrical representations. Mr. Otis opposed the repeal. It was on this occasion Samuel Adams said he "thanked God that there was one young man willing to step forth in the good old cause of morality and religion."

In 1796 he was chosen to represent Boston in the State Legislature, and the same year he succeeded Fisher Ames in Congress; about this time he was appointed United States District Attorney for Massachusetts. From 1803 to 1805 he was Speaker of the Massachusetts House of Representatives. In the political struggle of the Massachusetts Senate, 1805, by a vote of nineteen out of thirty-seven, he was chosen by the Federalists its President, and continued in that office several years. What an array of talent was seen in 1811, when Elbridge Gerry was Governor of the State, Joseph Story Speaker of the House, and Harrison Gray Otis President of the Senate!

At the bar, meantime, Mr. Otis was, especially before juries, a man of transcendent power. If he had not the massive learning and strength of Parsons, or the majesty of Dexter, he fascinated his hearers " by his honeyed flow and brilliant sparkle." In the celebrated trial of Fairbanks for murder in Dedham, Otis and Lowell occupied six hours, with their wonted powers of persuasion, in ingenious efforts to save the life of the prisoner, although the unsurpassed eloquence of Otis failed of its aim.

Among the recollections of my boyhood are conversations upon the duel between Hamilton and Burr, which resulted in the death of the former. In our Federal family the name of Aaron Burr, of course, ever afterward, was a spell to conjure up all that is corrupt in politics and base in character. No greater contrast could be drawn than that between him and Hamilton, and that he should have brought death to that pure man, that noble patriot, that exalted genius, the friend of Washington, the model of all excellence, was too much even for the mind and heart of a boy. Trained amid such traditions, with the high regard we entertained for the Otis family, it seemed to us all, as we listened to the account of that day, that no man living could have done greater justice to the memory of Hamilton than Harrison Gray Otis. When he rose in King's Chapel, July 26, 1804, to pronounce a eulogy on that great man, in the presence of so many distinguished citizens of Boston, and with Rufus King among his auditors, it was indeed a memorable occasion. The nation was in mourning, and party feeling seemed, we are told, allayed at that moment. We may envy those privileged to hear the gifted orator of the day, as with consummate grace he portrayed the signal virtues, the masterly intellect, and the high and patriotic services of Alexander Hamilton. It was but just that near the close of his eulogy he should give this picture of the public feeling: "The universal sorrow, manifested in every part of the Union upon the melancholy exit of this great man, is an unequivocal testimonial of his public worth. The place of his residence is overspread with a gloom which bespeaks the pressure of a public calamity, and the prejudices of party are absorbed in the overflowing tide of national grief."

During the War of 1812 Mr. Otis was continuously either in Congress or in one of the legislative branches of his State, where he was often at the head of the one or the other. The people looked to him as their guide in all the trying scenes of that period. With a cultivated mind and commanding eloquence, he was easily first among his equals, ready alike with his voice and his pen.

No impartial judge can now say his purposes were not pure. He was the last man — although then charged by his opponents with that crime, and although his example was quoted by one section of the country in the late Civil War — to favor a combination, by discussion, still less by bloodshed, to bring on, through discord and strife, a dissolution of this noble fabric, this glorious Union, consummated by the wisdom and sacrifices of our fathers.

In 1814 he was a member of the Hartford Convention of the New England States, to consider some mode of defending these States and arresting the grievances produced by the war with Great Britain. This convention was in session from the fifteenth of December, 1814, to the fifth of the following January. Their proceedings, it is true, were conducted with closed doors, and yet nothing was done unfriendly to the peace and harmony of the country. In the call to it the members were expressly enjoined not to propose measures "repugnant to their obligations as members of the Union." After twenty days' deliberation they published an Address to the People. It spoke of the evils of the existing war, of the enlistment of minors and apprentices, of the national government assuming to command the State Militia, and of the proposed system of conscription for both the army and navy; and yet it contained these very words: "Our object is to strengthen and perpetuate the union of these States, by removing the causes of jealousies." Not to overthrow, but amend the Constitution, was their aim and labor. They would equalize the representation in Congress, by basing it on free population; they were opposed to embargoes and non-intercourse laws, and would make the President ineligible for a second term. I remember well the abuse and crimination heaped upon them by their opponents in my own town; " enemies of their country," " traitors," and many other forms of calumniation were often in my ears; but when the Massachusetts legislature adopted their report, and sent such men as Harrison Gray Otis, Thomas H. Perkins, and William Sullivan commissioners to Washington, asking Congress to consent to the measures of a convention containing the names of George Cabot, Harrison Gray Otis, Samuel S. Wilde, Nathan Dane, William Prescott, Joseph Lyman, Stephen Longfellow Jr., Daniel Waldo, George Bliss, Hodijah Baylies, Joshua Thomas, from Massachusetts, and others of equal ability and the same stern patriotism from other New England States, even we youth of the day felt somewhat the wisdom, uprightness, and purity of the purposes of that convention, which father and grandfather daily commended in our earnest ears.

In 1814 Mr. Otis was appointed Judge of the Court of Common Pleas of Massachusetts, and held that office until 1818, when he was elected to the

JOHN LOVELL.

FIRST LATIN SCHOOL, SCHOOL LANE.

United States Senate; and he continued in that body until 1823. That year he was opposed to William Eustis as candidate for governor of Massachusetts. Eustis had won fame as a surgeon in the Revolution, and in subsequent civil capacities. Otis was strongly opposed, among other things, for his theological views, being an avowed Unitarian; while Eustis was of the Orthodox faith, and widely supported by that denomination, which gave him success at the polls. Mr. Otis, on meeting him in the street the next day, after the result was known, said to him, "I have no doubt you believe now in the doctrine of election." I recall the figure and face of Mr. Eustis at the age of seventy-two, grave and bowed with years, and that his clubbed, white hair gave him a venerable appearance.

In the election of governor, 1823, Otis was defeated by Eustis; but, like many wise men in similar situations, he remarked long afterward: "My failure in this contest was a mortification and a severe disappointment to me at the time, but I look back upon it now without regret. I regard it as the most fortunate event of my life. I have been a happier and better man, since I was thrown out of political life, than I should ever have been had I remained in it."

I have spoken of the pleasant relations between Mr. Otis and Mr. Josiah Quincy. These continued throughout their lives. When Mr. Otis, as mayor, was inspecting the excavation of earth where the gravestones of William Paddy and human bones were discovered, Mr. Quincy, standing by, said to Mr. Otis: "In the whole of my administration I have never been accused of disturbing the bones of my ancestors;" to which Mr. Otis, complimenting Mr. Quincy for his great energy of character, replied with a smile: "Why, Mr. Quincy, I always supposed you never made any bones of doing anything."

In 1829 Mr. Otis became Mayor of Boston, and held that office until 1832, when he retired from public life, although he occasionally took part in meetings to consider subjects of general interest.

When, in 1834, the Catholic convent at Charlestown was burned by a mob, and the outrage brought the citizens of Boston to a meeting at Faneuil Hall to express their indignation, I rejoiced to hear the voice of the "old man eloquent," Harrison Gray Otis, with that of Josiah Quincy, and other just and good men, advocate a remuneration for those hapless women and children who were driven by the fury and the flames from their home at midnight. The conduct of Bishop Fenwick in restraining his people from violence, the bold and Christian stand in behalf of the Irish Catholics taken by Father Taylor in a public address at that time, the earnest efforts of Chief Justice Shaw and of the Governor of the State to bring the offenders to justice, all combined to make those days memorable to all of us who would not only advocate but practise the religion of charity to every sect, party, and people in our own and in every land.

Never losing his interest in public measures, in 1839 Mr. Otis headed a petition for the repeal of the famous "fifteen-gallon law," believing it unfriendly to the true interests of temperance. His old profession retained its hold upon his love to the end. At a late period of his life he consented to argue a case in court, when he was overheard by a friend of mine to say, " I thought I would come once more to the bar, and see if I had any of my old tact left."

On the eighth day of September, 1836, the Alumni of Harvard College assembled in Cambridge to commemorate the two-hundredth anniversary of the establishment of that institution. The authorities of the college fittingly invited Harrison Gray Otis, one of the oldest living graduates of the college, to preside at the dinner on that occasion. To all of us who had listened to that eloquent orator, — of whom it was not, perhaps, too much to say that he was never surpassed in power of language and graceful utterance by any scholar and statesman of his native State, excepting his noble kinsman, James Otis, and perhaps the accomplished Fisher Ames, and him who stood that day at Harvard in the place of Mr. Otis, — it was a sad disappointment that a heavy domestic bereavement prevented his presence with us at that time. It required a substitute no less cultured and fascinating than Edward Everett to satisfy our high expectations.

Happily for us who knew Mr. Otis, yielding to

the request of his old friend President Quincy, who gave the Anniversary Address at that time, he permitted his remarks, intended for the table, to appear in the record of the proceedings of that occasion, published in Mr. Quincy's invaluable "History of Harvard College." Mr. Otis, after speaking of the prospects of the country with a fervent patriotism, closes by referring to the indispensable need of the education of the mass of the people, and a due preparation of men in the universities and colleges, to enlighten and guide public opinion, and help in preserving the moral purity of the nation. "Let us," he says, "cultivate and adhere to the principles taught here, and not trust to the promises of the conductors on the modern intellectual railroad, to grade and level the hills of science and take us along at rates that will turn our heads and break our bones. Let us eschew the vagaries and notions of the new schools, and let each of us, reminded of a quotation which Burke did not think unworthy of him, be ready to say :

'What though the flattering tapster Thomas
Hangs his new Angel two doors from us,
As fine as painter's daub can make it,
Thinking some traveller may mistake it?
I hold it both a shame and sin
To quit the good old Angel Inn.'"

Mr. Otis then gave the following toast: "Harvard College,—' the good old Angel Inn,' where the intellectual fare is served up in the old family plate, from which our ancestors and ourselves have been regaled for the last two hundred years."

Among the patriotic deeds of this family should be named the generous public services of Mrs. Harrison Gray Otis, Jr., to whose influence we owe it that the birthday of Washington was made in Massachusetts a legal holiday.

WILLIAM FOSTER OTIS, son of Harrison Gray and Sally (Foster) Otis, was born in Boston, December 1, 1801; entered the Latin School in 1813; and graduated at Harvard College, 1821. He read law with Harrison Gray Otis, Jr., a brother, and Augustus Peabody, and became a counsellor-at-law. He married Emily, daughter of Josiah Marshall, Esq., a selectman of Boston, May 18, 1831; she died August 17, 1836, aged 29.

Mr. Otis was a member of the Ancient and Honorable Artillery Company in 1828; a major in the Boston Regiment, a judge-advocate, a representative to the State Legislature, and President of the Young Men's Temperance Society. At a public Festival in Faneuil Hall he gave an oration before the Young Men's Association of Boston, after the delivery of which, at the dinner, the following sentiment was given: "The Orator of the Day, rich in the hereditary possession of the virtues and talents of his ancestor, — far richer in possessing the hearts of the present generation." I do not think this compliment was undeserved; for, after hearing the father repeatedly, I can testify that a large portion of his oratorical gifts descended upon his son. He had not the personal beauty and grace of that rare man; but he had a strong face, a dark and piercing eye, and great energy and decision of manner. He was at one time in the State Legislature, and while he was there I heard from him an eloquent speech on a very important financial measure, to relieve the pecuniary distress of the hard times of that period. Various propositions were brought forward for that purpose. Mr. Otis spoke of the urgency of the situation, and employed in his argument, as I remember, a very striking illustration. "While we sit here," said he, "with our multiplying schemes to aid the community in their suffering, I am reminded of a case in which two surgeons, called to perform a critical operation, stood over the patient, after the amputation, discussing the best method of tying up certain arteries, while, in the heat of their talk, the subject in their hands was fast bleeding to death."

A passage from his oration to the young men is so pertinent to our own day that I cannot forbear to cite a part of it: "We are asked, upon what is our reliance in times of excitement, — what compensation for human infirmities, what substitutes for bayonets, dragoons, and aristocracy? I answer: The religion and morality of the people. Not the religion of the state; not the morality of the fashionable. Our trust, our only trust, is where it ought to be, — the religion and morality of the whole people."

Referring to the marriage of Mr. Otis, I cannot forbear speaking of his companion, that celebrated Boston beauty, "the observed of all observers," Miss

Emily Marshall, whom I could never meet in society, or elsewhere, without a fixed admiration. With a manner immediately fascinating, and a face blending the charms of the red and white roses, she had an eye full and lustrous, a mouth of rarest chiselling, opened only to disclose teeth of perfect evenness and color. Her smile had a sweetness which was in accord with the expression of every other feature; her voice was the appropriate instrument of a rich soul; her whole bearing was accompanied by a simplicity never betraying the least consciousness of her beauty. This rare lady, the companion of Mr. Otis, was called away, alas, in the very prime of a life pervaded, as those nearest her testified, with all that is pure, gentle, kind, and winning. We were not surprised that the stricken survivor soon followed her to their upper and enduring home.

In looking upon family faces and portraits we often trace striking resemblances in personal beauty or strength. Both the husband and wife just named illustrated this truth. If grace and loveliness of expression were transmitted on the side of the wife's mother, there were traits to be traced back to that of the father. The portrait of Colonel James Otis, born in 1702, gives us one of the rarest combinations of strength and beauty. To a manly and noble figure he united a face beaming with intelligence; self-devotion was written in every lineament, broad-heartedness was joined with an energy of character, fitting him for the work he so well performed for his age. One can see, in the outspeaking countenance, why he was, as history records, "a very popular man," and can only wish to have had a place in that company who voted to "carry their address in person," testifying the enthusiasm and veneration they felt for his generous services to the country.

And nothing else can we say of his son, "James, the Patriot." When we fix our gaze on that remarkable figure of him on canvas in Faneuil Hall, we are carried back to the days in which he lived. We are kindled by the bold, terse, and convincing argument and remonstrances with Great Britain, placed on record by his pen. We can see in him the embodiment which Cicero gives of "The Orator," in whom not the voice only, but the eye, the hand, the whole man, are instinct with power. Webster comes before us with his inspiring description of true eloquence; the portrait stands out from the canvas, a living form, and we are ready to join in the loud and universal applause.

James, oldest son of Colonel James Otis of Barnstable, and in the fifth generation from John Otis of England, was born in West Barnstable, February 5, 1725. He was prepared for college by Rev. Jonathan Russell of West Barnstable, and entered Harvard College, in June 1739. In his junior year he began to show great talent and power of application. He took his first degree in 1743, at the age of nineteen, and the degree of Master of Arts three years afterward. He devoted his college vacations to books, and was little known near his father's home. Although grave and abstracted in his turn of mind, he would at times manifest that keen wit which marked his subsequent character. After leaving college he spent a year and a half in general reading and culture, and regretted afterward that he had not devoted more time to such literature before he entered upon his professional studies. He advised every law student to prepare himself for such study by a general acquaintance with other arts and sciences than those pertaining directly to the law. Mr. Otis began the study of law in 1745, with Jeremiah Gridley, one of the first lawyers and civilians of his time. He began the practice of his profession in Plymouth in 1748, and, after two years residence in that town, removed to Boston. His business soon became extensive, and he earned a reputation for learning, wit, eloquence, and strict integrity. He kept up his classical knowledge, and thought little of those who could only quote the English poets. To a young friend he remarked: "These lads are fond of talking about poetry and repeating passages of it; but do you take care that you don't give in to this folly. If you want to read poetry, read Shakespeare, Milton, Dryden, and Pope, and throw all the rest into the fire."

Mr. Otis partook of the filial respect common in his time, but in this latter part of the nineteenth century, threatening to become quite obsolete.

"Honored Sir" may seem to us rather stiff and formal, and we do well to substitute our ordinary address, "My dear Father;" but it is to be hoped that obedience to parents, so conspicuous in the youth of Mr. Otis, is not to vanish with our age.

In 1755 James Otis married Ruth Cunningham, who died November 15, 1789, aged sixty years. Their children were: (1) James, born 1755, a very bright boy, a midshipman in the Revolution, who died, it is said, on board the Jersey Prison Ship in 1777, at the early age of twenty-one years. (2) Elizabeth, who married a Captain Brown of the English army, previously wounded at the battle of Bunker Hill, with whom she resided abroad, making only a short visit to this country in 1792. She was living, a widow, in England, 1821. Her marriage offended her father, and he left her in his will but five shillings. (3) Mary, who was born in 1764, and married Benjamin Lincoln, son of General Lincoln, who graduated at Harvard College in 1777. He was a lawyer of great promise, but died at the early age of twenty-eight. His widow, a lady of excellent talents and very agreeable character, who had married Rev. Henry Ware, Professor in Harvard College, died suddenly at Cambridge in 1807. Benjamin Lincoln had two sons, Benjamin, a physician, and James Otis, a lawyer, both of whom died in early life,— Benjamin in August, 1813, and James Otis in August, 1818, the latter leaving a widow and two children.

In 1761 James Otis pleaded with great power against the Writs of Assistance which the customhouse officers had sought from the Judges of the Supreme Court. Of this speech John Adams said: "Otis was a flame of fire; with a depth of research, and a rapid torrent of impetuous eloquence, he hurried away all before him. American Independence was then and there born." He was at this time chosen a member of the Massachusetts Legislature, where he had a commanding influence by the power of his reasoning, his large intellectual resources, his wit and eloquent manner. Of a fearless temper, he signed a remonstrance against the aggressions of the parent country.

His letter to Mauduit, agent of the Massachusetts Assembly in London, dated June 13, 1764, in reply to a proposition of Great Britain for compromise, says, with his accustomed insight and sarcasm: "The kind offer of suspending the stamp duty amounts to no more than this, that if the Colonies will not tax themselves as they may be directed, the Parliament will tax them."

He was a member of the "Stamp Act Congress" held at New York in 1765, in which year his "Rights of the Colonies Vindicated" was republished in London, for which he was threatened with an arrest. With a patriotic spirit he resigned, in 1767, his office of Judge Advocate, which he had held six years.

August 14, 1768, the principal men of Boston

met at Liberty Hall to celebrate the repeal of the Stamp Act; they had a band of music, and the much admired American Liberty Song was enthusiastically sung. This song had just been received by James Otis from its author, John Dickinson. It was first printed July 4, 1768; and is the earliest of the Revolutionary lyrics, advocating *independence and union*. It was sung to the tune "Hearts of Oak." A few stanzas of it are contained in Drake's Revolutionary History.

In 1769 Mr. Otis, finding the Commissioners of Customs had sent to England charges of treason against him, denounced them most bitterly in the "Boston Gazette." He met one of these commissioners, the next evening in a public room, where he was assaulted by a band of ruffians and covered with wounds, having a sword-cut in the head. Although this attack was not fatal, and in a lucid interval he forgave those who had assaulted him, and relinquished the five thousand pounds sterling which had been awarded him, his reason was shaken, his usefulness at an end, and he lived mentally in ruins for several years.

He saw that event towards which his efforts had primarily contributed, but could not fully enjoy it, the Independence of America. In a lucid interval he went from Andover to Boston and resumed the practice of law, but soon returned to the country. In 1770 he retired to reside permanently in the country, but was the next year chosen Representative. Nearly all the remainder of his life he was insane. On the 23d of May, 1783, as he was leaning on his cane at the door of a friend's home in Andover, he was struck by a thunderbolt and instantly killed. President Adams, then Minister in France, wrote of him: "It was with very afflicting sentiments I learned the death of Mr. Otis, my worthy master. Extraordinary in death as in life, he has left a character that will never die while the memory of the American Revolution remains, whose foundation he laid with an energy and with those masterly abilities which no other man possessed."

While in the prime of his vigor he published several volumes: in 1760, "Rudiments of Latin Prosody," and also a "Dissertation on Letters, and the Principles of Harmony in Poetic and Prose Compositions;" in 1762, "A Vindication of the Conduct of the House of Massachusetts Representatives;" in 1764, "The Rights of the British Colonies Asserted;" and in 1765, "Considerations on behalf of the Colonists." He was of an irritable temper, but easily conciliated, although his course often appeared inconsistent, in consequence of this infirmity.

CHAPTER III.

ADAMS FAMILY.

The field opened to our minds by the mention of this name is extensive. To the historian of America, it is large ; to the biographer, still wider. It is with diffidence that I enter upon it in any form. The plan of this work restrains me to what seems narrow and meagre, compared with the abundant and rich materials of the subject. My personal recollections of this illustrious family pertain mainly to one member of it, JOHN QUINCY ADAMS.

And yet I must refer briefly to two other relatives of his — one his distinguished father. A classmate and warm friend of mine, George Whitney, a native of Quincy, and afterward minister of the Unitarian Church at Jamaica Plain, often spoke to me, while in college, of the then aged and venerated JOHN ADAMS. Their conversations led him to relate many anecdotes concerning this patriarch. He once told my classmate that he had kept a journal through nearly his whole life. He began it when he was but ten years old. Looking over one day the first two volumes, they

ADAMS OPPOSING THE STAMP ACT FROM THE OLD STATE HOUSE.

seemed to him so small, their contents so childish, and the occurrences related in such a simple and poor way, that he "shut them up in disgust, and committed them to the flames." "But," said he, "I have again and again been sorry for it, and have often felt, as I do now, that I would give the best farm I ever owned if I could once more see and possess them." Who of us all has not, in some hasty moment, destroyed papers, perhaps the letters of dear friends, or some other memento of the past, for the restoration of which no price would seem too great?

Too much credit can hardly be given to John Adams for his spirit and energy in fostering the temper of the Revolution. The refugees, whether we call them Tories, or by the milder name of Loyalists, dreaded Mr. Adams's influence probably more than that of any other one man in America. Chief Justice Oliver, himself rewarded for his flight to England, by royal favor and promotion, pronounced John Adams "one of the most dangerous men to British domination in America."

The perpetual absorption of Mr. Adams in our cause justified this remark. On one occasion while he was minister at the Hague, after dinner, he was observed in an abstract frame of mind, when suddenly raising his head, his face brightening with thought, he exclaimed to one sitting at his side: "Yes, it must be so; *twelve sail of the line supported by a proportion of frigates.*

When America, my friend, shall possess such a fleet she may bid defiance, upon her own coast, to any naval power of Europe." This anecdote illustrates what a place his country had in the depths of his heart in those dark and distressing days. We may smile at the small defence it promised to our naval protection; but it is almost enough to draw tears, when we think of the picture it exhibits of the poverty and straits and sacrifices of our people at that gloomy period.

It was John Adams who said, early in the Revolutionary struggle, what brought our needs into a photograph: "There are four pillars essential to a republic, Church, School, Trainband, and Town." He should have added, in our case, a fifth, — Navy. The schools, — even in the day of John Adams, — had done a great work for our people. They were, in one respect, miserably poor; but in another, in the intelligence and determination of their character, they had an inexhaustible wealth.

The ignorance of the mass of the English in regard to America and the character of its inhabitants, at the time of the Revolution, is almost incredible. A traveller, riding in a London coach, overheard two ladies talking on this wise. "I have seen," said one of them, "a wonderful sight — a little girl born in a place called Boston, in North America; and what is very astonishing, I pledge you my word it is true, she speaks English as well as any child in England; and, besides, she is perfectly white." "Is it possible?" exclaimed the other, astonished at the statement. "Many of the people of England suppose us," says the narrator, "to be a nation of Indians, negroes, or mixed blood." This account of the English ignorance of our people is matched by a fact related by Professor Andrews Norton, while I was in the Cambridge Divinity School, in 1826. Being in Exeter Hall at a public meeting that year, he saw on the platform a colored man, who was introduced to the audience as an American. "There," said a well-dressed lady to a companion at her side, "I have always told you the Americans were negroes." And so late as 1843 I met in a coach, among the English lakes, an intelligent man, an innkeeper, who, as he sat by my side, on learning from me that I came from the United States of America, replied: "The United States — that is in Canada, is'nt it?" But, I suspect, since the late Civil War, the English nation, even the common people, have ascertained that we are not all either negroes or Indians.

Who of us that lived at that time can ever forget the sensations occasioned by the event that took John Adams and Thomas Jefferson from this world on the very same day, — and that day, too, the fiftieth anniversary of our National Jubilee? On that occasion, July 4, 1826, my classmate Rev. George Whitney was appointed to give an oration in Quincy. Preparatory to that celebration Mr. Whitney was deputed to visit Mr. Adams and ask him for a sentiment to be offered at the dinner. He did so. On the 30th of June he called at the house of the veteran, then very feeble, and on Mr. Adams being requested to furnish a sentiment, " I will give you," said he, " Independence Forever." He was asked " if he would add anything to it," his reply was, " Not a word." And it was well he did not. For, as his grandson, Hon. Charles Francis Adams, says, in his graphic account of this scene: " In that brief sentiment Mr. Adams infused the essence of his whole character, and of his life-long labors for his country."

To have been the contemporary of Adams and Jefferson, and to have heard Daniel Webster's discourse, August 2, 1826, in Faneuil Hall, in commemoration of their lives and services, was a privilege for which I have never ceased to be grateful.

JOHN QUINCY ADAMS, born July 12, 1767, inherited many qualities from his father. Both had an intelligent countenance, expressing moral courage; both were endowed with a strong physical constitution, had a firm and dignified walk, and took remarkable care of their health. They rose early, and had habits of indefatigable industry. John Quincy Adams rose in the summer at 4 o'clock; and, when President of the United States, he bathed in the Potomac River, walked after it several miles, and continued the practice for years of translating a few verses in the Hebrew Bible before breakfast. Like his father, he was always temperate. I noticed, in dining at his table, that he took two glasses of wine, and have been told that this was his daily practice, and never exceeded.

During his presidency, my classmate Whitney was ordained; and Mr. Adams was present and sat on the Council, as a delegate from the church in Quincy. His dress was plain but neat. He was of middling stature, of a full bodily habit; his eyes were dark and penetrating, and, when he was not conversing, they were usually downcast and fixed. Being introduced to him, I inquired of him in regard to the Unitarian Society in Washington, at which I had heard he was a constant attendant. He spoke very kindly of Rev. Cazneau Palfrey, who was then its pastor. "I go there to church," he continued, "although I am not decided in my mind as to all the controverted doctrines of religion."

Mr. Adams expressed this same view when, several years afterward, I met him on the occasion of an exchange with the minister at Quincy, at which time he invited me to dine with him. The subject of my sermon was the Indestructibleness of Christianity. On our way to his house he said : "I agree entirely with the ground you took in your discourse. You did not speak of any particular class of doctrines that were everlasting, but of the great, fundamental principles in which all Christians agree; and those I think are what will be permanent." I am inclined to believe that this was Mr. Adams's position to the close of his life. He was a truly liberal Christian, not in the sense of holding to liberty as an end, but as a means, its value depending wholly on the use made of it. This did not make him a sectarian; to that he was earnestly opposed. Still less did it leave him in a state of intellectual or spiritual indifference.

It is interesting to know the church-going habits of the venerable Adams family, who owned, it seems, pew number one in the old church edifice until it was taken down in 1828. Then the owner was President John Quincy Adams. The former owner, President John Adams, died July 4, 1826, in his ninety-first year. He was never absent from church, forenoon or afternoon, when in Quincy. His son, the President, was as punctual at church. He had by nature, inherited probably from both parents, a religious disposition. I have it on good authority, that of his personal statement to another, that he continued through life to repeat, before closing his eyes for the night, the comprehensive verse taught him in childhood by his mother, taken from the New England Primer: —

>Now I lay me down to sleep,
>I pray the Lord my soul to keep;
>If I should die before I wake,
>I pray the Lord my soul to take.

I was interested by meeting at Mr. Adams's table a man whom I was told he often invited to his house, and who was celebrated in Boston business circles, P. P. F. Degrand. Mr. Degrand had during his life edited a commercial paper some ten years, had been a stock and exchange broker for twenty years, and died leaving some $100,000, to be given by his will chiefly to benevolent objects. He was more of a Protestant than his countrymen, the French, usually were at that time. Being asked one day what meeting he attended,—" Meeting? Oh yes," he replied, " Mrs. Pierce goes to Brattle Street." She was the landlady who provided for his temporal wants, and he probably thought it was her duty to supply the spiritual wants of her boarders, so far as they felt the need of it. This was quite convenient, as she kept a boarding-house fronting the Brattle Street Church, on the spot where the Quincy House now stands. Mr. Degrand understood the French, English, Spanish, and Italian languages, and united to a French precision in business a Yankee shrewdness which made him helpful to his thrifty friend Adams.

The wisdom and thoroughness of Mr. Adams's education were tested by its influence throughout his whole life. The boy had in his character those elements and traits which marked the man in every station, duty, and service. He had, both by nature and domestic education, a remarkable courage in supporting everything right and true. He possessed, as has been said, "a lion heart which knew not the fear of man." When he had made up his mind what he ought to do, he did not stop to ask what others would think of him, but went straight forward and performed his duty. No man had a higher standard of conduct, and few ever acted up to their standard so nobly. He did not hold his good principles loosely, so that others could take them easily from him; but he grasped whatever he thought right with a firm hand, and trusted himself to it on all occasions. I do not say that he was a perfect man; he was human, and his judgment might sometimes err; but I do say that he did uniformly what at the time he thought was right. He was a man of strong feelings, and if in the warmth of the moment he either said or did what proved to be wrong, he was ready to change his position when convinced of his error.

He was from his boyhood deeply interested in the subject of human freedom, and he did as much perhaps for that cause, in his way, as any man that has lived. His interest in the emancipation of the enslaved grew deeper and deeper the longer he lived. But a few months previous to his death, when smitten with that disease the repetition of which proved fatal to him, he expressed a regret that he had not done more for freedom and humanity. His devotedness to this subject in his closing years, the moral courage he displayed, and the dangers he encountered for it, are worthy of all praise and emulation. The old tree seemed to root itself more firmly, and to gather new strength, as blast after blast assailed its majestic form.

The most striking trait in this rare character was an indomitable resolution. We are told that Fichte, the great German philosopher, when but seven years of age, once threw into the river a fascinating book he was reading, because he found it took off his mind from his studies. We can imagine young Adams doing similar deeds. He would allow nothing to stand between himself and his duty; he learned very early a certain contempt for ease and enjoyment, and never gave way to their seductions. As the coral insect, by unremitted perseverance, raises at last an island in the ocean, so did he, step by step, accomplish every work to which he had once set his hand. He never tampered with a good purpose, moral or intellectual; irresolution, he well knew, creeps on its victim with a fatal facility. If he saw that serpent in the bottom of the cup before him, no earthly consideration could induce him to taste its poison.

What he would become afterward was manifest in his earliest years. There was never an instance in which it was truer that "the child is father of the man." That sun which shone so brilliantly at noonday, and which went down with a heavenly serenity and glory, had risen from a dawn full of beauty and promise. He did not, like most men, "need the sting of guilt to make him virtuous, nor the smart of folly to make him wise." In his very childhood he saw that there is nothing so valuable on earth as firmness of purpose and purity of heart. For these he then and there resolved to live. Wealth and honors he did not despise, but he never, for one moment, made either of them the great object of his life. Before he was ten years of age, he wrote a letter to his father asking his advice in regard to his studies, expressing his desire to "keep his resolution to improve," and closing with these words: —

I am, dear sir, with a present determination of growing better, Yours,

JOHN QUINCY ADAMS.

Go back to the age of fifteen, when he went out as private secretary of Francis Dana, minister to the government of Russia, and follow him to the day when he expired at the Capitol in Washington, you find him everywhere and always the same person, intellectually and morally, marked by his individuality, clear-sighted, scholarly, firm, bold, —earnest in youth, in middle life a vigorous writer and convincing speaker, and to the very last "the old man eloquent."

I have spoken of the mother of John Quincy Adams. The life of this woman was so remarkable from her early days, especially her first acquaintance with her future husband, that I give a chapter of it in this place. It may be somewhat colored by the writer; still the main facts of it show that full often truth is stranger than fiction, and we are compelled at last, in real life, to rely upon that as veritable which would at first view seem only romance. I give this account the more readily, as the aged and revered Rev. Jacob Norton, successor of Mr. Smith, the father of our subject, was a relative by marriage, whom I visited while in college, and whose wife was a person whom to know was both to respect and love. He confirmed the account here given. The article is entitled " Courtship of the Elder Adams."

Some ten years ago I spent a college vacation in the town of Weymouth, Norfolk County, Massachusetts. While there, I attended church one Sunday morning at what was called the Old Weymouth Meeting-house, and heard a sermon from the venerable pastor, Rev. Jacob Norton. About the same time, I made Mr. Norton a visit, and became much interested in the old gentleman. I mentioned my agreeable visits to an aged lady of the parish, whose acquaintance I had made. She informed me that Mr. Norton was ordained their pastor when he was about twenty-one years of age, and that he had been with them nearly forty years. She observed that most of his parishioners could remember no other pastor; but that she could well remember his predecessor, the Rev. Mr. Smith, and that he and Mr. Norton had filled the same pulpit for the better part of the last eighty years.

" Mr. Smith," said she, " was an excellent man, and a very fine preacher, but he had high notions of himself and family; in other words, he was something of an aristocrat." My informant said to me one day: " To illustrate to you a little the character of old Parson Smith, I will tell you an anecdote that relates to himself and some other persons of distinction. Mr. Smith had two charming daughters — the eldest of these daughters was Mary, the other's name I have forgotten — who were the admiration of all the beaux, and the envy of all the belles of the country around. But while the careful guardians of the parson's family were holding consultation on the subject, it was rumored that two young lawyers, both of the neighboring town of Quincy, a Mr. Cranch and a Mr. Adams, were paying their addresses to the Misses Smith. As every woman and child of a country parish in New England is acquainted with whatever takes place in the parson's family, all the circumstances of the courtship soon transpired. Mr. Cranch was of a respectable family of some note, was considered a young man of promise, and altogether worthy of the alliance he sought. He was very acceptable to Mr. Smith, and was greeted by him and his family with great respect and cordiality. He was received by the oldest daughter as a lover. He afterwards rose to the dignity of Judge of the Court of Common Pleas in Massachusetts, and was the father of the present Hon. Judge Cranch of the District of Columbia.

"The suitor of the other daughter was John Adams, who afterwards became President of the United States; but at that time, in the opinion of Mr. Smith and family, he gave but slender promise of the distinction to which he afterwards arrived. His pretensions were scorned by all the family, excepting the young lady to whom his addresses were especially directed. Mr. Smith showed him none of the ordinary civilities of the house; he was not asked to partake of the hospitalities of the table; and it is reported that his horse was doomed to share with his master the neglect and mortification to which he was subjected, for he was frequently seen shivering in the cold, and gnawing the post at the pastor's door, of long winter evenings. In fine, it was reported that Mr. Smith had intimated to him that his visits were not acceptable, and he would do him a favor by discontinuing them. He told his daughter that John Adams was not worthy of her,—that his father was an honest tradesman and farmer, who had tried to initiate John in the arts of husbandry and shoe-making, but without success, and that he had sent him to college as a last resort. He, in fine, begged his daughter not to think of making an alliance with one so much beneath her.

"Miss Smith was among the most dutiful daughters, but she saw Mr. Adams through a medium very different from that through which her father viewed him. She would not, for the world, offend or disobey her father; but still John saw something in her eye and manner which seemed to say 'persevere,' and on that hint he acted.

"Mr. Smith, like a good parson and an affectionate father, had told his daughters, if they married with his approbation, he would preach each of them a sermon on the Sabbath after the joyful occasion, and they should have the privilege of choosing the text.

"The espousal of the eldest daughter, Mary, arrived, and she was united to Mr. Cranch in the holy bonds of matrimony, with the approval, the blessing, and benedictions of her parents and her friends. Mr. Smith then said: 'My dutiful child, I am now ready to prepare your sermon; what text do you select for next Sunday?' 'My dear father,' said Mary, 'I have selected the latter part of the 42d verse of the 10th chapter of Luke: "Mary hath chosen that good part which shall never be taken from her."'

"'Very good, my daughter,' said her father, and so the sermon was preached.

"Mr. Adams persevered in his suit in defiance of all opposition. It was many years after and on a very different occasion, and in a resistance of very different opposition, that he was supposed to have uttered those memorable words, 'sink or swim, live or die, survive or perish, I give my heart and hand to this measure.' But, though the measures were different, the spirit was the same. Besides, he had already carried the main point of attack, the heart of the young lady, and he knew the surrender of the citadel must soon follow. After the usual hesitation and delay that attend such unpleasant affairs, Mr. Smith, seeing that resistance was fruitless, yielded the contested point with as much grace as possible, as many a prudent father has done before and since that time, and Mr. Adams was united to the lovely Miss Smith. After the marriage was over, and all things settled in quiet, Mrs. Adams said to her father: 'You preached Mary a sermon on the occasion of her marriage; won't you preach me one likewise?'

"'Yes, my dear girl,' said Mr. Smith; 'choose your text and you shall have your sermon?' 'Well,' said the daughter, 'I have chosen the 33d verse of the 7th chapter of Luke': "For John the Baptist came neither eating bread nor drinking wine, and ye say he hath a devil."'"

The old lady, my informant, looked me very archly in the face when she repeated this passage, and observed, "If Mary was the most dutiful daughter, I guess the other had the most wit."

I could not ascertain whether the last sermon was ever preached.

The integrity, conscientiousness and stern justice of John Quincy Adams were conspicuous in every station, and in the multiplied and responsible offices he filled. At the age of fifty-eight — the same with that of the first five Presidents of the United States when they entered on that office — he was inaugurated as President. With no partisan temper, he selected for his Cabinet men of different political opinions. He was too impartial in all things to secure his own re-election as the candidate of his party. While in Congress he espoused the cause of the freedom of the enslaved, and, with more and more decision and moral courage, battled for the "Right of Petition," on the side of Emancipation, to the last day of his long career in the National House of Representatives. For the whole fifty-three years of his public service, faithfulness was his motto; and when, in 1836, I saw him in his seat in that House, where he was always, early and late, at his post, I felt a reverence which no other moral hero of our whole country could awaken. The grandest historic citizen of America, it was a study to look at that venerable man in the House of Representatives in Washington, and think over the events of his long and distinguished life.

It was difficult to realize that he was nine years old when the Declaration of Independence was adopted; that he had gone abroad when a boy with his father, John Adams, and might have heard Chatham, Fox, Burke, and Sheridan in the British Parliament; that he had seen George the Third and most of the crowned heads and eminent statesmen who had lived in the preceding fifty years; that he had seen and conversed with Washington; had been intimate with Jefferson and Madison; had been Secretary of State to James Monroe; and finally, that he had been President of the United States.

On the day of his burial there might have been seen at the Capitol of this country, in which he died, February 23, 1848, a long funeral train, consisting of many of the wisest and ablest men in the land, following to the tomb the mortal remains of this great and good man. Eloquent voices had pronounced his eulogy on the floor of Congress, and the high and the honored accompanied his relics, as in one vast procession they were borne from city to city until they reached the metropolis of New England. All felt that a mighty man had fallen, and reverently assembled to pay their last tribute of respect to the memory of the dead. And then with solemn rites those relics were laid in their final resting-place in his native town, from which he had recently departed, never more to greet there those kindred and neighbors and friends, among whom he had passed, at intervals, more than fourscore years.

Under the portico of the new church, dedicated November 12, 1828, rest in a granite tomb, the remains of President John Adams and Abigail, his wife. The remains of President John Quincy Adams and his wife are deposited in the same place.

John Quincy Adams was a striking illustration of the continuous spirit of some of the best families of the Revolution. Born in the same town, and almost on the very spot of his father's birth, he once said of the old family house at Mount Wollaston: "It has a peculiar interest to me as the dwelling of my great-grandfather, Quincy, whose name I bear. He was dying when I was baptized, and his daughter, my grandmother, present at my birth, requested that I might receive his name. The fact, recorded by my father, has connected with that portion of my name a charm of mingled sensibility and devotion. It was the name of one passing from earth to immortality. These have been among the strongest links of my attachment to the name of Quincy, and have been to me through life a perpetual admonition to do nothing unworthy of it."

The lineage of this branch of the family is so exceptionally distinguished that I cannot forbear to give a few outlines of it. Their American progenitor was Henry Adams, who, in 1639, fled from oppression in England, and came to Mount Wollaston, the present town of Quincy, with eight sons, one of whom returned to England, four removed to Medfield and the neighboring towns, two to Chelmsford, and one became an original proprietor of the town of Braintree, incorporated in 1639. His great-grandson, John Adams, President of the United States, erected a monument to Henry Adams and his descendants, "from a veneration of the piety, humility, simplicity, prudence, patience, temperance, frugality, industry, and perseverance of his ancestors, in hope of recommending an imitation of their virtues to their posterity." How well did the spirit of this family shine forth, not only in their domestic relations, but still more brightly in their noble work as American patriots, in founding and preserving the free institutions of their country.

John Adams, second President of the United States, born in Braintree, now Quincy, October 19, 1735, married, October 25, 1764, Abigail Smith, daughter of the minister of Weymouth, a lady whose intellectual abilities, social virtues, domestic worth, and entire sympathy with her husband did much to enhance the lustre of his family. One of their children, — JOHN QUINCY ADAMS, named for his mother's grandfather, John Quincy, — was born July 11, 1767, and became the ornament and pride of the family. He married, July 27, 1797, Louisa Catherine, daughter of Mr. Joshua Johnson of Maryland, consul in France and afterward in England. They had several children, of whom CHARLES FRANCIS, born in Boston, August 18, 1807, alone survived his father. He was educated at the Latin School, and graduated at Harvard College in 1825. He studied law with Daniel Webster, and was admitted to the bar in 1828. In 1829 he married Abby Brooks, daughter of Hon. Peter C. Brooks, of Boston. In 1831 he was chosen Representative to the Massachusetts Legislature, which office he held three years, and the next two he was in the Senate. In 1848 he was candidate for Vice President, with Martin Van Buren as candidate for President. He has been a contributor to the North American Review and Christian Examiner; and edited the writings of his grandfather John Adams in ten volumes, the first entitled "Life of John Adams." He also edited the writings of his father, John Quincy

Adams. He was minister at the Court of St. James, and distinguished by his wisdom and discretion, respected alike by his own country and England, at the trying period of our Civil War. He was a member and President of the Board of Overseers of Harvard College, President of the American Academy of Arts and Sciences, and is a member of the Massachusetts Historical Society and other literary associations. In 1864 he received from Harvard College the degree of LL. D., and that of D. C. L. in England. His taste and culture are shown in his library, one of the richest private collections in the country, numbering some 20,000 volumes.

Having been with him three years in Harvard College, and since enjoyed his acquaintance, it has given me pleasure to witness his course, marked by the traits of his wise, patriotic, and renowned ancestry.

It is a privilege to have spent even a single day under the roof of that venerable house in Quincy occupied by the generations of such distinguished men. What an array of talent and official eminence has gone forth from that spot! Two Presidents of the United States of America; three Ministers to the Court of that nation who claims to rule the seas, and on the sound of whose drumbeat the sun never sets; and two Ministers to that Power who, with her millions upon millions of people, and almost limitless territory, is perhaps alone feared at the Court of St. James.

Another member of this honored family, foremost among the patriots of his country, whose faith in free institutions prompted him to be ever active in promoting its liberties, himself "organizing the Revolution," and who was, as has been truly said, "the personification of the American Revolution," was SAMUEL ADAMS.

The mightiest events in human history can often be traced to apparently the humblest beginning. It is not, perhaps, too much to say that Samuel Adams, James Otis, Joseph Murray, Paul Revere, and a few other kindred spirits, meeting day after day at the Green Dragon Tavern in Boston, did then and there, amid all the clouds and darkness and distress of the prospect, plan the gigantic enterprise of the American Revolution. It was Samuel Adams who moved at a town-meeting in Boston, October 28, 1771, that a Committee of Correspondence of twenty-one persons be chosen to assert, in the face of Great Britain, "the rights of the Colonists, and the infringements thereof."

The testimony of his kinsman, John Adams, who knew him thoroughly, and labored with him in the interests of freedom, should be imprinted on the nation's memory. "Samuel Adams was the father of the Revolution, and a man of steadfast integrity, exquisite humanity, genteel erudition, engaging manners, real as well as professed piety, and a universal good character."

Language like what Webster ascribed to John Adams, his relative, Samuel Adams actually used: "We will submit to no tax. We will take up arms, and shed our last drop of blood, before the King and the Parliament shall impose on us, or settle crown officers, independent of the colonial legislature, to dragoon us." His thirst for independence was branded by his Tory associates as an original sin. "This unhappy contest," he once said, "will end in issues of blood, but America may wash her hands in innocence."

I have before me a portrait, by Copley, of Samuel Adams at the age of forty-nine, which expresses all that is contained in the strong language of his relative. He is represented as of the ordinary height, of muscular form, erect in person, with light-blue eyes and light complexion. He wore a tie wig, cocked hat, and red cloak. He was a forcible speaker, his manner very serious; and he had a tremulous motion of the head, which gave emphasis to his speech and became associated with his eloquent voice. He voted in favor of adopting the Constitution, although in politics he opposed the administration. At the age of seventy-two, May 1794, he was elected Governor of Massachusetts and remained in office three years. By his pen, his tongue, and, best of all, his example, he then, as before, did all in his power to establish the principles of the Revolution, and staked everything dearest to him upon its issues.

Samuel and John Adams, illustrious fellow-laborers in the Revolution, had the same great-grandfather, an emigrant from England and a son of Henry Adams. Samuel Adams was born in Boston, September 27, 1722, of a renowned family in that town, and he died there October 2, 1803, at the age of eighty-one.

My personal interest in this family is enhanced from the several circumstances that he, with John Hancock, was proscribed from the offer of pardon to all rebels in this country, made in 1775 by General Gage; and that, being with Hancock, on the Provincial Committees of Safety and Supplies, at Wetherby's Black Horse Tavern in Menotomy, the eighteenth of April 1775, they fled the evening before the Battle to my native town, Lexington, for safety; and that it was on a hill familiar to my boyhood that he uttered to his companion John Hancock, while they were on their escape from the British troops, as they saw the sun rise on the memorable nineteenth of April, 1775, that immortal sentence: "What a glorious morning this is for America."

By a singular good fortune there came into my hands certain memorials of the family of Mr. Adams, in the form of personal expenditures, worthy of a permanent record. I am permitted by a descendant of William Donnison, executor of the will of Samuel Adams, dated December 29, 1790, to give the following receipts to the public.

It has been truly said that Samuel Adams, with all his power and patriotism and eloquence, both by pen and voice, "was no man of business." This was indicated in his boyhood, when, being placed with a merchant, he did not succeed. The story is circulated that he was once taken from the hands of a sheriff by his friend John Hancock. It is certain that at his death he left real estate of a moderate value, and personal property, according to the inventory, worth only $665.70. The following is the receipt of earliest date before me : —

The estate of the late Hon. S. Adams to Charles Jarvis, to visits and attendance on the family in eight years $150

BOSTON, Oct. 14, 1803.

Received the above in full of all demand of John Avery, esq., attorney to the executrix Mrs. Elizabeth Adams.

CHARLES JARVIS.

This charge for eight years, — a mysterious delay, — of medical attendance on a whole family, is extremely low, owing probably to one or both of two causes, — either the remarkable health of the family or great consideration and kindness on the part of the physician. When we remember that in those days medicine was usually furnished by the doctor and included in his bill, the charge appears marvellously small.

The next receipt is as follows : —

BOSTON, October 6th, 1803.
The Estate of his Honner
Samuel Addams Late Governor Deceas^d
To Henry Lane . . Dr.
For the Interment of his Boddy
to Cash pay^d the Sextons . . . $12
to horse hir and expences out of town   5
to Opening the tomb Use of Pall to-
gather with my attendance . . 13
                                      ―――
                                      $30
Received payment of Mrs. Elizth Adams Execut^x to the above Estate
                                HENRY LANE.

The charges in this account, if estimated in the metallic currency of that period, appear high, but if reckoned by the paper values of the day they were not unreasonable.

The tax bill of the same year is interesting, as showing the valuation of Mr. Adams's property, with certain customs then prevalent.

Ward No. 11.
To SAM^{EL} ADAMS Esqr.

Your Commonwealth Tax.		Your Town and County Tax.	
	Doll's. Cts.		Doll's. Cts.
Poll,	27	Poll,	1. 48
Real Estate,	2. 76	Real Estate,	16. 56
Personal Estate, Income &c. }	3.	Personal Estate, Income &c. }	18.
	6. 03		36. 4
			6. 3
			42. 7

You will please to notice, that by paying the above Tax in Thirty Days from this date, there will be made a

Discount of *Five per Cent.* and within Sixty Days *Three per Cent.* and within One Hundred and Twenty Days *Two per Cent.* and, if not paid within Six Months, Prosecution will ensue.

Errors excepted.   BENJAMIN SUMNER, Collector.

BOSTON, Octr. 1803.

Several questions here arise. On what scale was the Poll tax assessed? And for what number of persons? Who were the separate owners of the Real Estate? Mr. Adams's Personal Estate was valued after his death, as we have seen, at only $665.70, and his income is known to have been very small. Could the tax on the above sum have been, with that on his income, so little as $3 in the one column, or so great as $18 in the other? And yet on the back of the bill we find this endorsement: —

Amount,	$42.07
Discount,	2.10
	$39.97

Nov. 16, 1803.

Rec^d for BENJ^N SUMNER Collct.

$39. 97 JA^s SUMNER.

This shows that the bill was paid in thirty days, and apparently without objection, as it bears the further indorsement " paid by Mrs. Adams."

Mrs. Adams died in 1808, at the age of seventy-four. After this the following bill was rendered and paid : —

The Estate of Mrs Eliza[th] Adams Dec[d]
to Samuel Danforth Dr.
1808 To a visit on Consultation Jany 18, . $5
    To Ditto in March 3
                                        ———
                                         $8

BOSTON, July 11, 1809.

Received payment of the above act
                            SAMUEL DANFORTH.

These charges appear, in our day, exceedingly low. A few persons still living may recollect the name and reputation of Dr. Danforth. He was a very skilful physician, but quite brusque and eccentric in his manners and conversation. Being consulted once as to his opinion of the best way of preparing cucumbers for the table, he replied: "Pare them nicely, cut them into thin slices, put on a good quantity of pepper, and then — give them to the hogs."

Among the legacies in the will of Mrs. Adams, dated December 15, 1807, are the following: "To Mr. William Donnison I give $200, and to his wife $10, to buy a ring." This testimonial of regard to Mr. Donnison was doubtless made from his refusing any compensation for his long and faithful services both to Mrs. Adams and her distinguished husband. The gift of a ring was a very frequent bequest in those days, and the price was almost uniformly fixed at ten dollars.

Mr. Adams had the fortune to be strangely misunderstood abroad. As an illustration of the errors and misstatements of the English, we read in one of our journals of that time: —

An extraordinary compliment to Samuel Adams, at the expense of his kinsman John Adams, appears in the London Morning Post, of 1779. "The dismission of John Adams from the rebel embassy at the court of Versailles indicates a decline of the influence of the northern faction, and bodes no good to American independence. John Adams is the kinsman and creature of Samuel Adams, the Cromwell of New England, to whose intriguing arts the declaration of independence is in a great measure to be attributed."

What a relief it must have given to those who credited this and similar language to read in the same paper, shortly after, that the downfall of this tyrant — perhaps we should say his political suicide — had actually been accomplished: —

November 12, 1779. — This day, being Sunday, the famous Samuel Adams read his recantation of heresy, after which he was present at Mass, and we hear will soon receive priests' orders to qualify him for a member of the American Sorbonne.

Many anecdotes, illustrating the customs of his day, might be cited from the Journal of Samuel Adams. One day, on his journey to Congress, he dined, he tells us, in Orange County, New Jersey — this was in 1777 — at a Mr. Brewster's, grandson of one of the adventurers at Plymouth. "The manners of the family," he says, "were exactly like those of New England people; a decent grace before and after meat; fine pork and beef, and cabbage and turnips."

Of the five delegates appointed in June, 1774, by the General Court, to attend the Continental Congress in Philadelphia, two were Samuel Adams and John Adams. The different economic habits of these two men are seen in the following slight incident. Mr. Samuel Adams, in rendering his account of expenses in a bill directed to the Colony of Massachusetts Bay, inserts this item, "For three months' shaving and dressing, one hundred and seventy-five pounds," which was duly paid; while Mr. John Adams, in a very long list of charges, makes no mention of any sum due him for " shaving and dressing."

THE OLD SOUTH CHURCH.

CHAPTER IV.

QUINCY FAMILY.

A PERSONAL acquaintance with HON. JOSIAH QUINCY, son of the patriot, Josiah Quincy Jr., especially during his presidency of Harvard College, leads me to devote a few pages to his prolonged and distinguished life, and that of members of his family.

Mr. Quincy's name stands in a long line of men, prominent in American history. Edmund Quincy, of Wigsthorpe, Northampshire, England, married Ann Palmer, October 15, 1593. Their son Edmund was baptized May 30, 1602. He married, July 14, 1623, Judith Pares.

Edmund and Judith Quincy came from England in the reign of Charles I., to escape persecution. They reached Boston, September 4, 1633; he was made Freeman in 1633. In 1634 he was chosen Assessor, and in May, the same year, was Representative to the First Colonial General Court, and on a committee to purchase the peninsula Shawmut of Mr. "Blaxton." He had an allotment for a farm at Rumney Marsh, December 4, 1635, and was among the first to receive from Boston, in 1635, a grant of land, afterward called the "Quincy Home," at Mount Wollaston. Soon after he died, at the early age of thirty-three years; yet he had already been one of the first Representatives in the General Court of the Province. He led the way of a long line of descendants—magistrates, judges, and officers civil and military. It was with this line that, subsequently, the patriot Hancock became connected by marriage.

Mr. Hancock was familiar in the Clark Mansion, at Lexington, partly doubtless from his engagement to a connection of that family. Their marriage is thus recorded in a New York journal, dated September 4, 1775:

August 28th, was married at the seat of Thaddeus Burn, Esqr., at Fairfield, Connecticut, by the Rev. Andrew Elliot, the Hon. John Hancock, Esq., President of the Continental Congress, to Miss Dorothey Quincy, daughter of Edmund Quincy, Esq., of Boston. A brave Roman purchased a field in a certain territory near Rome, which Hannibal was besieging confident of his success. Equal to the conduct of that illustrious citizen was the marriage of the Hon. John Hancock, who, with his amiable lady, has paid as great a compliment to American valor, and discovered equal patriotism, by marrying now, while all the Colonies are as much convulsed as Rome when Hannibal was at her gates.

Edmund, son of Edmund, born in England in 1627, came to Mount Wollaston, and settled there on his father's estate. In 1670-3-5, and in 1681, he was Representative to the General Court. He died March 15, 1697. He had two sons, Edmund

JOHN HANCOCK.

and Josiah. His son Edmund was born in Braintree, October, 1681, graduated at Harvard College in 1699, and was Judge of the Supreme Court of the province; he died in London February 23, 1738, aged fifty-six years. The inventory of his estate, goods and chattels, valued at £2073 12s. contained "housing, outbuildings, and Farm he lived on, valued at £1400; Moore Farm and housing upon it, £200; one negro man and a woman and 3 boys, £100; Plate, £44; 1 Pair silk curtains, £2 10s; 70 sheep, £24; 8 cows, £24; 4 steers and 3 heifers, £19 10s. = £67 10s. besides 8 yearling calves and 3 horses, value, £15."

It was in honor of Colonel Josiah Quincy, who occupied the Mount Wollaston farm, and in 1670, built a house upon it, that the town of Quincy received its name. He was distinguished as the Representative of that place in 1717, 1719, 1722, 1729, and 1741, and was Speaker of the House in 1729 and 1741. The people of this town, under the lead of the Quincys and many of their stamp, were hopeful and far-reaching in their anticipations, and in their straits they aided the colonies in establishing free schools, and in founding the college at Cambridge; and, impelled and directed by their broad and spiritual faith, they built churches and worshipped, one and all, in them.

The second tomb built in the old cemetery of Quincy, Massachusetts, in 1699, was that of Edmund Quincy. Fairfield's Diary has this record in regard to his burial there: —

January 10, 1697-8. Helped dig Mr. Quincy's grave. Frost is one and near two feet thick.

January 11, made an end of digging, bricked the grave, weather warm. [This must have been an old fashioned "January thaw."]

September 16, 1699. I carted stone for Mr. Quincy's tomb.

To us it seems almost incredible, with our care for the resting-places of the dead, that this ancient cemetery, like many others of that period, should have been left uninclosed and used as a pasture for cattle. Yet so it was for more than a century and a half, until a few reverent spirits in 1809, — among them was Josiah Quincy, — raised by subscription one hundred and fifty dollars, with which they purchased of certain others the right of herbage and pasturage in the cemetery. This privilege was afterward presented, with a deed, to the inhabitants of Quincy, on condition that no " horse or cattle of any description shall be allowed to run at large in the cemetery, a fence shall be maintained around it," and, with what to us seems a singular provison, " no trees shall be permitted to grow within the said ground."

Edmund Quincy had a son Daniel, whose only son John Quincy, born 1689, was great-grandfather of John Quincy Adams, who derived his name from him. He was Speaker of the House of Representatives, and was a member of the Council forty successive years.

In 1675 we find in the will of Leonard Hoar,

third President of Harvard College, the following item: "I give to my dear sisters, Flint and Quincey, each a black serge gown." This latter lady must have been the wife of Colonel Edmund Quincy, who, with "other principal gentlemen and gentlewomen of the Town of Boston," attended at "Brantry," May 25, 1723, the funeral of the widow of President Hoar.

Josiah Quincy, youngest son of Edmund, was born in Braintree in 1710, and graduated at Harvard College in 1728. He died in Braintree 1784. Edmund, eldest son of Josiah, was born in Braintree in October, 1733, and graduated at Harvard College in 1752. He died at sea, March 1768, aged thirty-five. JOSIAH QUINCY, Jr. was born in Boston, February 23, 1744; he graduated at Harvard College in 1763; studied law, and was eminent in the practice of it. He took a firm and bold stand as a writer and actor in the cause of his country's freedom. Ill health compelled him to go abroad to England, where he labored for his native land. He was returning home to work heart and hand for her independence, but died near the coast, April 26, seven days after the Battle of Lexington. His last prayer was for his country, and his name is immortalized among those who laid the foundation of her liberty and the cause of freedom throughout the civilized world.

JOSIAH QUINCY was the only child of Josiah Quincy Jr., the Patriot, living at his father's death. His widowed mother believed it her duty to send

6

him at the age of six to Phillips Academy in Andover. When he was censured or punished he found rest for his sorrow and tears in the home of his good friend Rev. Mr. French. He describes the old meeting-house in Andover : " A three-story building, with two tiers of galleries, and the tything-man with his long pole, with which he would rap on the wall ever and anon, to the terror of mischievous boys and sleeping elders." He spoke often of the kindness of Mr. French at this time.

Rev. Jonathan French, of South Parish, Andover, who was distinguished for his self-sacrificing patriotism. heard of the Battle of Bunker Hill, Sunday morning. and started for the battle-field with musket in hand, and his case of surgeon's instruments and medicines, — the clergy were sometimes half physicians in those days,— and no doubt, as became a minister, with his Bible also. He rendered valuable aid that day, caring for the wounded, and administering comfort and consolation, physical and spiritual.

When his meeting-house was remodelled in 1821, stoves were put in. It had previous to this a Noon House, where distant members ate their luncheon, and in winter warmed themselves and filled their footstoves, for afternoon service in the cold meeting-house, with live coals from the great wood fires, blazing at both ends of the house.

My first direct knowledge of Mr. Quincy was on the visit of Lafayette to this country in 1824. Being then Mayor of Boston, he accompanied the

QUADRANGLE, HARVARD COLLEGE.

nation's illustrious guest when he visited Cambridge, and did the honors of his office there, as in his own city, with that dignity and patriotic affection which became the occasion. He was then fifty-one years of age, a fine figure, his face indicating a mind which combined a Roman gravity with an Attic wit, and in society he had a fascinating smile. Harvard College honored him this year, 1824, by conferring upon him the degree of LL. D., an honor which he amply repaid by his long and distinguished services as president of that institution, commencing in 1829, and continuing until 1845.

During this period I was brought into official and personal relations with Mr. Quincy. As president of the college he became one of the trustees of the Hopkins Classical School in Cambridge, of which body, as chairman of the school committee, I was also a member. He paid me also the unsought, long-continued honor of a place on committees for examining the students in college, an office quite different, as regards the frequent association of its incumbents, from that bearing the same name now. He called at my residence, then in Cambridgeport, to ask if I would accept the position. A carriage was sent on each day of examination to bring the members of the committee to the college, and one was provided for such as desired it to take them home. We were invited to a dinner, at which always the professor whose department we had visited, and often other committees, with the instructors in their several branches, were present. President Quincy invariably attended the examinations, and was with us as the host at the dinner table. His manner on these occasions was cordial, courteous, and affable. I recollect many striking and facetious remarks of his which space forbids me to relate. The country was then agitated deeply on the subject of slavery. On one occasion Dr. Rufus P. Stebbins had the day previous preached in the College Chapel a sermon on the text: "Whosoever committeth sin is the servant of sin." "The emancipation spoken of yesterday morning," said the President "was one of whose need we all agree, whatever we may think of negro emancipation."

Mr. Quincy's residence was in the old Wadsworth Mansion, where the presidents of that period lived. There we were always welcomed, not only by the host, but by his gracious companion. It would be unjust to history to pass unobserved the memory of her who partook with Mr. Quincy in his spirit, and adorned her station at his side, whether in the social circles of Boston, or in the literary atmosphere of Cambridge. I cannot recall her presence, her personal dignity and attractiveness, without a sense of our obligations to her on her own merits, and as a representative of that sex to whose signal patriotism, back to the earliest American history, we are so much indebted. Be it a legend or be it truth — and I think the latter is the probability — it was fitting that a woman's foot should be the first that pressed the rock of Plymouth, at the landing of the noble company who, in faith, fortitude, and affection, began here the glorious work of God and man in the great cause of civil and religious liberty. It was a presage of the heroic spirit and self-denying and adventurous labors of that sex in all our subsequent history. How often, by her tender care of the suffering, and her sharing in all the perils and privations of the times, woman rendered a service to the country never yet fully appreciated.

The devoted wife of John Adams was a right arm of strength to her illustrious husband, in every hour where sound judgment as well as untiring affection could minister to his necessities. Her invaluable "Letters" show both a wisdom and a patriotism not eclipsed by the brightest records of woman's influence in history, ancient or modern.

We extol the Father of our Country in unmeasured terms, but no pen, I believe, has yet given a true and just picture of the influence on our national destinies of Mary the mother and Martha the wife of Washington; of the latter of whom Mr. Quincy says, commenting on her matronly beauty, and her services to her husband and her country: " Of her it might be as truly said as ever it could be of woman — she was of her own sex the glory, and of the other the admiration."

Mrs. Quincy was a model in hospitality, and her genial smile and courteous manner made their weekly receptions most agreeable, not only to the officers of the college, but to the students at large. In this regard, as in others, Mr. Quincy's was a joyous administration. After long years of regret at the single life of his predecessor, good Dr. Kirkland, we were delighted to meet our esteemed and cordial president, surrounded by a family circle so cultivated and honored.

An extraordinary energy pervaded the whole character and life of Mr. Quincy; whatever his hand found to do he did with his might. This trait was seen in his emphatic mode of conversation. I often noticed a reaction of this intensity. He would express himself with great clearness and force, and, notwithstanding he was a thorough gentleman and full of courtesy, he would in a few moments — even while one perhaps was responding to his words — from the power of his temperament, be sometimes lost in oblivion, and, seeming unable to resist the tendency, even close his eyes as if overtaken by sleep.

To this peculiar temperament, I think, was owing in part his occasional lapse of memory. He often forgot the names of those he knew perfectly well, even of college students, whom he wished specially to address aright. The story was told, probably without a sure foundation, that he went one day to the Cambridge post-office for his mail, and, upon his asking if there were any letters for him, the clerk, being that day a new-comer in the office, asked, "For what name, sir?" "For what name,"

Mr. Quincy replied, " you know me of course." In his absence of mind, as the story went, he for the moment actually forgot his own name. Turning away he was met by a friend who thus accosted him : " Good-morning, Mr. Quincy." "Ah, Quincy," said he, returning to the clerk, " are there any letters for Mr. Quincy?" I think those who had known and enjoyed the benefit of the remarkable memory for names of his predecessor, Dr. Kirkland, liked to repeat, and would sometimes exaggerate, anecdotes of this kind.

The industry of this rare man was as remarkable as his intellect and eminent virtues. I remember in a conversation upon the dangers and evils of the prevalent excessive reading of newspapers, he once said : " For myself, I devote but ten minutes a day to the papers." Perhaps this will appear to many a meagre allotment of time for such reading. But it reveals that marvellous economy of time which enabled him, not only to read so many solid books, but to write volume upon volume himself, in addition to his practical labors, as a lawyer from 1793, as a business man, the discharge of his manifold offices as representative in the State and National legislatures, on the bench as mayor for six years of a rapidly growing city, for sixteen years as president of Harvard College, beside working elsewhere in the cause of education, and in many other distinguished and useful occupations.

I well remember the joy we felt when it was known that Mr. Quincy had been elected to preside over our beloved university. He was a man eminently marked for the position. The financial affairs of the institution needed, many thought, a practical man at its head, some said a layman. Here was one whose ability, as well as experience, fitted him for the exigency. Certain reforms in the administration of the college were called for. He had the energy, united with the good judgment, required for the place. His interest in education, and the work he had done for it in the case of the public schools, no less than his own culture and literary attainments, pointed to him as the best candidate for this office. He had exhibited both social and moral traits which fitted him for this place. In his relations to other public men he had shown an elevated spirit. A marked trait of Mr. Quincy had been his magnanimity. For example: toward Harrison Gray Otis, in their lives both friends and rivals, he had always maintained a noble attitude. After his success over Mr. Otis in their opposition as candidates for the mayoralty, he said at a public political meeting, in the presence of Mr. Otis, that his own election over his opponent was after all a compliment to Mr. Otis: "It demonstrated the conviction, on the part of our fellow-citizens, that to degrade Mr. Otis by such a comparatively subordinate office would be like making a common drag-chain of a diamond necklace."

When he came to the college and gave his inaugural address, we saw that wisdom was to be justified by her own children, by this faithful son of Harvard. The transition from the mayoralty of Boston to the academic seclusion of the college grounds was well portrayed, in his fine Latin inaugural Address, as a passage, "ex pulvere ac strepitu urbis" from the tumult of the one place to the quiet of the other, to his noiseless and comparatively retired home. I was struck in his address that day with the same Roman vigor and classical and lucid terseness which had marked all his public literary and civic productions. Among these was his memorable oration of the Fourth of July, 1826, delivered before the city authorities of Boston. He was then in his prime, about fifty-four years old, at which time Stuart painted a portrait of him, which combines the fire of the patriot with the mental strength and moral beauty of the man. In this address he spoke in an eloquent strain of "John Adams, that eminent citizen of Boston, that patriarch of American independence, of all New England's worthies on this day the sole survivor." By a coincidence, rare in all human history, while Mr. Quincy was uttering his noble testimonial to the aged patriot, that man was fast sinking in the arms of death. The venerable ex-President was still alive, but before the festivities of the day were over, his spirit had passed away.

Those same qualities characterized his subsequent able and patriotic oration at the second centennial celebration in Boston, September 17, 1830. His experience and success as Mayor of

Boston naturally turned all eyes toward Mr. Quincy as the fit orator on that occasion. The commemoration took place appropriately in the Old South Church. A poem was read by Charles Sprague, and an ode contributed by John Pierpont, then minister of Hollis Street Church. The Mayor, Harrison Gray Otis, and the Aldermen and Common Council met for the first time in their several rooms in the Old State House, afterward the City Hall. They subsequently convened in the Common Council Chamber, where the Mayor delivered an address of some length. The City Government then moved to the State House, where a procession was formed, under the direction of General William Sullivan, Chief Marshal of the day. It included the Historical Society and other historical and literary associations. The procession, under the escort of the Ancient and Honorable Artillery Company, moved down Beacon Street, entered the Common, and passed through two lines containing several thousand children of the public schools, and, marching through the chief streets of the city, arrived at the Old South Church. I thought Mr. Quincy appeared that day at his best. Although his oration occupied two hours, its great interest commanded the close attention of the crowded audience who heard it. While listening to the oration of his great-grandson, Josiah Quincy, on commencement day, at his graduation from Harvard College in 1880, I was reminded of the noble figure, the resonant voice, the

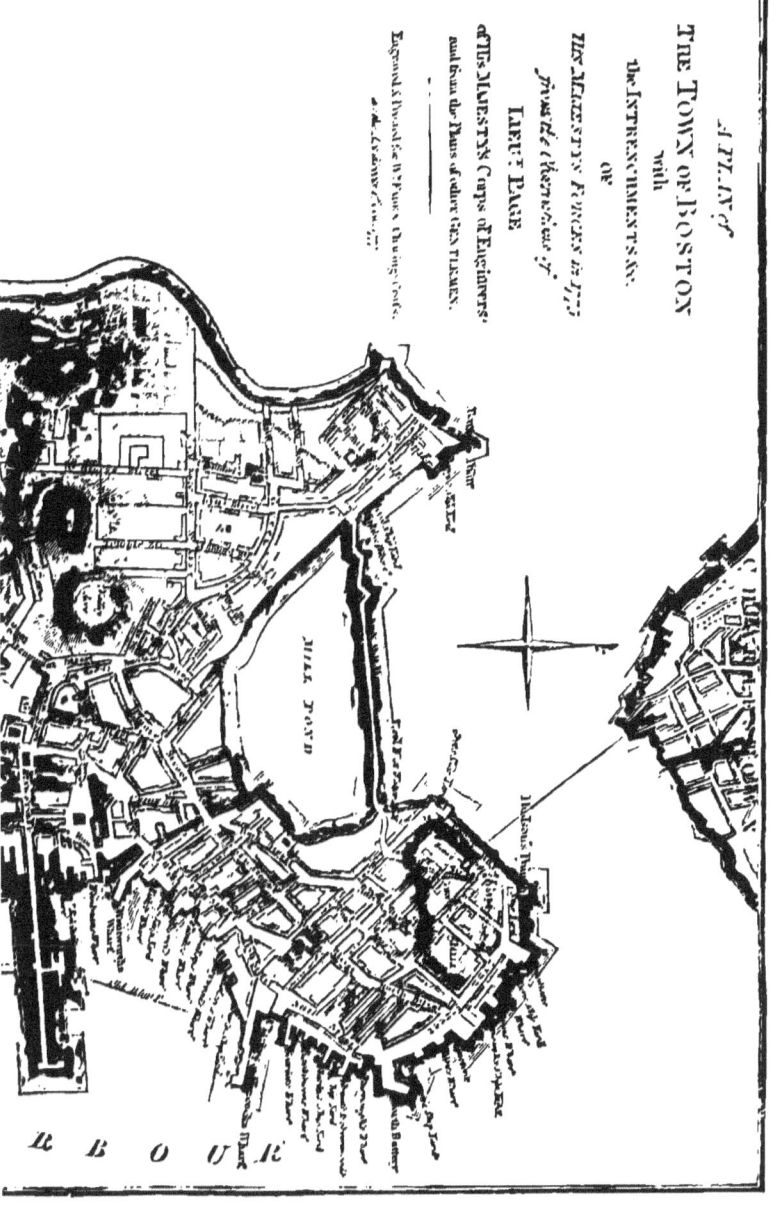

eloquent and high-toned principles of his distinguished grandparent, and of the noble patriotism of the long line of Quincys.

In Mr. Quincy's brief speech at the dinner table after the re-interment, April 19, 1835, of the men killed in the Battle of Lexington, whose remains at this time, after an eloquent address by Edward Everett, were placed in a sarcophagus under the monument in that town, I was impressed with his earnest, though modest and dignified manner, and his spirit so in harmony with that of the protomartyrs whom we that day commemorated. By request I had prepared the sentiment intended to draw from him what followed. It was in these words : —

Josiah Quincy, Junior, who died April 26, 1775, among the first-born of the champions of American Liberty: like the martyrs whose memory we this day venerate, he saw but the dawn of that light he prized higher than life. "His sons come to honor, but he knoweth it not." Peace to his ashes!

Mr. Quincy, then President of Harvard College, being called upon for a sentiment, remarked that, after what had been said by distinguished gentlemen, in the church and at the table, it would not be expected of him that he should make a display or a speech. It was a time for feeling, — a time for thought, — not a moment to applaud; he should, therefore, simply reciprocate the sentiment of the chair: "The town of Lexington — where brave men are raised, and brave men honored."

The patriotism of Mr. Quincy shone out on every occasion suited to call it forth. He was filled with the spirit of the Revolution. It will be remembered that when the signers of the Declaration of Independence met for that momentous service, John Hancock said, as he affixed to it, the first in order, his own name: "We must be unanimous; we must hang together." "Yes," said Franklin, " or hang separately." I heard President Quincy, at a public dinner, give this sentiment, which was received with unbounded enthusiasm: "The times of the Revolution, when the only question was — shall we hang together, or hang separately."

His characteristic energy and wisdom were manifested during his whole administration of the college. He held personal intercourse with the students. He reformed the state of the Commons, made the fare of the students better, and thus broke up that old source of rebellions among the classes. The studies became more systematic, and electives began to take the place of compulsory work. The College was expanded to a University; the Law School was reorganized; Gore Hall was built, and the Library enlarged and made more secure from fire; an Observatory was established, and the quickened movements in other directions justified the subsequent remark of President Walker that " Mr. Quincy was the Great Organizer of the University."

Mr. Quincy, in speaking of the class of 1790, of Harvard College, of which he was a member, and its first scholar, says: "The most talented, taking light literature as the standard, was Joseph Dennie. His imagination was vivid, and he wrote with great ease and felicity." It was, I think, at this time that, although Mr. Dennie resided in Boston, he frequently visited Lexington, and he and my father, of about the same age, became acquainted with each other. I often heard him speak of Joseph Dennie as a delightful companion, full of mirth and repartee; his society was most agreeable to one of the same facetious disposition. He was a perfect gentleman, and attracted great interest among the ladies of that quiet town. I believe he married one of these his youthful associates.

Knowing well Mr. Quincy's public course in subsequent years, I can readily conceive his friendship in youth for those noble men of Boston, Samuel Dexter, George Cabot, Fisher Ames, Harrison Gray Otis, the Lowells, (father and son), Theophilus Parsons, John Adams and his eminent son, John Quincy Adams, and others of their circle. One who knew him later, and witnessed his Christian principle and rare magnanimity, cannot question that, in the heat of party strife, when the last named of this bright train left the Federal ranks, in which he and Mr. Quincy had always been the closest friends, Mr. Quincy wrote of his companion to his own wife: "I am glad you enter into no asperities such as you hear upon the character of John Quincy Adams. He has just as good a right to his sentiments as I have to mine. He differs from his political friends, and is abused. Let us not join in the contumely. It can do us no good, and may do him some hurt." He could not always agree with Mr. Adams in his public course, but when he had been stricken down at the Capitol, and was no more, how touching and noble were these words taken from his daily journal: —

February 25, 1848. — I have to record the loss of the friend of my youth, of my manhood, and of my old age, John Quincy Adams — on the spot where his eloquence had often triumphed, and where his varied powers were so often shown, and are now acknowledged. Friend of my life, farewell! I owe you for many marks of favor and kindness. Many instances of your affection and interest for me are recorded in my memory, which death alone can obliterate.

The interest of Mr. Quincy in the Antislavery cause, partly for its dangers to our national liberties, began in his early life. While in the Massachusetts Senate, 1804-5, he took part in a movement for eliminating from the National Constitution the article which permitted the Slave States to count three fifths of their slaves as a part of their basis of representation. He more than once said to friends in conversation, in presence of one of his sons: "You and I may not live to see the day, but before that boy is off the stage, he will see this country torn in pieces by the fierce passions which are now sleeping." So true were the prophetic instincts of this great man in regard to the day and the scenes of our recent Civil War.

The services of this devoted man cannot easily be exaggerated. The nation owes him a large debt. While he was in Congress the country was distressed by measures of the Democratic administration creating commercial restrictions, by the embargo, and by our being plunged into war with Great Britain. Mr. Quincy, a warm Federalist, took his stand firmly as a bold and eloquent opponent of all these measures. He represented with decision the feelings and the judgment of his constituents. He drew up the strong address of the minority of Congress; and his speeches were delivered with that dignity, power, and point which we, who in subsequent years heard his voice at home, feel sure must have made a deep and — on all who were not arrayed against him by party hostility — a convincing impression. They are among the best political records of those eventful times. His broad and wise views, his mastery of all financial questions, his demand for a more perfect protection of our maritime rights, his just appreciation of our foreign relations, and the high-toned patriotism which pervaded his whole course, will excite the admiration of future generations. Among the very able men of those days he stood shoulder to shoulder, in counsel and in conduct, a peer of whom Rome or Sparta might have been proud.

During his Mayoralty in Boston, he was earnest

in every good work for the improvement of the city. He reorganized the Fire Department, established the House of Reformation for juvenile offenders, and the Girls' High School, under charge of Mr. Ebenezer Bailey; but the noblest of his benefactions was the erection of the great Quincy Market-house, at the cost, eventually, of three hundred thousand dollars.

He was indefatigable in the use of his strong and cultivated intellect in the production of several valuable works by his pen: the Life of his father, Josiah Quincy. Jr.; the History of the Boston Athenæum, 1851; the Life of Colonel Samuel Shaw; the Municipal History of Boston, in 1852; the Life of John Quincy Adams; and the elaborate and complete History of Harvard University, in two large volumes. It is not saying too much to affirm that no man, in the cluster of distinguished benefactors in our history, has combined in himself more rare excellences as a patriot, a statesman, a vigorous and classical writer, or broader views on the great subjects of education, philanthropy, social economy, and the wide financial and public good of the community, with a practical illustration of sound principles in their best action, than Josiah Quincy.

His personal character, not only intellectual, but moral and thoroughly Christian, will stand the test of history. Future generations will respond to the testimonial given by his cotemporaries, on the recommendation of Mayor Cobb, October 11, 1879, and from the fund left the city by Hon.

Jonathan Phillips — in the erection of that imposing statue in Boston, which will speak of his virtues to the eye that looks upon it, in the midst of the thronged city for whose welfare he labored so faithfully and with such success. And so of that other beautiful figure in Memorial Hall, Cambridge, which shows him in his office as the head of our University, an example and an inspiration to those who in coming years shall resort to its walls for literary instruction, and who will be sure to honor the place of their education if they carry from it the integrity, the earnestness, the patriotic and Christian virtues, which marked his character and will perpetuate his influence.

It is a remarkable circumstance that there have been six in this family named Josiah, several of them to be noticed for their ability and public services, and three at least very prominent. The oldest was born April 1, 1710. His son, Josiah Quincy, Jr., was born in February, 1744. His intense, almost agonized, spirit is embodied in the address of a Committee to the Provincial Congress, dated July 26, 1774, and written by their Chairman, Josiah Quincy, Jr., — the tone of which seems to resound along the illustrious line of that family: "You, gentlemen, our friends, countrymen, and benefactors, may possibly look toward us at this great crisis. We trust that we shall not be left of Heaven to do anything derogatory to our common liberties, unworthy the fame of our ancestors, or inconsistent with our former professions and conduct. To you we look for that wisdom, advice, and example, which, giving strength to our understanding and vigor to our actions, shall, with the blessing of God, save us from destruction."

In an edition of President Quincy's most valuable and interesting memoir of his father, which was prepared by his patriotic and gifted daughter, Miss Eliza S. Quincy, we have a note which exhibits an instance of the noble spirit of her father: —

Two thousand pounds sterling were bequeathed by the will of Mr. Quincy to Harvard College, in case his son should die a minor. His son lived and became president of the University in 1829, held that office sixteen years, and survived to the age of ninety-two years. Unwilling that the college should lose the bequest of his father, he gave, in 1848, ten thousand dollars, as an equivalent for the loss the institution had sustained by the continuance of his own life. He gave this donation to the publishing fund of the Observatory founded by his exertions during his presidency, and directed that the following sentence should be inscribed on the titlepage of every volume the expense of which was defrayed from this source: "Printed from funds resulting from the will of Josiah Quincy, who died April 26, 1775, leaving a name inseparably connected with the history of the American Revolution."

After a prolonged life of most active service to his country, to the interests of education, and, by his pen, to the cause of good letters, Mr. Quincy still showed his interest in the welfare of the college over which he had so long and so faithfully presided. The very last year of his life he attended its Commencement, and it was a touching spectacle to see that venerated man, disabled both by age and an unfortunate accident, supported by his eldest son, a model of filial respect and affection, as he entered the audience room. The vast company rose as one man, with a salutation that found expression in the heartiest applause; and we were thrilled, at the dinner table on that day, to hear the voice of the aged patriot still loyal to the memories of his best days.

"I want," said the sage, hero, and patriot within a few months of his death, " to live to see this War of the Rebellion through." But, although he was called to his reward before seeing that issue, dying July 1, 1864, it must have cheered his closing days to reflect that he had lived to see a grandson in that war, General Samuel M. Quincy, who served in it with distinction, and survived among those who received the honor and gratitude of the country they did so much to save.

I should do injustice to this family not to name, among its departed worthies, Edmund, son of President Quincy, born February 1, 1808, and graduated at Harvard College in 1827. An early advocate of the Antislavery cause, he never hesitated to speak and to act whenever he could advance its interests. Who that ever saw him can forget his noble figure, his benevolent face, the urbanity of his manner, and his pleasing address? I never conversed with him, I never saw him, without being reminded of his honored father.

His self-possession and dignity, his logical acumen, his union of sound sense with keen wit, were seen in public speech. In consecration to the great interests of liberty, in his manly defence of the humblest who needed its shield, in his literary culture, and his political and miscellaneous writings, especially in that model biography he has left us of his distinguished father, we have abundant materials for a respectful, pleasant, and never fading remembrance of him. We may well say of this, his closing production, breathing as it does the spirit of this grand old family, — whether we regard the writer or his subject, — the tribute of a worthy son to a worthy sire. We find his name in the old Massachusetts Antislavery Society, where he labored with zeal in its most trying period. The officers of that society were, for many years, Francis Jackson, president, Edmund Quincy, corresponding secretary, and Robert F. Walcott, secretary, and still living.

CHAPTER V.

LINCOLN FAMILY.

A PERSONAL acquaintance with many members of the large Lincoln family: with Luther B. Lincoln, as a schoolmate in the academy of Westford where I was prepared for college, a young man of most amiable and attractive qualities of character, who won "troops of friends" wherever he was known, who stood high as a scholar, was a pattern of application and earnestness in every literary pursuit, and successful afterward as a schoolteacher; with Rev. Calvin Lincoln, a cotemporary in the Christian ministry, whom I knew well as the secretary for some years of the American Unitarian Association, not less loved as a man than honored for his consecration to his work, his excellent judgment and practical ability in all business affairs; with my good friend, Hosea H. Lincoln, the friend of a whole generation passed by him at the head of one of our Boston schools; and with others whom my limits forbid me to name, — and, not least, the circumstance that of the stock of Thomas Lincoln "the husbandman" came my maternal grandmother, Rachel

Lincoln, who exhibited in herself the rare qualities of this good old lineage, in patriotic sympathy with her husband, a Revolutionary officer, her life spared to the advanced age of eighty-six, wise, dignified, beloved by the large circle of her kindred, and sought as a kind neighbor, an intelligent adviser, her hand as ready to help as her heart was to prompt it in daily offices of love and good-will, — all these associations make the writer deeply interested in this ancient family.

The origin of the Lincoln family can be traced back to the Countess of Lincoln, England, as early as 1619. Dr. Young in his " Chronicles of the Pilgrims," says : " The Lincolns had a more intimate connection with the New England settlements, and must have felt a deeper interest in their success, than any other noble house in England." This opinion is confirmed by Cotton Mather in his " Magnalia ;" he speaks of the family as " religious," and " the best family of any nobleman then in England."

Governor Dudley wrote to the Countess of Lincoln, from Newtowne (Cambridge), under date of March 28, 1631, in relation to recent losses by fire, and says, in " our new town, intended this summer to be builded, we have ordered that no man there shall build his chimney with wood, nor cover his house with thatch." It is fortunate, with our taste for genealogy, that we can go back to so early a date. We in the East do not sympathize in this respect with the habit of some other portions of the country. Abraham Lincoln, when in Boston, was questioned by some of the Lincoln family about his ancestry. "Well," he replied, "I don't know much about that; few people out West care to go any further back than their grandfathers."

Most of the early settlers of this country, named Lincoln, came from Norfolk County in England, and they were all more or less related to each other. They were then designated by their several occupations. Thus we have Thomas the Husbandman, Thomas the Weaver, Thomas the Miller, and Thomas the Cooper Of these Lincolns, Thomas the Weaver came from Hingham, Norfolk County, England, and his brother Samuel from Norwich, the chief town of the same County. Samuel came first to Salem, Massachusetts, and went thence to Hingham. Samuel had a son named Mordecai, born at Hingham in 1651; he settled in Scituate in 1700. Mordecai had a son named Jacob; Jacob had a son named Solomon.

Thomas the Husbandman came from Windham, Norfolk County in England, and settled in Hingham, Massachusetts. This town was named for Hingham, a market-town and parish in Norfolk County, England. Windham, five and a half miles west-northwest of Hingham, is now Wymondam, so called from a prominent family in the original place, named Wymond, the syllable *ham* signifying "home," the "home of the Wymonds." Hingham, Massachusetts, was formally settled September 18, 1635, by Rev. Peter Hobart and twenty-nine others who drew houselots on that day. Within three subsequent years large numbers were added to these, embracing, with the first comers, nearly all the old families which have been conspicuous in that town.

In 1638 Thomas the Husbandman, — made Freeman in 1637, — and Stephen his brother, — who also came from Windham, and went first to Salem, thence to Hingham, — received grants of houselots. Thomas the Husbandman has numerous descendants in Hingham, in the County of Worcester, and in other parts of Massachusetts. There are distinguished men of this family, who have rendered valuable services to their communities in civil and military offices.

Thomas the Husbandman, born probably in 1616, had four sons, Joshua, Thomas, Caleb and Luke.

Joshua, son of Thomas, was baptized May 3, 1645.

Thomas, son of Thomas, was born December 22, 1652.

Caleb, son of Thomas, born May 8, probably in 1654, married Rachel, daughter of James Bates. Their children were Joshua, Peter, Caleb, Jacob, Solomon, Thomas, and Ebenezer.

Luke, son of Thomas, born March 27, probably in 1698, in Scituate, removed to Leicester, where he held public office, being selectman in 1747; he married Lydia Loring, daughter of David Loring of Barnstable.

The children of Luke and Lydia (Loring) Lincoln were five in number.

(1) William was born May 23, 1738.

(2) Rachel, born August 7, 1741, married, January 21, 1768, Colonel Timothy Boutelle of Leominster.

(3) Loring, born May 6, 1744, married Dorothy Moore. They lived in Greenboro, Vermont. He was a captain in the battle of Bunker Hill, and was eight months in the Continental army.

(4) Lydia was born January 18, 1746.

(5) Mary, born October 10, 1754, married, in 1778, Asa Meriam of Oxford, Massachusetts. They had only one child. The town of Oxford is remarkable as the place in which, in 1636, thirty families of the Protestant refugees from France took up their residence, in consequence of the Revocation of the Edict of Nantes by Louis XIV. in 1634.

Stephen Lincoln, son of Stephen, who came from Windham, England, had only one son, Stephen. Stephen, son of Stephen, son of Stephen, had three sons: Stephen, born probably in 1666, who had a descendant in Hingham, Alexander Lincoln, who died October 7, 1879; David, born September 22, 1668; James, born October 26, 1681.

The descendants of Stephen Lincoln, brother of Thomas the Husbandman, many of whom are now (1882) living, have been confined largely to the limits of Hingham.

Isaac Lincoln, born Jan. 18, 1701–2, was a graduate of Harvard College in 1722, and for a long term of years a public school-teacher in Hingham.

Abner Lincoln, born July 7, 1766, was a graduate of Harvard College in 1788, and the first preceptor of Derby Academy. He was an accomplished scholar and a successful teacher.

Rev. Perez Lincoln, born February 9, 1767, was a graduate of Harvard College in 1795, and was a minister in Gloucester.

Rev. Calvin Lincoln, born in Hingham, November 1800, died September 11, 1881, aged eighty-one years and ten months. He fell from paralysis in his pulpit, and while in the act of devotion on the day set apart for prayers in behalf of President Garfield. He graduated at Harvard College in 1820; was minister at Fitchburg many years; resigned in 1855, and was Secretary of the American Unitarian Association a few years. He was afterward settled over the First Parish in Hingham — its church edifice being, it is said, the oldest still used for worship in this country, — and its sole pastor till his death, excepting three years, when Rev. Edward Augustus Horton was his colleauge. Beloved by all denominations and all classes, he had the reverence and confidence of all who knew him. He was a devout, earnest, and faithful minister, and the oldest living pastor in his denomination at the time of his death.

Hon. David Wilder, in his History of Leominster, says of Rachel Lincoln: " She was the wife of Colonel Timothy Boutelle of this town, a daughter of Captain Luke Lincoln of Leicester, and her genealogy may be traced back to a near relationship with the late distinguished General Lincoln of Hingham." This is unquestionably true. Although all the Lincolns did not come from the same town, Hingham, in England, they did come from the same county, Norfolk, and were living but a few miles from each other at the time of their emigration to this country. Their family attachments have always been strong from the earliest accounts we have of them. They all clustered in a near neighborhood to each other in the Old World, there is the best reason to believe, as they have in the New. Their characteristics have borne in every branch of the family a striking resemblance. Friends of good learning, a large number of them have been graduates of Harvard and other colleges,—patrons and earnest supporters of our public schools and academies, and men of high principles, public-spirited and uniformly patriotic. It is but justice to dwell on individuals who have honored the name.

Our subject leads us to speak of BENJAMIN LINCOLN of Revolutionary fame. His military career stands out brightly in the annals of that war which established our national independence. His father held a colonel's commission in England. The son was born in Hingham, January 24, 1733, and died May 9, 1810, aged seventy-seven years. His direct ancestor, Thomas Lincoln the Cooper, came from Hingham in England to Hingham in Massachusetts in 1636. Benjamin Lincoln was a farmer until forty years old. He held many civil offices, and was a major-general of the State militia early in the Revolution.

At the time of the battle of Bunker Hill, General Lincoln led a company, although not its commissioned captain, from Hingham to that vicinity.

An incident shows the deplorable destitution of some of our men at that period. On his return home, Israel Beal, Chairman of the Committee of Public Safety in Hingham, said to him: "Well, General, did you see the red-coats?" "Yes," was the reply. "Did ye get a shot at 'em?" "No." "Well, it seems to me, General, I would have got one shot at 'em." "The fact is, Mr. Beal," said Lincoln, " we had no ammunition."

Lincoln was in 1776 a brigadier-general, and soon after was made a major-general in the Continental army; he joined Gates's command, opposed Burgoyne's advance, and aided in his final defeat and capture, and held many important commands during his long service. From his sound judgment, cautious, yet brave, determined, and indefatigable, he secured in a marked degree the confidence of Washington. In the battle of Bemis's Heights he received a wound in his right leg, which eventually rendered it two inches shorter than the other, caused him great suffering, and compelled him to walk lame the remainder of his life.

In September, 1778, he was placed at the head of the Southern Army, with 1100 men. At Fort Moultrie he was compelled to surrender; but although unsuccessful also in the attack on Savannah and the defence of Charleston, he had through the whole campaign the confidence of Washington, of Congress, of the army, and all the patriotic men of the South. He possessed wit as well as wisdom. While on the Savannah River, two ropes having been broken in the attempt to hang a deserter of his command, Lincoln, when applied to for directions, replied, "Let him go; I always thought he was a scape-gallows."

After the siege of Yorktown, in 1781, having had a full share in the operations at that place, he, in common with Lafayette and Steuben, was publicly thanked in Washington's general orders, October 20. On the surrender of Cornwallis, that haughty nobleman was compelled to accept the very same terms of capitulation, in manner and style, which he had imposed upon General Lincoln at the siege of Charleston. On his march to the North with a portion of the army after the surrender of Cornwallis, General Lincoln received notice of his appointment by Congress as the first Secretary of War, on a salary of four thousand dollars per annum, being allowed at the same time to retain, without pay, his rank in the army. In October, 1783, when Congress accepted his resignation as Secretary of War, they voted "that he be informed that the United States in Congress Assembled entertain a high sense of his perseverance, fortitude, activity, and meritorious services in the field, as well as his diligence, fidelity, and capacity in the execution of the office of Secretary of War, which important trusts he has discharged to their entire approbation."

Governor Bowdoin, in 1787, placed General Lincoln at the head of the militia to suppress the Shays Rebellion, which had assumed formidable proportions. January 20, with forty-four hundred men he marched rapidly through Worcester, Hampden, and Berkshire counties, and, although the rebels were decided and in force, he succeeded, by his wise, firm, and yet cautious movements, in dispersing them completely without a drop of blood being shed by the men under his command; although, in the sequel, about eight hundred persons were brought as insurgents before a commission consisting of Benjamin Lincoln, Samuel Phillips, Jr., and Samuel A. Otis, a name ever honored in the hour of peril to the country and state. Some thirteen men were convicted of treason and sentenced to death, but afterward pardoned. As a curious relic of barbarous punishment, a seditious member of the Legislature was sentenced to sit on the gallows with a rope about his neck, and to pay a fine of fifty pounds.

Lincoln was chosen lieutenant-governor of Massachusetts in 1788, and was a member of the convention which ratified the Federal Constitution. He was early a member of the American Academy of Arts and Sciences, and of the Massachusetts Historical Society, and was president of the Massachusetts Society of the Cincinnati from its organization until his death. The confidence bestowed by Washington upon Lincoln, from his entrance on public life to the close of his active career, is remarkable. So early as 1776, during the siege of Boston, his military capability, as major-general of the State militia, was noticed by Washington. The same year he was sent by Massachusetts to Long Island to join the commander-in-chief. He was in the battle of White Plains and at Morristown, and was by State influence raised to the rank of major-general in the Continental service. After prominence in the army at several other places, he joined Washington in 1781 on the Hudson, and co-operated in the siege of Yorktown with distinction. After the surrender of Cornwallis, the honor of receiving the sword of the British commander, was given by Washington to Lincoln. On the establishment of the Federal government his friends were anxious he should have an office in it. Among these was Rev. Joseph Jackson of Boston, who called on Washington to speak in his favor: "I will give you," said he with his usual decided economy of time, "fifteen minutes to talk." He began by naming Lincoln. "You need not go on," said the President; "I know all about General Lincoln." Washington at once gave the first appointment of collector of Boston, the best office in New England, to his old friend and favorite, in which office Lincoln remained until about two years before his death, showing in it a clear judgment, spotless integrity, and practical sagacity which fitted him eminently for the situation. His keen sense of honor led him to offer President Jefferson, from whom he differed in politics, his resignation, although he was induced to withdraw it.

General Lincoln retained the plain and simple habits of his early farmer's life to the last. He was accustomed, when in the Boston collectorship, to return to his home in Hingham at night by the packet from Long Wharf. Walking one day from his office on State Street down to the packet, he was met by his young friend Samuel May, who saw him coming, lame and limping from a wound which he received at the taking of Burgoyne, with a pair of boots in his hand. Young May, feeling it out of place for a man in Lincoln's high position to be carrying such things in his hand, asked the privilege of taking them to the vessel for him. "No, thank you, my dear," said the General; "when I get so old I can't carry my own boots I'll go without." His wit was always ready. Dr. Waterhouse of Cambridge, a warm friend, often called at his office, and on one occasion inquired of him if his daughter Mary was still in Hingham. "No, sir," was the reply. When about leaving, the Doctor again remarked: "Then you said, General, that Mary was not in Hingham?" "No, sir," was the answer, "she is there, but not still in Hingham, — she is never *still* anywhere."

Between Generals Knox and Lincoln, who resembled each other in person, there was great intimacy. Knox, who was rich at one time, named for his friend Lincoln a township he owned. Engaging afterward in Eastern land speculations, and being withal of expensive habits, he became greatly involved, and Lincoln kindly endorsed his notes. He was urged to evade his responsibility, but he refused to do this. His old friend Israel Beal came forward, and said to Lincoln : "General, I have a hundred silver dollars in my house that you are entirely welcome to." To which the veteran replied, with eyes full of tears: "Mr. Beal, I thank you, but it would be a drop in the bucket." We are glad to know that Knox, having lands transferred to him in Maine, finally relieved Lincoln of his burden.

The correspondence of Knox with Washington, Lafayette, and other distinguished men, amounting to fifty-six folio volumes, has recently, 1882, been presented to the New England Historic Genealogical Society, and will be to future generations a testimonial of inestimable value to the services of General Knox, General Lincoln, and his other associates in the toils, perils, and sufferings, by which our National Independence was achieved, the foundations of our government securely laid, and its work commenced.

General Lincoln's home was in Hingham to the last, and the house in which he was born and died is now owned and occupied by his grandchildren, who are the seventh generation who have lived there. The estate has descended in a direct line from the ancestor who settled there in 1636. Six generations of Lincolns have been born on that spot, and each family had a son named Benjamin. The General died May 9, 1810, a little more than seventy-seven years of age. His remains were followed to the tomb that stands on an elevation in the cemetery — near the unique old meeting-house built in 1680, within whose walls he had so long worshipped — by a long train of relatives, friends, and surviving companions in arms.

CHAPTER VI.

PARKER FAMILY.

The name of Parker has many claims to notice in a biographical work on the Revolution. On the roll of the men in Captain John Parker's company which stood on Lexington Common, April 19, 1775, there were four of this name: John the commander of the company, Jonas who fell in the battle that morning, Ebenezer a corporal, and Thaddeus; of whom the two latter were afterward in the Continental service, — one for eight months, the other at Cambridge the month following the battle of Lexington, — and the last, Thaddeus, was in the battle of Bunker Hill. I recollect John, the son of Captain Parker, well; and his grandson, the distinguished Theodore Parker, was a schoolmate with me at Lexington.

The ancestor of this family, THOMAS PARKER, born in 1609, came from London, England, March 11, 1635, and settled in Lynn the same year. He was made Freeman in 1637. He removed to Reading, where he aided in establishing a church, of which he became deacon. By his wife, Amy, he had eleven children. Of these Joseph, born in 1642, died 1644. Nathaniel was born May 16, 1651. Jonathan, born May 18, 1656, died in 1683, aged twenty-seven; his wife died January 15, 1690.

Hananiah, the second son, born in 1638, married first, September 30, 1663, Elizabeth Brown. She died in 1698, and he married second, Mrs. Mary Wright, widow of Deacon John Wright, of Watertown. He died March 10, 1724; she died January 4, 1736, aged eighty-seven years. He lived in Reading, and had the then honored office of Lieutenant. They had seven children, of whom the first, John, born in 1664, came to Lexington about 1712. According to a deed, dated June 25, 1712, he bought the original family estate in Cambridge Farms, afterward Lexington, containing "one small mansion, and sixty acres of land." He must have been a prominent man in town, since in "seating the meeting-house," in which reference was had to age, property, and rank, he was placed in the second seat, with the most highly respected citizens. His wife died March 10, 1718; and he died January 22, 1741, aged seventy-eight years. They had five children, of whom Josiah, born April 11, 1694, married December 8, 1718, Anna Stone, daughter of John and Rachel (Shepard) Stone. He was honored with the office of Lieutenant, and filled several town offices, being chosen town-clerk four years, an assessor from 1726 to 1755, with intervals, and selectman seven years. Josiah Parker and wife were united to the church, August 13, 1719. He died October 9, 1756, aged sixty-two; she died September 8, 1760. They had eight children, of whom, John, born July 13, 1729, married May 22, 1755, Lydia Moore. They joined the church October 31, 1756.

JOHN PARKER was a prominent man in Lexington. He was chosen assessor in 1764-65-66-74. When, in 1774 and early in 1775, the town of Lexington made an effort to organize a company of minute-men, we have a record over his signature in this language, which shows his military leadership, and seems the first note of preparation for the bloody drama so soon to be enacted:—

Agreeable to the vote of the town I have received by the hands of the Selectmen the drums — there were two — provided by the town for the use of the Military Company, in this town, until the further order of the town.

JOHN PARKER.

LEXINGTON, March 14, 1775.

But his greatest distinction was the part he took in the beginning of the military operations of the Revolution. Ten British officers rode up from Boston on the evening of April 18, toward Lexington, hoping to intercept any news of the movement of troops toward Concord. They dined on their way at Cambridge.

The Provincial Committee of Safety — Orne, Lee, Gray, and Heath — had adjourned from Concord to Menotomy, now Arlington. On the arrival there of the British troops, at midnight, they waked, and ran, without dressing, into a field to elude them. Dr. Warren, a member of this committee, was meanwhile in Boston, watching the movements there. Both sides were anxious to avoid firing the first shot. The Continental and the Provincial congresses cautioned their committees, and the people generally, to use great forbearance.

John Parker commanded the company who stood bravely at their post on the 19th of April, 1775, — some seventy men, confronted by six hundred British regulars. Although the company contained such men as Lieutenant Edmund Munroe, and Ensign Robert Munroe, who had held commissions in the French War, with some twenty or thirty, both soldiers and officers, who had seen service in the field, Parker commanded such confidence that he was chosen above them all; and the issue showed they had committed no mistake. He was firm, cool, and determined in the trying hour. He ordered his men to load their guns, but not fire unless fired upon first. When some few seemed inclined to falter, he said: "I will cause the first man to be shot down who quits the ranks without orders." Of Parker's company seventeen out of seventy were either killed or wounded. This shows that they stood their ground, and must have been fired upon at close range. Although eight of his men had been killed and several wounded in the morning, he rallied his company in the afternoon to meet the foe on their return from Concord, and fired upon them with execution.

Captain Parker led a detachment, forty-five men, of his company to Cambridge, upon call of the Provincial Congress, where they served from May 6 to May 10, 1775. And again, on the day of the Battle of Bunker Hill, he marched with sixty-one of his company to Cambridge, ready for action.

Although his health was feeble at the time of the battle of Lexington, and a fatal disease continued its invasion of his physical strength, he marched to Cambridge in the following month, and again on the seventeenth of June, resolute for the defence of his country. It must have saddened his heart, after the heroic part he had taken in the beginning of the great struggle for liberty, that he could not live to witness its happy issue. He died September 17, 1775, at the age of forty-six.

In the Massachusetts State House there were placed two muskets, memorials of Captain Parker, the gift to the State of his grandson, Rev. Theodore Parker. On one is inscribed: —

THE FIRST FIRE ARM
CAPTURED IN THE
WAR OF INDEPENDENCE.

and on the other: —

THIS FIREARM WAS USED BY
CAPT. JOHN PARKER,
IN THE BATTLE OF LEXINGTON,
APRIL 19TH,
1775.

These invaluable mementoes were received by the State authorities with appropriate ceremonies, and are conspicuously suspended, for public view, in the Senate chamber of the State House.

The children of John and Lydia (Moore) Parker were seven, of whom John the 3d, born February 14, 1761, married, February 17, 1785, Hannah Stearns, born May 21, 1764. He died November 3, 1835, aged seventy-four; she died May 15, 1823, aged fifty-nine years. They had eleven children, the youngest of these was THEODORE, born August 24, 1810. He married, April 20, 1837, Lydia D. Cabot of Boston, daughter of John and Lydia (Dodge) Cabot, born September 12, 1813. They had no children.

My earliest acquaintance with Theodore Parker dates back to the days of our boyhood. Living in the central district of Lexington, — where, as the wages of the school-teacher were higher than in the outside sections, and the appropriations equal, our portion was soonest exhausted, — I was sent by my parents to finish the winter's schooling at some one of the outer districts. One season it was my lot to go a few weeks to the same school with Theodore. He was a very bright boy and a pleasant companion. His schoolmates found it needed a spur to keep pace with him in his rare progress. I remember well the old family mansion, which had been a homestead back to 1712. There was the well of the fathers, with its high mounted sweep and its "old oaken bucket," in use, I believe, to this day. And there, near the house, stood the old belfry building which, on the site of the present monument on the Common, rang forth the alarm that called Parker and his company to arms on the memorable nineteenth of April, 1775. This venerable relic was obtained by his family, and removed to the ancient estate where it is in part still standing.

In November 1879, I visited the old Parker homestead, then occupied by a nephew of his name and family, and entered the old workshop where Theodore's father long labored at his bench; and where the son, no doubt, must in his early days have worked with his own hands. What memories clustered around that belfry workshop! Here the child and the youth, surrounded by field and wood, in the simple home-life of his venerated and wise mother, and his modest, faithful father, must have meditated great thoughts and pious resolves, and been trained to become afterward the world-renowned preacher and writer, whose words have gone out so far and sunk so deeply into thousands of revering minds and loving hearts. I brought away with me, the gift of the kind nephew, as a precious souvenir, a block of one of the very timbers that supported the bell which, April 19, 1775, rang forth the first summons to battle in the cause of American freedom and independence.

Theodore Parker came of a family who were farmers or mechanics. His father not only cultivated the land, but bored pumps, in which occupation I often saw him employed at my father's house, — a plain man of quiet manners, and endowed with the good sense of his ancestors. Theodore worked on the farm and in the carpenter's shop, and in 1830, at the age of twenty, entered Harvard College; but, from his narrow pecuniary resources, he could not pursue his studies there, and remained at home studying as he could, "keeping school" — having begun at the age of nineteen — in the winters. He afterward took a private class in Boston, and went on with his studies, yet not in such form as to secure a degree from Harvard College. His vast love of knowledge prompted him to fill every leisure hour with the study of Latin, Greek, Hebrew, German, French, and Spanish. He opened a private school in Watertown in 1832, and had fifty scholars. Meantime he was studying theology to prepare for the ministry, and entered the Cambridge Divinity School in 1834, and took up the Syriac, Arabic, Danish, and Swedish languages, and soon added the Anglo-Saxon and modern Greek.

After preaching in many pulpits he was settled at West Roxbury, in June, 1837. In 1840 he received from Harvard College the degree of Master of Arts. He gradually changed his views of the inspiration of the Scriptures, and in 1841, May 19, he preached an ordination sermon at South Boston, on "The Transient and Permanent in Christianity," in which he advocated the simple humanity of Christ and a complete anti-supernaturalism. He became involved in a widespread controversy, which led at length to his preaching at the Boston Melodeon, where he was installed over a new society in 1846. Previously to this time he had occasioned much censure by preaching in Unitarian pulpits, whose ministers had consented to such exchanges. The writer was among those who committed in this way what some of his friends regarded as an offence. We were settled near each other. I was attached to him, and we sympathized in our love of liberty, civil and religious. I exchanged pulpits with him, not as agreeing wholly with him in his theology, but feeling that he was honest and reverent, and entitled to respectful and kind treatment in the pulpit, even from those who differed from him on many contested points in regard to the inspiration of the Scriptures and the nature and character of Christ.

His treatment of the Bible seemed to many of us very free, although at the present day he has been far outstripped in that direction, and to some of those who write on the same topics now, abroad and at home, he appears quite conservative. The Progressives of our age would have startled Mr. Parker, denying or doubting, as they do, in not a few instances, those great truths which were fixed in his mind as firmly as his own being, — the existence of a God, wise, kind, paternal, and that immortality, of which he said he was personally conscious, and for which logic as well as feeling furnished, he affirmed, a sure basis.

On the day of our exchange I remained and took tea at his house, some half-mile west of his church, with him and his wife, a most pleasing and amiable person. They had no children, and seemed to be truly all in all to each other. It was a most happy meeting, and may well recall those ten resolutions we find entered on their wedding day, in Mr. Parker's since published journal : —

1. Never, except for the best of causes, to oppose my wife's will.
2. To discharge all duties for her sake, freely.
3. Never to scold.
4. Never to look cross at her.
5. Never to weary her with commands.
6. To promote her piety.
7. To bear her burdens.
8. To overlook her foibles.
9. To love, cherish, and forever defend her.
10. To remember her always, most affectionately, in my prayers. Thus, God willing, we shall be blessed.

Mrs. Parker survived him until April 9, 1881, to the age of sixty-seven years.

I subjoin an autograph letter, which led to the above mentioned exchange : —

WEST ROXBURY, 9 Feb. '46.

MY DEAR SIR : — You and I have never exchanged. I write not to request but to *suggest* one. If you have any objection on the score of *conscience*, as some, or of *expedience* which *is* the conscience of some, say "nay" plainly, and at once. But if you feel scruples from neither source, I shall be glad of an exchange, and the sooner the better, as I have none *past, present, or to come*, for since the 11 of July I have had but six exchanges, one for half a day only.

Yours very truly,

THEO. PARKER.

Mr. Parker was a devout man, as all who ever attended his services, or have read the volume of his prayers, must acknowledge. Like all other men he had his limitations. He was sometimes exasperated by the illiberal treatment he received, and used sharp and incisive language in public regarding those whose alleged crimes or faults, and what he deemed errors of thought or conduct on the questions of reform, deeply stirred his spirit. But he had still a kind heart, and sympathized with all the suffering, oppressed, and friendless, and labored in season and out of season for their relief; and he was, in my judgment, for these reasons, entitled not only to charity but strict justice.

To the writer it seems very narrow in one who claims to be a liberal Christian not to accord cheerfully to Theodore Parker the virtues of thorough honesty and sincere piety, however differing from him in drawing the line or believing in a line between the natural and supernatural. We all can afford to go as far in this direction as Dean Stanley, who said: " The theology of the times is more indebted to Theodore Parker than to any of his contemporaries," and who recently entertained as his guest, Ernest Renan, from many of whose theological opinions he widely dissented.

As an evidence of the intellectual tastes and culture of the American branch of the Parkers, it is interesting to note that, so far back as the year 1826, no less than fifty-nine of this family had graduated at New England colleges. So early as 1661 John Parker graduated at Harvard College, at which period we find this record on the Steward's Books: "walter hooke, Debitor &c. pay^d by John Parker of Boston."

England sent over many valuable ministers to this country in our early history. Rev. John Woodbridge, afterward the highly prized minister of Andover, came to New England, Boston, in 1634, in company with his uncle, Rev. Thomas Parker, who settled at Newbury, and was one of the best scholars of his day, and generally had more than one student in his charge. Rev. Shubael Dummer, minister of York, Maine, was fitted for college in Newbury, his native place, by Rev. Thomas Parker.

The Hon. Charles Hudson told me, as we stood together in the old Lexington burying-place, November 11, 1879, that Theodore Parker, with Captain Jonathan Parker and himself, while standing on a lot in that ground by the side of gravestones marked with the name of Stearns, the family name of his mother, said: "Here all my father's and grandfather's family were buried, and when I die, I wish to be buried on this spot." If this spot is thus clearly identified by the burial there of the remains of Captain John Parker, a monument ought to be erected upon it in honor of that brave and patriotic man, the first who commanded an organized force arrayed against the British Empire in that memorable Revolution which led to our national independence. A large space of land is now, 1882, vacant of tombstones, and these centennial years ought not to pass without at least some modest memorial being raised, to commemorate one so clearly entitled to the veneration, not only of his own town and State, but of the whole country.

It should be said in justice to the many devoted friends of Theodore Parker, that they erected a commemorative stone in Lexington on the spot where the old house stood in which he was born. This stone is of Concord granite, three feet square and three and a half feet high, resting on a base four feet square and one foot high. On the front, in raised characters, is the simple inscription:—

Birth Place
of
Theodore Parker,
1810.

I am glad to know that, by the liberality of Mr. N. C. Nash, who contributed for this object $5,000, and with additional subscriptions, a statue of Mr. Parker is to be erected in the city of Boston.

Unhappily his wish in regard to his burial-place could not be gratified. In 1859, he was enfeebled by incessant labors, and a hemorrhage from the lungs obliged him to suspend his work. He, by the advice of his physician, embarked for the West Indies, and after a time sailed for the South of Europe. But nothing could arrest his disease, and he died at Florence, Italy, May 10, 1860. His great heart yearned for the emancipation of the colored race, but he "died without the sight." Yet, when he was near the borders of the Heavenly land he said, with a prophetic instinct: "There is a glorious future for America, but the other side of the Red Sea." He was buried in a small Protestant cemetery, outside of the city walls, which I well remember visiting some years before his death. The grave is enclosed by a border of gray marble, and at its head is a plain stone of the same material, with this inscription: —

Theodore Parker,
Born at Lexington, Mass.,
United States of America,
Aug. 24, 1810.
Died at Florence, May 10, 1860.

Andrew Parker, born February 14, 1693, son of John Parker, born 1664, married August 2, 1720, Sarah Whitney. She died December 18, 1774, aged seventy, and he died April 8, 1776, aged eighty-three years.

They had twelve children, one of whom Jonas Parker, born February 6, 1722, was one of the martyrs of liberty who fell on Lexington common, April 19, 1775. His name stands second on the noble roll of the eight martyrs who fell on the morning of that eventful day. Edward Everett, in his address, April 19, 1835, says of him: "Roman history does not furnish an example of bravery that outshines that of Jonas Parker. A truer heart did not bleed at Thermopylae. He was next door neighbor of Rev. Mr. Clark, and had evidently imbibed a double portion of his lofty spirit. Parker was often heard to say, 'Be the consequences what they might, and let others do what they pleased, he would never run from the enemy.' He was as good as his word, — better. Having loaded his musket, he placed his hat, containing his ammunition, on the ground between his feet, in readiness for the second charge. At the second fire from the enemy he was wounded and sunk upon his knees, and in this condition discharged his gun. While loading it again upon his knees, and striving in the agonies of death to redeem his pledge, he was transfixed by a bayonet, and died on the spot."

Thaddeus Parker, born September 2, 1741, son of Josiah, born April 11, 1694, married May 27, 1759, Mary Reed, daughter of William and Abigail (Stone) Reed. He died February 10, 1789, aged forty-eight; she died October 9, 1811, aged seventy-three years. Thaddeus Parker was one of the selectmen of Lexington in 1770–71–73–77, at a period when that board were required to perform most important duties. He was a member of that brave company who, under the command of his brother, John Parker, stood before the British forces April 19, 1775. He was afterward, true to his principles, in the service for eight months.

Ebenezer Parker, son of Thomas, son of Andrew, married, December 3, 1772, Dorcas Munroe. They had three children, baptized in Lexington: Abijah, baptized May 30, 1773; Quincy, baptized April 30, 1775; Lucy, baptized July 22, 1781. He and his wife were dismissed to the church in Princeton, November 9, 1788. He was a corporal in the company of his relative, Captain Parker, and was with them April 19, 1775, — also on the sixth of May following, and on the seventeenth of June at Bunker Hill.

FIRST MEETING-HOUSE IN SALEM.

CHAPTER VII.

MUNROE FAMILY.

WHEN some one spoke to Colonel William Munroe of Lexington, — member and officer in Captain John Parker's company, April 19, 1775 — of the bravery of the Munroes in the War of the Revolution : " No wonder, at all, sir," he replied : " they have Irish, Scotch, and Yankee blood in their veins." We trace this family back to Ireland. The original name was spelt with one syllable, Ro ; the first person of this stock whom we find in history is Occon, or Ocon Roe, whose son Donald, born in Ireland, went to Scotland, in the beginning of the eleventh century, to assist King Malcolm II. in his war against the Danes. The King gave him for his services certain lands in Scotland, which were named by the King the Barony of Fowlis. His descendants added to the original name the syllable *Mon*. At subsequent periods this name was spelt variously Monro, Munro, Monroe, and Munroe. The present name of a clergyman and popular writer of this family is spelt Roe. He undoubtedly is a descendant from the original Ro of Ireland.

The same traits of character may be found in

all ages, the heritage of the heroic, shrewd, honest, firm, and courageous old stock of Ro.

We should never lose sight of the grand military record of this family. George Munroe, Ninth Baron of Fowlis, was slain at the battle of Bannockburn, under Robert Bruce of Scotland, in 1314. Robert Munroe, Twenty-first Baron, was killed in the service of Gustavus Adolphus of Sweden, defending the civil and religious liberties of Germany, in 1633. Sir Robert, Twenty-fifth Baron, was a zealous Presbyterian, and being remarkable for size and corpulency, — the same figure with Colonel Munroe of our Revolution, — he was nicknamed "the Presbyterian mortar-piece." His grandson Sir Robert, Twenty-seventh Baron, who succeeded his father in 1729, was greatly distinguished for his military services. He was in the battle of Fontenoy. He would order his men to throw themselves upon the ground and receive the enemy's fire, and then rise and rush upon them, as they did with fatal effect; but he himself stood upright under fire. Being asked afterward why he did this, he replied that " though he could throw himself on the ground, like the young and leaner men, his great bulk and corpulency would not suffer him to rise instantly and rush upon the enemy." In the battle of Falkirk he was slain. Two of his brothers, Dr. Munroe and Captain George Munroe, were also in that engagement, and the former was killed.

Up to the year 1651, there had been three generals, eight colonels, eleven majors, thirty captains and five lieutenants of the Munroe stock. At the battle of Worcester, where Cromwell was victorious, several Munroes were made prisoners, and some of them were bound out as apprentices to farmers in America. Among these is supposed to have been William, the ancestor of the family in this country. In the two great wars on this soil, in the eighteenth century, their name is prominent. In the old French War, Sergeant William Munroe served in 1754–55; Lieutenant Edmund Munroe in 1757, 1758 and 1761; Jonas Munroe in 1755–57; James Munroe in 1757–58–59; Ensign Robert Munroe in 1758 and 1762; David Munroe in 1757–59. To these we must add Thaddeus, John, Abraham, Stephen, and Josiah, eleven of one family name in the French War; while in that of the Revolution there were no less than fourteen who bore arms, of whom one, Ensign Robert Munroe, is enrolled among the eight whose names are on the monument at Lexington as killed in the battle.

Colonel William Munroe — with whose stalwart form and determined movements, slightly enfeebled by age, I was familiar from my boyhood — was born October 22, 1742. He married first, Anna Smith, daughter of Benjamin and Anna (Parker) Smith, who was born March 31, 1743, and died January 2, 1781, aged thirty-eight years. He married second, widow Polly Rogers of Westford, whose first husband was killed at the battle of Monmouth. Colonel Munroe was an officer in the Revolution, —

one of the noble company who met the British on Lexington Common, April 19, 1775, and at that time was orderly sergeant. He was a lieutenant in the Northern army at the taking of Burgoyne, in 1777. He was a prominent man in Lexington, was selectman nine years, and Representative to the Legislature two years, was a colonel in the militia, and engaged in suppressing the Shays Rebellion. He kept the Munroe Tavern, where the British troops refreshed themselves April 19, 1775, on their return from Concord, and where they committed many outrages, murdering in cold blood John Raymond, as he was quietly leaving the house. It was here President Washington dined in 1789, when, on his visit to New England, he came to Lexington to view the first battle-field of the Revolution. Colonel Munroe died October 30, 1827, aged eighty-five years. His second wife died January 10, 1839, aged seventy-three years. The children of William and Anna (Smith) Munroe were six in number.

(1) William, born May 28, 1768, who married Susan B. Grinnell of New Bedford, was killed at Richmond, Virginia, in 1814, by the upsetting of a stage-coach.

(2) Anna, born May 9, 1771, married Rev. William Muzzey of Sullivan, New Hampshire, September 20, 1798. Both died in Lexington, — he, April 16, 1835, aged 64, and she in 1850, aged 79 years.

(3) Sarah, born October 21, 1773, married Jonathan Wheelock of Connecticut; she died at the age of seventy-seven years.

(4) Lucinda, born April 9, 1776, died unmarried, June 2, 1863, aged eighty-seven years.

(5) Jonas, born June 11, 1778, married, March 17, 1814, Abigail C. Smith. He lived on the homestead in Lexington, — a man "of infinite jest," of popular manners, and known through the town by the familiar name of "Uncle Jonas."

(6) Edmund, born October 29, 1780, married first, Harriet Downes, second, Lydia Downes, third, Sophia Sewall. He was a broker in Boston, and died April 17, 1865, aged eighty-four years and six months.

This ancient family were among the first to embrace the Reformation, and were zealous supporters of it. As I read the old record of these men, I am constantly reminded of their honored descendants of Lexington. They were "all remarkable for a brave spirit, full of love to their native land, and of distinguished zeal for religion and liberty, — faithful in their promises, steadfast in their friendships, and abundant in their charity to the poor and distressed."

William Munroe, the ancestor of the Lexington family, was born in Scotland in 1625, and came to this country in 1652. He lived first in Menotomy, now Arlington, and then a part of Cambridge. We first find his name in the records of Cambridge in 1657. He settled at Cambridge Farms, now Lexington, then a part of Cambridge, about 1660. Several of his sons, of whom he had six, settled near him at first. Mrs. Sanderson, his great-granddaughter, who died at Lexington in 1853, aged one hundred and four years, said that his old house looked like a ropewalk, so many additions had been made to it to accommodate his sons, as they successively settled in life. Adopting the custom of the Scottish clans, he kept the Munroes much together, and made them, for some time, a kind of distinct people. The section of Lexington they occupied was, and still is, known by the name of Scotland, in honor of the first settler on that spot. He died January 27, 1717, at the age of ninety-two. He had three wives. The third was Elizabeth Wyer, widow of Edward Wyer of Charlestown. He must have married for love and not money, for, among the papers he left is an inventory of the property which belonged to her, the whole of which is " one bed, one bolster, one pillow, one chest, one warming-pan, one pair of tongs, and one pewter platter."

Edmund, grandson of William Munroe, was born February 2, 1736, and married, in 1768, Rebecca, daughter of Jonathan and Abigail (Dunster) Harrington. She was a sister of Jonathan Harrington, who died in 1854, the last survivor of the battle of Lexington. Edmund Munroe entered the Provincial service at an early age. He was ensign in a corps of Rangers under Major Rogers, which performed signal service in the French War. In 1761 he was acting adjutant in Colonel Hoar's regiment at Crown Point. In 1762 he received a commission, from Governor Bernard, as lieutenant in his Majesty's service, and continued with the troops at Crown Point, Ticonderoga, and its vicinity till the peace of 1763. His services in these campaigns were of the most honorable character, and he was presented, as a reward of his bravery, with a sword captured from one of the French officers. This interesting relic is now in the possession of one of his descendants, Mr. E. S. Fessenden of Arlington.

On the nineteenth of April, 1775, he was one of the Lexington minute-men, and was present at the battle on that day. As early as August, 1776, we find him on his way to meet the British on the same field where he had co-operated with them to subdue the French and Indians. He was commissioned lieutenant on the twelfth of July, 1776, in Colonel Reed's regiment. On the sixteenth of the same month he was appointed a quartermaster, and sent to the northern frontier. On the first of January following, he received a commission as Captain in Colonel Bigelow's regiment. He was with the northern army, under Gates, at Stillwater, Saratoga, and Bennington, and so distinguished himself, that after the capture of Burgoyne, he was presented by his superior officers with a pair of candlesticks, a part of the travelling equipage of General Burgoyne. They are now in the possession of a lady in Arlington.

On the capture of Burgoyne, Captain Munroe was sent with his regiment to New Jersey, where he served under Washington. When he entered upon the command of a company, he had with him fifteen men from Lexington. He was killed by a cannon-ball, while in line of battle, on the field of Freehold, commonly called the battle of Monmouth, June 28, 1778. The oath of office of Captain Munroe, witnessed at Valley Forge by the Baron de Kalb, May 18, 1778, is now in the possession of Dr. Francis H. Brown, a descendant of Captain Edmund Munroe.

Captain Munroe was deliberately brave, without rashness. His knowledge of military matters and his sterling traits of character rendered him a valuable aid in the struggle of the Revolution, and his services were eagerly sought in the formation of the American army.

He was forty-two years old at the time of his death. His widow survived him, and died in 1834, at the age of eighty-three years.

THE HANCOCK HOUSE, BOSTON.

CHAPTER VIII.

BROWN FAMILY.

FRANCIS BROWN came of the good old yeoman stock of New England. His ancestors, coming from England in 1632, in the persons of "John Brown and Dorothy his wife," settled in Watertown, in company with the uncles Richard and Abraham. Anterior to this date, for eight generations, and for nearly three hundred years, their ancestors had been landed gentry in the East of England, where they left memorials of upright lives and honorable positions in the society of the day.

John Brown brought with him his son, of the same name, then a year old, who at the age of twenty-four married Hester Makepeace of Boston; and from their union came this branch of the family. Their grandson, Francis Brown, was born in 1738. At the time of the battle of Lexington, he was living in that portion of the town known as Scotland. His grandfather had removed to Lexington in 1709, and the family has been represented there from that time. The knowledge we have of the Lexington minute-man is such as to show that he was a man of great decision of character, and well fitted by nature and training to meet the impending crisis. He was of middle size, strong and active. He was a man of true courage, of the calm and reliable class, which does not rush unnecessarily into danger; but when duty called, he would not flinch or hesitate. He was a person of good executive qualities in all situations in life, ackowledged by common consent and choice as a leader among his neighbors and friends. In 1764 he married Mary Buckman of Lexington, sister of John Buckman, who was the village innholder in 1775. She was born in 1740, and died in Lexington in 1824. She is represented as small in stature, quiet and retiring, of great refinement and considerable culture. She had a then rare taste for painting, fine needlework, and embroidery, and other accomplishments, which gave her a superior position in the community in which she lived.

James Brown, whom I recollect from my boyhood, the oldest son of Francis and Mary, was a mere child at the time of the battle of Lexington. He remembered the trepidation which he witnessed in his parents and their fellow townsmen, but could not well appreciate, at the coming of the British troops. The hasty concealment of their household treasures, and the retreat of the family to the woods, made an impression on his infant mind which years could not efface. At the time of the battle, the minute-men of Lexington included in their number the principal men of the town. John

Parker, then forty-six years of age, commanded the company in which Francis Brown was a sergeant. On the study walls of one of our city homes hangs an old-time cartridge-box, having the inscription, "F. B., 1774." At a later date Brown was captain of the same company, and did good service at Cambridge, in the fortifications around Boston, at Ticonderoga, and elsewhere.

The similarity of names in the old rolls of the company indicate that several of the minute-men were closely related by ties of family, as well as by those of a common interest, and that they thus stood up as one family to offer the first armed resistance to British oppression. The spirit of unrest which pervaded the neighborhood of Boston in the spring of 1775 did not fail to reach the inhabitants of Lexington. Everything indicated an immediate crisis, and the information brought by watchful Patriots during the night of the eighteenth, found the minute-men prepared for the emergency.

Sergeant Brown was one of the band who guarded Hancock and Adams at the house of Parson Clark on the memorable night of the eighteenth, and accompanied them to the place of safety they sought on the morning of the nineteenth of April. He was present with the company on the Common at the time of the attack by the British troops, and in the afternoon followed them to Concord. After leaving the Common he proceeded up the old Bedford Road, now

Hancock Street, in advance of a squad of the regulars sent up to search the old Clark house. He was seen and pursued by a mounted officer, who struck at him with his sword, and demanded his surrender. Brown managed to keep the horse at the length of his musket, and the sword of the officer only fell on the barrel. Seeing the soldiers drawing near to him, and that his position was becoming perilous, he took advantage of a favorable moment, leaped a high rail-fence, and ran down into a swamp at the side of the road. He escaped the bullets of the soldiers, which clicked among the leaves of the trees above his head. Here he found a number of fellow minutemen, who had preceded him in seeking this place of temporary shelter. After this escape, he joined in the pursuit of the British troops, keeping near enough to do his part in harassing them, and exchanging shots with them as occasion offered. On the return from Concord, in the town of Lincoln, he fell in with three of the regulars, and while stepping out from behind a rock, was seen and fired upon, the ball wounding him in the neck. With that singular good fortune which so often attends wounds in this region, no important parts were injured, and the ball found a lodgment beneath the skin at the back of the neck, and was removed a year later.

Francis Brown left his home, his wife and children, to meet the demand of his country for brave hearts and freedom-loving spirits. He outlived the dangers and the thraldom of the period, and enjoyed for many years a happy home and the respect of his fellow townsmen. He died in 1800. His body rests in the cemetery at Lexington, beside that of his faithful wife. The stones above their graves tell the simple tale of life and death. His son James married Pamelia, born in 1773, daughter of Captain Edmund Munroe.

CHAPTER IX.

KIRKLAND FAMILY.

The names of Samuel and John Thornton Kirkland figure somewhat largely in American history. They were separated in their special offices and functions, the one as missionary among the Indians and chaplain in the Revolutionary War, the other as pastor of a church and president of the oldest college in the country; and yet they were united, we shall find, at many interesting points.

Of a common stock, we may look a moment at their ancestry. The name Kirkland, that is Churchland, indicates their Scotch descent. John Kirkland is said to have come to this country directly from Silver Street in London. He had a son John who was the father of ten children, of whom Daniel, the father of Samuel, was the youngest but one. Daniel was born in Saybrook, Connecticut, in 1701, graduated at Yale College in 1720, and was ordained as the first minister of the Third Congregational Church in Norwich, December 10, 1723. In 1753 he resigned his pastorate, and was for a short time settled at Groton, Connecticut, but returned to Norwich in 1758, and died there in May, 1773. He bore the reputation of being a devoted minister of Christ, a man of native abilities, a good scholar, of a facetious turn, and a most amiable disposition. In many respects his character seems to have foreshadowed qualities conspicuous in his grandson, the President of Harvard College.

SAMUEL KIRKLAND, born December 1, 1741, was a student at Rev. Dr. Wheelock's school at Lebanon, Connecticut, in 1761. In the autumn of 1762 he entered Princeton College, New Jersey, and received a degree in 1765. Many of the students at Princeton, including Indian youth, were then preparing themselves to be teachers or missionaries among the Indians. This circumstance had its influence probably in deciding Samuel Kirkland to become afterward himself a missionary to that race.

At the early age of twenty-three he was marked by his great physical vigor, his benevolence, his courage, his devotion to the cause of Christ, and zeal for the conversion of the heathen, as a fit man to be sent as missionary to the Senecas, a tribe of savage and bloodthirsty warriors. He spent a year and a half among these Indians, and his journeys through forests, and especially snows in the month of January, were attended with extreme sufferings and perils. On his arrival, one of the chiefs made a friendly speech, and advised his "brothers" to receive the young man kindly.

"He loves Indians," were his words, "he wishes to do them good." After a long silence another chief, of an opposite character, uttered himself in a different strain: "This white-skin," said he, "has come upon a dark design, or he would not have travelled so many hundred miles. He brings with him the white people's Book; they call it God's Holy Book. You know this book was never made for Indians. The Great Spirit gave us a book for ourselves. He wrote it in our heads. He put it into the minds of our fathers; and gave them rules about worshipping him; and our fathers observed these rules, and the upholder of the skies was pleased, and gave them success in hunting and made them victorious over their enemies in war. Brothers, attend! Be assured that if we Senecas receive this white man, and attend to the book made only for white people, we shall become miserable. The spirit of the brave warrior and the good hunter will be no more among us. We shall be sunk so low as to hoe corn and squashes in the field, chop wood, stoop down and milk cows. . . . Of this are we not warned by the sudden death of our good brother and wise sachem? Brothers, listen to what I say. Ought not this white man's life to make satisfaction for our deceased brother's death?"

After much discussion, and finding in Mr. Kirkland's knapsack no magic powder that could have killed their lost brother, and after the head sachem had made a long speech, and advised them to "bury the hatchet deep in the ground," the opposition was withdrawn; there was a general shout of applause, and the head sachem said, "Our business is done, I rake up the council fire."

Mr. Kirkland began his missionary labors about the first of August, 1766, and continued them, with occasional interruptions, for forty years. In 1769 he married Jerusha Bingham, a niece of Rev. Dr. Wheelock, a lady of fine intellectual and moral qualities and deeply interested in his missionary work. By her he had two sons, twins, born August 17, 1770, and named in honor of two of his esteemed friends and benefactors, George Whitefield and John Thornton. They resided some time in Oneida, and the Indians at once adopted the boys into their tribe, giving to George the name of Lagoncost, and to John that of Abganoiska, that is, Fair Face.

Mrs. Kirkland passed the winter of 1772-73 at Stockbridge, Massachusetts; and the unsettled condition of affairs among the Indians and the prospect of war with Great Britain making it unsafe for her to return to her husband, she occupied a small farm in Stockbridge, and, occasionally visited by him, she remained there until the peace of 1783.

Mr. Kirkland rendered important services to the country through the whole Revolutionary War. As early as July 18, 1775, a vote of Congress recommended that "the Commissioners of the Northern Department employ Rev. Samuel Kirkland among the Indians of the Six Nations, in order to secure their friendship and to continue them in a state of neutrality with respect to the present controversy between Great Britain and these Colonies." In this capacity he labored earnestly to keep the peace among them. He also received a commission from the Continental Congress as a chaplain in the army. At the siege of Fort Schuyler and the other posts in that vicinity he officiated with the pay and subsistence of a brigade-chaplain, and was instructed at the same time "to pay as great attention to the Oneidas and other Indians contiguous to them, as might be consistent with the above mentioned appointment."

He writes to his wife, from Fort Schuyler, September 15, 1776: —

I am to be faithful in improving opportunities of personal intercourse with the troops, to enliven their love of God and of liberty, and their readiness to do and to suffer for the cause of the country.

It was difficult to keep the Indians strictly neutral, and they insisted at one time on taking a part in the contest with Great Britain, and about two hundred and fifty warriors rendered great service to the cause under a remarkable Oneida chief named Skeneando. This chief was one of the most extraordinary men in all the Six Nations. Of a tall and commanding figure, his constitution was strong, and his countenance manifested great intelligence and dignity. Brave as a warrior, he became also a most noble and sagacious counsellor. For his interest in our people and his fidelity to all engagements with them, he was named among the Indians the White Man's Friend. So attached was he to Mr. Kirkland that he expressed a desire, and received a promise from the family, that he should be buried near him; that, as he said, " he might cling to the skirts of his garments, and go up with him at the great resurrection." He lived until 1816, and at his death, being then one hundred and ten years old, his remains were conveyed to Mr. Kirkland's former homestead in Clinton, N. Y., where a funeral service was held in the church, and his body was then deposited as he had requested. The Christian minister and the Indian chieftain now rest side by side in the old family orchard.

Mr. Kirkland was employed as a missionary under the patronage of a board in Scotland, and also of one in Boston; and he continued his services at the earnest request of the Indians themselves, after the close of the war, until the year 1787, when he returned to his family at Stockbridge. His children, then six in number, had been there educated under a most tender and faithful mother.

My limits prevent a full narrative of the missionary services of Mr. Kirkland. Suffice it to say that both his patriotism and philanthropy prompted him to continue his labors in this direction to the last of his life. He formed a plan of education, — to further which he visited Boston, it would appear, in 1791, to confer with the Board of Commissioners, who had that matter in charge. He took with him an Indian chief, Onondago, and they visited Cambridge at Commencement, where he was to meet two of the Board, President Willard and Rev. Dr. Wigglesworth. The chief was invited on Sunday to attend divine services. He objected, however, saying: "An Indian is a strange sight here. If I go to church, the people will look at me, and forget to worship the Great Spirit with the heart." He visited the library and philosophical apparatus, but said he was afraid his nation would not understand his account of the orrery, "the sun, moon, and star machine," as he called it; "they would be afraid it was some magic work." He was delighted and surprised "that the wise men of Cambridge, with their knowledge of everything about the works of the Great Spirit, could, nevertheless, turn their attention to the interests and happiness of poor Indians."

After Mr. Kirkland retired from his missionary work he showed his native hospitality and regard for this hapless race, who would come, scores of them at a time frequently, to visit their old and beloved friend. "Bodily infirmities," said he, "have occasioned some interruptions; but I think I have employed my time, exerted my talents, and spared no sacrifice to make myself useful among these poor Indians, my old and very dear charge."

Visiting the scene of this good man's labors at

Oneida, in the summer of 1826, I was exceedingly interested in spending an hour or two in one of those schools which, nearly a half-century before, Mr. Kirkland had done so much to establish. The bright faces of the little tawny boys and girls, their evident love of study, and their prompt and generally correct answers to their teachers' questions, gave me new encouragement and hope for the civilization of this unfortunate race.

Among the various plans and efforts for their advancement and elevation, I look with great confidence to the efforts of such men as Samuel Kirkland. He deserves a higher encomium than he has yet received for his devotedness to this noble enterprise, begun in his early life, and continued with unabated zeal so long as his powers of mind and body permitted.

Let us send men of his spirit and consecration to our Western territory, and let the Church and the State unite in giving them a generous sympathy and a just compensation, and we may feel assured that our own day and generation will yet do something to wipe out the stain that still remains almost hopelessly, under the old methods of dealing with this degraded, yet not irredeemable, portion of our people. To the shield of law, government, and social justice, we must add that best of all instruments and influences, a personal intercourse, pervaded with genuine sympathy and enforced by a persistent, humane, Christian treatment, and we shall no longer blush to read the record of our dealings with the wronged, hunted, and down-trodden Indian.

JOHN THORNTON KIRKLAND, the second son of Samuel Kirkland, was born at Little Falls, New York, August 17, 1770, and died in Boston, April 26, 1840. He inherited a large share of the self-devoted patriotism of his father. Although but five years old when the Revolutionary War began, he must have been stirred to take an interest in what he saw and heard about it, — especially as his father, so early as July 18, 1775, was recommended by the Continental Congress as adapted to labor among the Indians and preserve their neutrality during the war, and at once engaged in that arduous and responsible work.

From a mother of distinguished public spirit, energy, wisdom, and devotedness, he received the rudiments of a high intellectual and moral excellence. At the age of thirteen he was sent to Phillips Academy at Andover, where he acquitted himself creditably as a student, and by his exemplary deportment. Entering Harvard College in 1785, his course there was commendable both in scholarship and character. His patriotic spirit showed itself in 1787, when, at the early age of sixteen, suspending his studies, he joined a military corps for the suppression of the Shays Rebellion. We see here the germ of that interest in military tactics, and desire to encourage the formation of military companies, which he felt in his subsequent life. He evidently regarded this form of service as important to the welfare of the republic. In my college life during his presidency, there existed the Harvard Washington Corps, to which I belonged; and I recollect the pleasure with which he welcomed the West Point Cadets, when they visited the University, and invited them to dine with us in our Commons Hall.

After his graduation in 1789, he assisted in Andover Academy for a year, and purposed to take up the law as his profession. He thought it "good for exerting," as he said, "the virtues of integrity and patriotism." He expresses his regrets that "public spirit is decaying," and "that hardihood of character which becomes republicans." But he finally decided to enter the ministry, and studied for some time, in his preparation for that office, under Rev. Dr. West of Stockbridge, and afterward completed his professional studies with Professor Tappan, in Cambridge. The influence of Dr. West, a prominent and devoted patriot of that period, must have done much to strengthen his naturally patriotic spirit.

Dr. Kirkland had a strong historic taste, exhibited in many ways. He was elected in his early ministry a member of the Massachusetts Historical Society, was for some years one of its officers, and continued his membership for thirty-two years. He took a deep interest in the political condition of the country, and was an earnest member of the old Federal party. Some of his letters show the strength of his political convictions and feelings.

THE OLD AND THE NEW.

February 10, 1809, he wrote to one who had said he thought the Democrats must be soon led into better courses by "the bright lamps of truth and honor shining all around them." "What good," he replied, "will they, [the lamps] do those who choose false lights, or who are moles that sunshine cannot make see?" Writing again, April 12, 1810, to Josiah Quincy, then a Representative in Congress, he says: "The administration will not dare to repeat their outrageous measures; we are not to be made the quiet and harmless victims of their party passions, French politics, and Democratic feelings."

During his ministry in the Summer Street Church in Boston, he preached many sermons imbued with his decided views as a warm friend of his country, especially on occasions when the public mind was agitated by the political measures and the great national questions of the day.

Both by inheritance and early education Dr. Kirkland felt a deep interest in the character and prospects of the Indians. His views on that subject are especially noteworthy, amid the controversies of the present day in regard to that hapless race. In a volume of the Massachusetts Historical Collections, we have his answer to questions respecting the Indians, dated February, 1795, in which he discusses, with brevity and force, their situation, capacities and deserts. Three years previously he had resided in their neighborhood several months, and became acquainted with the Oneida Indians living a few miles south of Oneida Lake, with the Stockbridge Indians living near the chief Oneida village, and with the Brothertown Indians, living eight miles south of the Stockbridge settlement. He thinks that, " as the whites advance toward the Indians, the latter become vicious, intemperate, sickly, and dispirited, and in general diminish in numbers." While they acknowledge the importance of industry and the arts to their happiness, respectability, and even existence, they will add, " Indians can't work." " The character of parents is transmitted to the children, who grow up in all that indolence, listlessness, and intemperance which their predecessors exemplified, lamented, and condemned." Although Mr. Kirkland's view was at that time doubtless correct, some progress has since been made in their intellectual and moral culture, and their consequent civilization.

No view of Dr. Kirkland's character is complete which omits to notice that, with his substantial qualities he united a rich vein of wit and humor. At social gatherings, laying aside the cares and constraints of office, his conversation was free, his tone genial, and his spirit at times mirthful. The subject of the writing of sermons coming up at a ministers' meeting, one and another spoke of the gifts of certain preachers. " Oh," said he, " there is C. B. will write a sermon in twenty minutes and make nothing of it."

Dr. Kirkland resigned his office as President of

Harvard University, which he had held with great success for eighteen years, in 1828. After thirteen years of retirement he died at Boston, April 26, 1840, aged sixty-nine years, — having been honored, in every station he had filled, for his intellectual ability and culture, beloved by every one who knew his inexhaustible kindness, crowned with wisdom, purity, and self-sacrifice. Loved in life, he was lamented in death.

REV. SAMUEL KIRKLAND LOTHROP was admitted a member of the Massachusetts Society of the Cincinnati in 1868, under the rule adopted by the General Society, May 1854. He is a grandson of Rev. Samuel Kirkland, whom I have already noticed as a chaplain in the Revolutionary War from 1776 until the end of the contest. He was a son of John H., and Jerusha (Kirkland) Lothrop. He was born in Utica, New York, October 13, 1804, and graduated at Harvard College in 1825. He was ordained over the Second Church in Dover, New Hampshire, February 18, 1829; and, June 18, 1834, was installed pastor of the Brattle Street Church, Boston. He received the degree of D. D. from Harvard College in 1852; was a member of the Board of Overseers of Harvard College from 1847 to 1854; is a member of the Massachusetts Historical Society, and the author of a "Life of Samuel Kirkland" in Sparks's American Biography, a "History of Brattle Street Church," 1851, and " Proceedings of an Ecclesiastical Council in the case of Rev. John Pierpont," 1841, beside many articles in the reviews of the day, and sermons and addresses. Classmates in Harvard Divinity School from 1825 to 1828, we have enjoyed an uninterrupted friendship through our protracted lives.

DOROTHY HANCOCK'S RECEPTION.

CHAPTER X.

ELLERY FAMILY.

THE names of WILLIAM ELLERY and WILLIAM ELLERY CHANNING are properly placed in consecutive chapters. The men they unite stood, in more than one aspect, in a kindred relation to each other. Believing firmly in the doctrine of heredity, I have placed them in juxtaposition. Many of the traits of Dr. Channing may be traced to germs found in his distinguished ancestor. The one was born early in the same century which produced the other. They were alike in many of their qualities of character, in their deep and steadfast patriotism, in their devotion to truth and to liberty, and their faith in and loyalty to that great Being, the God of nature, of reason, and of revelation. Dr. Channing, it is true, stood preeminent in his genius as a writer and speaker, as a man to be marked through centuries for his rare intellect and his moral and spiritual exaltation. Yet both had the same consecration to the loftiest principles of thought and life.

William Ellery, whose earliest ancestor of whom we possess a record was William Ellery, freeman in 1672, and elected Representative of Gloucester in 1689, was born in Newport, Rhode Island, December 22, 1727. He was the grandfather of William Ellery Channing, who was born in the same place April 8, 1780, and lived near, and under the influence of, his grandparent. The great-grandfather of the latter, William Ellery, was born in Bristol, Rhode Island, October 31, 1701; and his life and character foreshadowed to a degree the eminence of his two descendants. He enjoyed, it is evident, the confidence of the community, as he was elected to the offices of judge, assistant, and deputy-governor. The inscription on his tombstone commemorates in Latin, not only his piety, and his many private virtues, but also his attachment to civil and religious liberty.

William Ellery, his son, graduated at Harvard College in 1747, and was one of eight of the name who had graduated at New England colleges up to 1828. Although engaged in mercantile pursuits at first, he was afterward a naval officer of the Colony. But, under the embarrassments of commerce through the revenue and non-importation acts, he gave up this office "when," as he says, "there was little or nothing for me to do but to join heart and hand with the Sons of Liberty."

In 1770 he entered on the practice of law. He was soon asked to defend the New York Committee of Inspection against a person who prosecuted them for burning goods brought into the city in violation of the non-importation agreement.

"You may depend upon my exerting myself," he says, "in your behalf in this suit, for the cause of liberty I always have had close at heart." In another letter he writes : "I rejoice that I had a share, however small it might be, in the repeal of the Stamp Act." This spirit was manifest in his whole character ; he was known for his good sense, his firmness and devotion to the public cause.

He had been placed on important committees to procure the repeal of oppressive revenue acts, and was in harmony with the men in other colonies who were preparing the people for a separation from the mother country, if it could not be honorably avoided.

His course inspired confidence in his fitness for a high public trust ; and in the memorable Continental Congress of 1776 he appeared as a delegate from Rhode Island. He took his seat in that body May 14, and his venerated colleague, Stephen Hopkins, and himself put their names, July 4, to the Declaration of Independence. His firm and beautiful signature contrasts strikingly with the tremulous character of his colleague's, whose limbs were shaken by age and illness, although his spirit was as intrepid and his perceptions were as clear as those of any around him. Mr. Ellery used, in his after life, to describe this scene with great animation. What must have been his sensations, knowing, as he did, that he then pledged himself to stand by an act so fearfully responsible that he might almost feel the very hand of the King's officer upon him for his audacious treason. "I placed myself," he tells us, "by the side of Charles Thomson, the secretary, and observed the expression and manner of each member as he came up to sign the Declaration." But we can see that, while he looks on so intently, it is with a calm and firm spirit, with the feeling that these men are equal to the crisis. Many of them evidently recognized the act with awe, perhaps with uncertainty as to its effect, but none with fear. "I was determined," he often said, "to see how they all looked, as they signed what might be their death-warrant. Undaunted resolution was displayed in every countenance."

He was naturally a quiet man, and strong in his attachments to home. "But," as he expressed himself at the time, "I placed my obligations to uphold liberty as high as those that bound me to my wife and children." Although cheerful, facetious, and no ascetic, Mr. Ellery was opposed to some of the popular recreations of those days. He says in one of his letters: —

I wish, while we are encouraging the importation of the amusements, follies, and vices of Great Britain, America would encourage the introduction of her virtues, if she have any. . . . This I am very clear in, that exhibitions of players, rope-dancers, and mountebanks have a more effectual tendency, by disembowelling the purse and enfeebling the mind, to sap the foundations of patriotism and public virtue, than any of the yet practised efforts of a despotic ministry.

He was on a visit to his family when the following resolutions passed through Congress; yet had he been in his seat, he would probably have given his vote for them: —

October 12, 1778. WHEREAS: True Religion and good morals are the only solid foundations of public liberty and happiness, — *Resolved:* That it be, and it hereby is, earnestly recommended to the several States to take the most effectual measures for the encouragement thereof, and for the suppression of theatrical entertainments, horse-racing, gaming, and such other diversions as are productive of idleness, dissipation, and a general depravity of principles and manners.

October 16, 1778. WHEREAS: Frequenting playhouses and theatrical entertainments has a fatal tendency to divert the minds of the people from a due attention to the means necessary for the defence of their country and the preservation of their liberties, — *Resolved:* That every person holding an office under the United States, who shall act, promote, encourage, or attend such plays, shall be deemed unworthy to hold such office, and shall be accordingly dismissed.

Enactments like these look strangely to our eyes, who find that, not only have members of Congress indulged in gaming quite freely, but taken special pleasure in witnessing horse-races; and as to theatrical amusements, I believe that not a single President of the United States has deprived himself of a seat, not to say a special seat, in the theatre.

Mr. Ellery was in the habit of keeping a diary

of his experiences on his journeys, which were on horseback, to and from Congress. Of one of these, in the autumn of 1777, he writes: —

November 1. We spent the Sabbath at Hartford. In the afternoon heard Mr. Strong preach a good sermon, and most melodious singing. The psalmody was performed in all its parts, and softness, more than loudness, seemed to be the aim of the performers.

This was probably very rare singing for those days. He writes at one time : —

Connecticut has collected and ordered taxes to the amount of one hundred thousand pounds more than she had issued. Brave spirits!

One day he gives us an idea of the old Revolutionary style of travel by great men : —

November 7. On our way to the ferry (North River) we met President Hancock in a sulky, escorted by one of his secretaries, and two or three other gentlemen, and one light-horseman. This event surprised us, as it seemed inadequate to the purpose either of defence or parade. But our surprise was not of long continuance; for we had not rode far before we met six or eight light-horsemen on the canter; and just as we reached the ferry, a boat arrived with as many more. These, with the one light-horseman and the gentlemen before mentioned, made up the escort of Mr. President Hancock. Who would not be a great man? I verily believe that the President, as he passes through the country thus escorted, feels a more triumphant satisfaction than the Colonel of the Queen's Regiment of Dragoons, attended by his whole army, and an escort of a thousand militia.

November 13. Met Mr. Samuel Adams and Mr. John Adams, about nine miles from Leven's, and hard by a tavern. They turned back to the inn, where we chatted, and ate bread and butter together. They were, to my great sorrow, bound home. I could not but lament that Congress should be without their counsels, and myself without their conversation.

Mr. Ellery won public confidence by his disinterested devotion to the country. His property at Newport was injured by the war, and even his own house burned to the ground. Still he adhered to the Congress, where he believed he could be, and was, useful, and left his possessions at home to the care of his fellow-citizens. His conduct was always straightforward and independent, — earnest, yet wise and prudent. He was a man to be trusted at all times, — honest, thoroughly good-principled, and therefore respected even by those who did not agree with him in opinions and measures. Throughout the war he had great influence, and after its close, in 1784, he was placed on the important committee appointed to ratify the articles of peace with Great Britain.

He had a Christian abhorrence of war; and still, while his country was involved in this calamity, he stood by her. In October, 1783, he was chairman of a committee of Congress who reported resolutions in honor of his fellow-citizen General Greene, and presenting to him two fieldpieces taken from the British army, in the southern department, as a testimonial to his wisdom, bravery, and military skill in that service. And in 1813, when another fellow-citizen had achieved a memorable naval victory, Mr. Ellery joined in the universal expression, saying: "Commodore Perry's exploit on Lake Erie is glorious."

No man could have been more modest than he in the appreciation of his own services to the country. "I was," said he late in life, "a member of Congress when Chatham eulogized that body, and possibly I might have been vain enough to have snuffed up part of that incense as my share; but the more I have known of myself, the more reason I have had not to think too highly of myself. Humility, rather than pride, becomes such creatures as we are."

His love of truth proved him a legitimate ancestor of the Rev. Dr. Channing. They both were slow in arriving at convictions on important subjects, and weighed justly the opinions of those from whom they finally differed. Both were distinguished for candor, fairness, and honesty in their views of all questions and the results which they reached. Mr. Ellery was indignant at the course of those who would lord it over others in matters religious or political. He speaks thus of reading two large volumes of sermons by Isaac Barrow: "I do not regret the time I spent in reading them, and I am about to read Calvin's Institutes. I think

I can read books of theology without being over-influenced by names. What appears to me to be right I shall embrace, and reject the chaff and stubble." He gave himself loyally to religious truth. Said he: —

I believe if party names were entirely disused, there would be more harmony among Christians. I heard a sensible minister of the Gospel inveigh, in a sermon against the Hopkinsians, as he called them, in such a bitter manner, that I dare say one half, at least, of his congregation would have avoided any writing of Dr. Hopkins as they would a most venomous serpent. And yet I don't in the least doubt that this same minister, if he had heard the first Episcopal clergyman in Newport declare, from the pulpit, that the breath of a Dissenter was infectious, would have severely reprobated it.

The tone and spirit of this language descended plenteously on his broad-hearted grandson.

Mr. Ellery found it difficult, however, to carry the same charity uniformly into his political sentiments. He was a Whig of the Revolution, and a Federalist of Washington's day; and, unlike the Democrats of that period, he held Napoleon Bonaparte in the utmost abhorrence. He feared that he might vanquish the Russians, and get possession of St. Petersburg. He writes: —

I wish I may be mistaken, and that Heaven may put a hook in his jaws and draw him back, and overthrow his immense army. How long this dreadful scourge will be suffered to lay waste and destroy, the Lord only knoweth. It is a matter of consolation, and even of joy, that the Lord reigneth.

In the midst of the convulsions at home and abroad, and all the public dangers and sufferings, this was steadfastly his final word: "The Lord reigneth." It will be recollected that his grandson inherited his strong feeling in regard to Napoleon. In his essay on that man he says: "Such a person should be caged like a wild beast."

Mr. Ellery, although quiet and undemonstrative, was a man of no ordinary powers and gifts. He did much for his country in her hour of greatest need; but his signal work, after all, was upon his own character. This was not the growth of original qualities, easily directed, and prone only to love, purity, and all moral excellence. He was not gentle from an inborn meekness, nor good from the force of outward circumstances. On the contrary he owed everything, we can see, to personal discipline, self-inspection, and self-control. This was to be noticed in his first attempts to speak in Congress. He used to say that it seemed to him when he rose, that he knew nothing, and he sat down very little satisfied with himself. But he resolved not to give way a moment to weakness or awkwardness; and in time "he became," as others testified, "not indeed an orator, but an easy and useful debater, and had always something to say to the purpose."

When his public life was over, he lived on, still interested in his country, regular and simple in his habits, fond of reading, and attractive in conversation,— carried along from year to year, with little loss of bodily vigor, and none of spirits, memory, or force of mind. His letters, written in the clear and firm hand of his early days, were full of affection, humor, and kind regard to others. In his eighty-fourth year he writes thus of the blessings reserved for that period of life: —

I do not think, notwithstanding the afflictive dispensations of Providence in the loss of friends, and the diseases and irritability to which old age is frequently subject, that it is so undesirable a condition as some have represented it to be. As to employment of time, I have experienced such instruction and delight in reading and investigating truth, that I mean, as long as my mind is capable of bearing it, to keep it in exercise, and doze as little as possible. There are those who think that the miseries of life are greater than its joys. I am not one of them, especially when I consider the numerous objects contrived and adapted to please our senses and our appetites, the discoveries which natural philosophy has made and is making, the improvements in arts and advance in science and in the philosophy of the mind, the profit and delight which attend reading and conversation, and compare the sources of pleasure, which kind Providence has furnished to entertain and instruct us in our pilgrimage, with the miseries of life. It appears to me that the latter are but just enough to constitute this a probationary state, — to prepare us, by the exercise of virtue and piety, for a mode of existence in which they who act according to the will of God will enjoy uncontrasted and eternal felicity.

The year before his death he writes again: —

There is no fence or guard that can secure us against the infirmities of old age. They must come, and it is our duty to bear them with patience, and not murmur at the condition on which long life is held.

February 10, 1820, his clergyman was with him an hour. They spoke of the prospect of death, and he said it was an event which for two years he had been fully prepared for, and even desired. The next day his doctor said to him, " Your pulse beats very well." " Charmingly," he replied. On another day he said that he knew he was dying; and in two hours he passed away, February 15, 1820, in the ninety-third year of his age. Happy in his life, happy in his departure from it, he was a genuine patriot, a true man, " an honest man, the noblest work of God."

BUNKER HILL MONUMENT.

CHAPTER XI.

WILLIAM ELLERY CHANNING.

THE centennial exercises in 1880, commemorating the birth of Dr. Channing, gave gleams from the inner life of that great man of intense interest. We had so long been quickened and elevated by his varied public productions that we earnestly desired to know more of his private thought and experience. It is much to see anything of the hidden motions of a spirit so sensitive to all that is pure, noble, broad, and tender in this our common life. We instinctively catch with eagerness every word that reveals to us the man himself.

This popular interest is enhanced in those who had a personal knowledge of Dr. Channing. Can we who knew him ever forget that slight frame gliding through the street in midwinter, muffled so closely against the air? We are not surprised that he regarded himself for long years as having but the slenderest hold upon life. No wonder we sometimes heard that from day to day it required the tenderest nursing to keep the soul in the body. See him on Sunday as he moves up the pulpit stairs. His debility fills you with sympathy and anxiety. He sinks exhausted on his seat; and, when he rises to give out a hymn, he is too weak, you fear, for the service. The single lock of his soft brown hair, as it falls across his forehead, contrasts strongly with its transparent paleness, and his thin, hollow cheeks are covered with pain-caused lines. The first tones of his voice, though feeble and low, are reverential, and stir the hushed congregation to devoutness. After a hymn, read with more strength, is sung, he rises for the sermon. A few sentences are uttered, when you feel that, out of all this weakness, there are coming words of a rare energy. His full eye kindles, his voice gains strength, and, forgetting his delicate figure, you are borne on, with increasing sway, assured that this man is a power to move, thrill, and inspire.

Perhaps there was never a more striking demonstration of the power of the human will over the body than in Dr. Channing. I met him often at councils for ordination and elsewhere; and his face usually bore the marks of his habitual introversion. It was his misfortune to be a bad sleeper; and we could read in the fallen cheek, and discoloring about the eye, proofs that often, in the midnight hour, he was a victim of wakefulness, that "tyrant of the burning brain." His intense thoughtfulness and strong concentration, and habit of rapid and fervid composition — to be afterward sedulously corrected — preyed at times fearfully on his delicate organization. He had, it is true, the advantage on one side, of a vigorous ancestry. His grandfather, William Ellery, lived to the age of ninety-three, and two of his own brothers reached a remarkable old age. We should give him credit, too, for great care of himself. His wise words may well be heeded by our students and writers : " The only true specifics for keeping health are exercise, temperance (in the large sense of the word), and cheerfulness."

He was indebted not only to his maternal grandparent, but to his own father, for germs of personal worth. William Channing, the father, was a business man of high integrity, a fit companion of Lucy Ellery, the mother. Both were faithful and friendly to all, self-reliant and of commanding qualities, alike energetic and benignant. The son inherited, on each side, a character conscientious, truthful, tender, elastic under trouble, and cheerful to the last.

The union of apparently conflicting elements in Dr. Channing was most striking. He combined great physical weakness with a still greater mental energy. In private conversation he seemed at times feeble, suffering, and dependent; his voice was low and his utterance difficult. One who did not notice his eyes would often think him languid, perhaps destitute of force. Being human, he, of course, shared the imperfection of our nature. Of a very ardent and excitable temperament, he was yet a model of self-control. I remember seeing but a single instance of the slightest loss of this power. At the council before the ordination of one of our young ministers he was strenuous for a written certificate of church-membership from the candidate. And as, for a strong reason, that document could not be presented to the council, he was unwilling to give his vote for the ordination to proceed. The discussion on this point elicited some feeling on his part. But however any of us might, at the present day, dissent from his position, this incident gave proof of his thorough conscientiousness, and that to an exalted spirituality he united a firm adherence to what he regarded as important ecclesiastical forms.

His was a truly liberal mind. I often saw him at conventions. I remember one of what was popularly called Come-outers, in Chardon Street Chapel, Boston, which he attended. He was fond of being present whenever any new light was even slightly promised. Some might have said he occasionally compromised his dignity in this way. But not so; you saw that he was in search of truth, and would recognize it wherever found.

Like his grandfather Ellery, he was intensely opposed to slavery. After the murder of Rev. Elijah Lovejoy at Alton, Illinois, he attended a meeting of indignant remonstrance in Faneuil Hall, December 8, 1837. Public opinion was then exceedingly sensitive on the agitation of the slavery question. But Channing did not fear its rebuke. Others might blench, but he remained firm. I see him, as I did that day — the bright rays of a winter sun shining on his noble head, — as he stood upon that platform. He attempts to speak amid hisses and jeers, and at length expresses his amazement that every man present does not join in a denunciation of this desecration of God's image, and insult to human justice. Calm himself, with a fearless voice and manner, he makes a solemn appeal to every lover of right, freedom, and justice, and then offers a series of resolutions, setting forth a protest against this trampling on a free press, and this deed of crime and bloodshed before the God of justice and under a government of equal laws. No wonder young Phillips — prompted by words spoken by another, that would justify the murderers at Alton and place them side by side with Otis and Hancock, with Adams and Quincy — rose and said he thought " those pictured lips," pointing to their portraits in the hall, " would have broken into voice to rebuke the recreant American, the slanderer of the dead." It seemed to me one of those occasions which carry us back to the very days and deeds of the noble fathers of the Revolution. Channing's moral courage was worthy a protomartyr. Then, as always in relation to all social wrongs, he not only felt an unfaltering interest, but took a public and bold stand against them.

He was, to a large extent, independent of criticism. I often saw him at the Boston Athenæum, and sometimes with a foreign review in his hand; but, it has been said, and, I have good reason to believe with truth, that he seldom read criticisms on his own publications: perhaps not those which were commendatory; certainly not, as in the case of the "Edinburgh Review,"—which once published a severe and caustic article on his thoughts and style,— those written against him. He evidently apprehended it might tempt him to shrink from the utterance of his own views fully and fearlessly on all points social, religious, or political. He said once, " he only regretted criticisms which would take from the power of his preaching."

Father Taylor once said to me, comparing him with one of our rare men who seemed at times somewhat cynical, " Dr. Channing is a sweet spirit." Reason and sensibility were never divorced either in his works or his character. To an unquestioned moral courage he joined a singular tenderness of spirit. He who was dauntless in every point of duty, and heroic in his public utterances, was as sensitive as a little child in private intercourse.

So earnest was he in conversation on certain topics, that I sometimes felt he must love disputation. There, again, he reminded one of his distinguished ancestor. He would question, and take the opposite side, and appear at times a Pyrrhonist, so full was he of doubts. But, all the while, his aim was to elicit the truth, and the whole truth, on the subject before him. The inquirer — seemingly almost the denier — in private, would, in this way, at last reach conclusions which, in his public discourses, we heard him maintain with moral enthusiasm.

His tender tribute to his personal friend, Rev. Charles Follen, LL. D. is an unconscious portraiture, in many of its touching passages, of his own character. To one privileged personally to know them both, sentence after sentence is a response of two noble spirits, who, we saw, must have drunk sorrows and joys from a common cup. Dr. Follen filled the pulpit of the Federal Street Church for a time, during the illness and absence abroad of its colleague pastor. Although not in full sympathy with Garrison, he was a decided abolitionist. He did not hesitate indeed to show this both in his writings on this subject and in his speech, public as well as private. Dr. Channing was in perfect sympathy with him, and he desired him as his temporary associate in the pulpit. He expressed this wish, it was said, to the standing committee of his society. " By no means," one of its prominent members is reported to have replied,— " by no means can we consent to have our pulpit occupied by an abolitionist." This account illustrates remarkably the state of public opinion at that time on the antislavery question, and shows the marvellous revolution produced in it by the subsequent emancipation of the colored race on our soil.

The prophetic spirit of Dr. Channing, everywhere discernible, is seen in one of his letters to Miss Aiken, in which he replies to a suggestion of hers in regard to American Slavery. He saw, in the power of Christian principles, a force that he felt confident must ultimately lead to its abolition. Referring to influences of a milder nature he says: "To effect great reforms, convulsions are sometimes necessary. If men resist a beneficent innovation, the same awful Providence which has in times past shaken the social state will again heave it from its foundations." But little did he, apparently, at that time imagine the end of American Slavery could be so near as it was.

One could not spend an hour with Channing without being struck with his singular modesty. So brave in public and fearless in uttering his opinions, in conversation he seemed to take always the attitude of an humble inquirer. Instead of protruding his own views, he studiously sought those of others. I have no doubt, from his air and manner, that he often gained quite as much, in preparing his lectures and discourses, from conversation as from books.

A passage in one of his letters is important as serving to correct an erroneous impression, held by some persons during his life, in regard to his estimate of himself and his own works. A friend once spoke to me of his undue self-esteem, and referred to his very frequent use of the pronoun in the first person singular. But this judgment was singularly unjust, as is made manifest in many ways. Why should not one speak of himself simply and naturally as he would of another? There is often more self-consciousness and real egotism in a studied avoiding to speak of self, than in a direct utterance of what is felt and thought. In one's private letters he is quite sure to give his true opinion of himself. And how is it in the case before us? "You ask," he says to Miss Aiken, "about my great work. I have nothing great about me but the undeveloped within." In another place he writes self-distrustfully, yet, as we now see, without good reason: "Pardon my egotism; I see far higher reputations fading away, and who am I that I should live? Providence is to raise up higher lights. . . . What better can we ask?" These words recall some of his grandfather Ellery's, almost identical with them.

His health was always delicate; and sometimes rendered his voice feeble. I recollect a Sunday when many of his hearers, having come from a chilling atmosphere, gave way to a sympathetic coughing. The preacher was manifestly disturbed. He at length paused, and requested that an effort should be made to suppress coughing, as he found it difficult to be heard. The effect was magical. An almost profound silence followed, and we had a new lesson of man's power over what are often considered wholly involuntary movements.

Dr. Channing, singularly just to other persons, was tried by the practice, not uncommon in his church, of many coming to the door and waiting until they saw whether he was to preach or another, when some, if disappointed, would turn away and leave. Perhaps to obviate this disrespect to his devoted colleague, he arranged to preach on some Sundays in the morning and on others in the afternoon. A friend once asked him, probably thinking it a compliment, "Are you to preach to-morrow, sir?" The quick reply was, "There will be divine service in the church."

Whenever able he attended church as a hearer. It was no slight ordeal to a young minister to preach with this great man sitting at his side in the pulpit. I recollect his kindness, after listening to a sermon which seemed to the speaker unworthy so distinguished a listener, — with what friendly words, while he approved of the general treatment of the subject, he criticised a fault of the discourse in not qualifying one of its parts which made, he thought, not too great account of consciousness as an evidence of the truth of Christianity, but too little of the evidence of miracles. He was to preach himself in the afternoon, and said to me, "I wish I could invite you home to dine with me, but I am obliged to-day to give up conversation, and spare all my strength for the service this afternoon." Within a few months afterward, spending an hour or two with him and his family, what I had lost on that Sunday was more than made up by his cordial reception, and the charm, freedom, and simplicity of his whole conversation and manner.

Usually he began his discourse in a calm and

quiet manner, and as he proceeded, gained in power, and at the conclusion flamed up with great zeal and fervor. But on one occasion, when his subject was Immortality, he entered at once, in a most eloquent tone, upon his favorite theme. It was like the launching of a noble vessel from its ways. His spirit kindled with the first sentence, and was borne on from topic to topic, each a fresh inspiration; and one felt as if lifted to a height of transfiguration, where it would be good to abide evermore. I think his readers will agree that one of the most striking of his discourses is that on the Future Life. No human production, perhaps, has given clearer views than this of the great unseen world; none privileged to hear him on this high topic but must remember the thrilling tones in which he spoke of it.

Channing reasoned cogently on this subject; His sermon on Immortality is a compact argument. It is, as was said of another production, " logic on fire." That on the Future Life is more intuitional. We seem, as we read it, to see heaven opened before us. I recollect being told of an occasion when Dr. Channing officiated at a funeral, and made it throughout his prayer a theme of thanksgiving that the pure spirit had entered its heavenly home. All tears seemed to be dried up in the bright sunshine of the everlasting world. His bosom friend, Dr. Tuckerman, who was present, congratulated him on lifting the mourning circle out of their griefs into the calm and joyous certainties of the celestial sphere. Often did one rise, as he heard him utter the word *Immortality* in the pulpit, into the same serene faith.

The impression he produced, when preaching, was that of a most exalted character. I can readily believe what was said of his influence at some such moments, even upon children. A little girl, meeting him at her home, and drawn toward him by his attractive manner in private, at length touched him, and said: " You are a man; I see you every Sunday in God's house, and I thought you was God."

Channing was a patriot, early and late, constant in his love, his labors, and his prayers for his own land. When he wrote, " I wish to see patriotism exalted into a moral principle," he gave the key-note of his own character, no less than the refrain of his national discourses. His Fast sermon during the War of 1812 has the ring of his maternal ancestor; and those wise and eloquent papers of his in the " Christian Examiner," on the perils of the Union, remind us strongly of the tones of that venerated man.

Whatever subject Channing takes up, if his treatment of it begins with our own country, it soon spreads out to other lands, and includes the entire race. At a moment when England and America were threatened with war, he gave a lecture on that curse of humanity, and said in the preface to it: " The relations between these countries cannot become hostile without deranging, more or less, the intercourse of all other communities, and bringing evils on the whole Christian world."

What I have said of the breadth of Channing's views in his public utterances was true also of his private conversation. In those gatherings of friends and acquaintances when topics of social interest were discussed, however wise the remarks of others, he usually had a wisdom beyond theirs. Men of large thought and liberal culture, and from various callings and professions, might be present and say excellent things. And yet you knew well, by the doubts he suggested, the limits he set up, his hard questions, his sharp criticisms, and bold objections, that he saw depths of the subject below your own best vision. He might at last come to acquiesce in your opinion; but it would be only after a delay, and after a firmness of opposition which, gentle and kind as his manner always was, promised anything but a final assent to your view.

Dr. Channing, instead of being narrowed, as many of us are, by advancing years, was less and less limited in his views and feelings. In that noble " Discourse on the Church," preached the very year before his death, we see how he spurns all ecclesiastical fetters and every mere denominational barrier. The same year he writes: " I speak as an independent Christian. . . . I can endure no sectarian bonds." Indeed one cannot but think that, had he and his grandparent Ellery lived to our day, both would rejoice in the growing indications of harmony and fellowship between the various liberal portions of long-separated Christian bodies.

Such men as Channing do not grow old with the lapse of years. We who saw him, on and on, from his early manhood to his closing days, remember how little he changed, even in personal appearance, with the approach of age. It seems to me, as I recall him in his meridian, that he showed more the effects of toil and time, and his face was more pallid and careworn, than in the last years of his life. At that time his countenance grew more radiant, and he manifestly felt more at ease, and enjoyed this world as he never had before. It is interesting to read his own language on this subject: "I enjoy fine weather as I did not in my youth. I have lost one ear, but was never so alive to sweet sounds. I am waking up more to the mysteries of harmony." That last summer, and when nearly sixty-three years old, amid the exquisite beauties of Lenox, he writes: "Here am I finding life a sweet cup as I approach what we call its dregs."

"Always young for liberty," he said of himself on one occasion, and we are not surprised at the glow of youthfulness in one so elastic and hopeful as Dr. Channing. Gloom had no resting-place in his nature. With his views of the all-embracing goodness of God, how could he droop and despond under his beneficent Providence? Looking, as he did, upon man as the child of a Heavenly

Father, and the whole race as embosomed in his love, the future was to him full of cheering anticipations. I might quote pages from the writings of his hopeful ancestor, William Ellery, of the same bright glow. In the high and broad development of his own character, and his conscious connection with the entire race, he could not but see tokens of its glorious capabilities and progress.

And here we reach the ground we have for believing that the works of Channing are to have a permanent place in the history of humanity. Their free spirit, the growth largely of our national institutions, makes us sure that their circulation is not to be limited to his own country, but will extend as far as the English language is spoken and written; and help forward everywhere the great cause of national liberty and independence. Nor will they stop here. Already they have been, wholly or in part, translated in France, Germany, Hungary, Italy, and even in Iceland, into their several languages. Many forces will contribute to their diffusion and perpetuity.

Writings which cover so wide a range of topics are suited to meet the wants of every people and every age. It is rare to find in so large a field so very little of a merely local or temporary interest. As I write, I can see the effect of his works on the great International Association which is aiming to establish a code of laws binding on the commonwealth of nations, by which their disputes shall be settled, like the differences of individuals, not by the sword, but by arbitration. Let Channing's abhorrence of war and his inculcations of righteousness and peace prevail, and then, through his and other Christian and pacific influences, the world will at last exhibit — what he yearned and prayed and labored, to accomplish — universal peace.

The impression Dr. Channing produced personally seemed to me not so much that of genius as of rare goodness. The corner-stone of his character was, I think, conscientiousness. He appeared not alone to do, but to think and feel, only what he regarded as right. With all his power and culture, and his mental superiority, he says, as he draws near the close of his life, "I am less and less a worshipper of mere intellect." The moral and spiritual nature, common to the lofty and the lowly alike, and its largest development, he more and more prized as the true end of man's existence.

It was fitting that he should close his life in the way he did. My thoughts had often reverted to the scene where he passed away, and a few years since I had the privilege of a temporary stay in that vicinity. A friend gave me, while at Lenox, the details of his visit at that place. Amid the exquisite scenery of Berkshire, and the refined, genial society he met there, Dr. Channing passed, as he himself said, some of the happiest hours of his life. In a building which we daily passed, he gave his grand address on the anniversary of emancipation in the British West Indies; but the effort of delivery overtasked his feeble frame, and I was told that after it he was but just able, with two friends for his support, to walk to a carriage. I went to the house at which he stopped, and saw the very window out of which he looked at the sunset hours. Unhappily, beyond question from imperfect drainage, it was on that spot he contracted the typhoidal disease which terminated his life. It seemed sad that such must be his lot, yet, judged by his glorious work, he had lived long; and therefore when, on that eventful October day, the tidings came that "the golden bowl was broken," while we shed some natural tears, we gave thanks to Him who had placed such power within that mortal frame, and permitted it to be exercised up to what is termed "the grand climacteric of man's life." We rejoiced that he had met the last call with an unfaltering trust, and entered those everlasting gates through which he had so long gazed, and for which his high inspirations had trained many a grateful spirit.

In this age of commemorations, when in all civilized countries monuments are erected to the departed great, I think this man, who was cosmopolitan in spirit, should have memorials set up in other lands to honor his name. It especially becomes this nation — the principles of whose government and institutions he lived, labored, and died to support — to build at its Capitol a monument that will do something to perpetuate the name and influence of William Ellery Channing.

CHAPTER XII.

SOCIETY OF THE CINCINNATI.

This association, formed by officers of the Revolution, for patriotic and social purposes, and to be continued through their posterity, has left records most valuable as materials for biographies of men associated with that eventful period. It brings before us, in its original members, a band of men, taken together, of rare military skill, science, and practical ability, and of high personal character. It includes not only American officers, but those of our generous allies, France, Prussia, Germany, with a few rare men of other nations of Europe, who sent us many commanders, and not a few in the ranks, who rendered noble service in their labors, sacrifices, and sufferings for the rights of the American Colonies, and the final emancipation and independence of these United States.

This society at once took a firm hold of the American people. When Lafayette revisited this country in 1824 he was received with enthusiasm and affection by all classes of the people. A public dinner was given him, at which the second toast, after "The United States," was, "General Washington." This was coupled with " The Cincinnati," showing that this body stood among the foremost in the love and honor of the nation. This latter sentiment was appropriately and immediately followed by, "The asserters and supporters of the rights of mankind throughout the world." The Cincinnati, thus early imbedded in the memories and grateful recognitions of the country, should hold its just place, as it did to the last with Washington; and its name, and those of all who have stood on its rolls, should remain through every generation of a people who owe so large a debt to the services of its members.

It adds to our interest in this society to know that the decoration of Cincinnatus, worn by Washington, was presented, in 1824, to Lafayette, with a request that it be afterward given to his second grandson, Edmond Lafayette. This decoration bears the date "A. D. 1783." It is of elegant materials and workmanship, supported by a sky-blue, watered silk "riband," edged with a white piping, in token of the alliance between France and America, and held together by a gold clasp. The "riband" used by Washington is half worn out.

Washington, in a letter to the Count de Rochambeau, dated October 29, 1783, speaks thus of the formation of the Society of the Cincinnati: —

SIR, — The officers of the American army, in order to perpetuate that mutual friendship which they contracted in the hour of common danger and distress, and for other purposes which are mentioned in the instrument of the association, have united together in a society of friends under the name of CINCINNATI; and having honored me with the office of president, it becomes a very agreeable part of my duty to inform you that the society have done themselves the honor to consider you, and the generals and officers of the army which you commanded in America, as members of the Society. . .

As soon as the diploma is made out, I will have the honor to transmit it to you.

The Society was at once placed on a firm foundation in France. The order met the approbation of the king, and a list of members was prepared comprising thirty-three officers. The whole number of the Society soon put on record was seventy-nine.

Lafayette was received at Boston, on his visit to this country in 1824, by the members of the Cincinnati, his brothers-in-arms, who extolled him, not only as the ally and savior of America, but as one who had "secured liberty to millions of freemen." At Staten Island his military associates in this Society, some of them then eighty years old, embraced him with tears of joy. Everywhere he had similar cordial greetings; and their spirit was transmitted to sons and grandsons of this order, at the recent reception, October 19, 1881, of our French and German guests, numbering in all twenty-seven persons, at the centennial celebration of the American victory at Yorktown. It gave me special pleasure to meet the Marquis de Rochambeau and his associates in the Massachusetts Senate Chamber on their recent visit to Boston, and to think of the devoted ancestors civil or military of those men, and of the many honors which their striking badges showed they had received from distinguished societies, both in France and Germany.

At the head of the Society of the Cincinnati we place GEORGE WASHINGTON. For his pre-eminent rank, in both military and civil services which he rendered to his country, this is his uncontested position.

His name takes us back to the meeting of the Continental Congress at Carpenter's Hall, Philadelphia, September, 1774 — a momentous occasion. Gathered from all the States, it was an illustrious array of patriotic men. Conspicuous among them was Samuel Adams, the master-spirit of the day. Beside him sat his younger kinsman, John Adams, bold, ingenious, determined, eloquent, a born leader of men. But look yonder! There sits a man only forty years old, in the prime of his energies. Others speak, but he is silent; and yet in his marked face, and especially in his firm mouth, there is an air of power and command that makes him a noteworthy man. His colleagues turn toward him with deference. So modest, he occupies a back seat, and yet he is the foremost man in the confidence of the assembly. This is the individual who has said in the Virginia Convention: " I will raise a thousand men, subsist them at my own expense, and march with them at their head for the relief of Boston." This can be no other than George Washington.

We are struck, early and late in his career, by the tenacity of his friendships. Not in his public offices and relations alone, but in his associations of a comparatively private nature with his companions in arms, and those in every subordinate civil capacity, it is most interesting to observe the depth of his affections. No man was ever surrounded by truer friends; and, as we often find in such cases, none had rivals so jealous and so determined as he. What with Royalists, — or, in the varied epithets of the day, Tories, Loyalists, Traitors, — military factions and political divisions and asperities, no man, in elevated office, ever suffered more than Washington from the injustice, open and concealed, of his contemporaries. This was true both in his own and the mother country. In the present universal admiration for his name and character, we find it difficult to conceive how this bitter spirit could have been exhibited toward one so exalted in purity, patriotism, self-sacrifice, and suffering for his country.

Among the traitors to our cause was one who appeared soon after Washington took command of the army at Cambridge, Dr. Benjamin Church. Up to this time he had stood high as a patriot and a friend of liberty. He was still a member of the House of Representatives, and had been just appointed Surgeon-General and Director of Hospitals. At this crisis he was suspected of a traitorous correspondence with the enemy in Boston. After thorough examination he was convicted, and expelled from the House of Representatives. Congress afterward resolved "that he be closely confined in some jail in Connecticut, without the use of pen, ink, or paper; and that no person be allowed to converse with him except in the presence and hearing of a magistrate or a sheriff of the county." Previously to the execution of this sentence he was confined in the former residence of Colonel Vassall, opposite the house occupied by Washington in Cambridge. I recently visited the room assigned to him, where the subsequent occupant, Samuel Batchelder, Esq., who has since died, 1880, at the advanced age of ninety-two years, politely showed me this room, in which I saw the name of Dr. Church, cut on the panel of a door by himself while imprisoned there.

At a distance from this dwelling is the house in which Burgoyne was confined after his defeat and capture at the battle of Saratoga. I never look on the house occupied by Burgoyne, in Cambridge, without contrasting his character, associated as it is with that dwelling, and the character of Washington, which forever permeates the atmosphere of the mansion he occupied when he took command of the American army, under the brave old elm that bears his immortal name. The same contrast I see between two pictures before me, as I write: one that of Washington seated, with his majestic figure, so modest, yet so grandly impressive, on his favorite horse, as he receives a salute on the field of Trenton; the other, a picture in an open book, of Burgoyne, the impersonation of haughtiness, — that defiant attitude, those disdainful eyes, the lips, especially the under one, projected in scorn, and the chin thrust forward to supplement its effect. How must this proud being have fretted himself when he thought of his titles and rank, and his pretensions a few months before, and saw himself now a prisoner at the mercy of those detested "Yankees!" One cannot pass that memorable building without recalling the pompous proclamation issued by Burgoyne when in his pride and power, and contrasting with it the reply of Washington. Burgoyne had threatened the Americans with all the outrages of war, enhanced by the aid of savages to be let loose on their prey. Washington, after saying, "The free men of America protest against such abuse of language and prostitution of sentiment," adds, speaking of the British domination, "This is a power we do not dread," and finally closes in this calm, dignified, and devout strain: "Harassed as we are by unrelenting persecution, obliged by every tie to repel violence by force, urged by self-preservation to exert the strength which Providence has given us to defend our natural rights against the aggressor, we appeal to the honesty of all mankind for the justice of our cause; its events we submit to Him who speaks the fate of nations, in humble confidence that, as His omniscient eye taketh note even of the sparrow that falleth to the ground, so he will not withdraw his countenance from a people who humbly array themselves under his banner in defence of the noblest principles with which He hath adorned humanity."

That a man of this stamp should have been so grossly misunderstood or misrepresented almost passes belief. Yet the record is clear. Not confining ourselves to the treason of Arnold, the cabal of Conway, the defection of Lee, and the known jealousies of military rivals, Gates and others, we find abundant and painful evidence of the calumnies spread in regard to Washington, not only in public journals and private documents, but among the daily fireside talks and gatherings of obscure individuals and the scandal of evil tongues.

We have only to take up some of the journals of the day to learn what incredible accounts were circulated in regard to the condition of our affairs, as viewed in the mother country. Incidents are narrated in the British newspapers, published during the Revolution, which betray an astonishing lack of knowledge in respect to the state of men and things in this country. Making all due allowance for the coloring of prejudice and passion, what are we to think of such accounts as the following, taken indiscriminately from journals and letters of that period? The first relates to two of the seven marked men who then resided on Tory Row, so called, in Cambridge: "Lieutenant-Governor Oliver, president of his majesty's council, was attacked at Cambridge by a mob of about four thousand, and was compelled to resign his seat at the Board, since which, upon further threats, he has been obliged to lease his estate, and take refuge with his family in Boston. . . Colonel Vassal of Cambridge, from intolerable threats and insolent treatment by mobs, has left his elegant seat there and retired to Boston, with his family, for protection."

The Loyalists in Boston are represented as suffering still worse things. In language not especially classic or Christian, we read this statement: "The fugitives from Boston are gone for Halifax; the people say, 'no d—d Tories shall be allowed to breathe in their air,' so that those ' d—ls ' can't find a resting-place there, which was the only place on the continent that they ever dared to hope they might stay in."

It is known that our commander was seldom alluded to by his military title. Even Thomas Hutchinson, American born, who had been governor of Massachusetts, sneeringly calls him, in his contribution to history, " Mr. Washington." and the following would make it appear that, viewed in his domestic relations, neither he nor his were entitled to very great respect: ": Mr. Washington we hear, is married to a very amiable lady, but it is said that Mrs. Washington, being a warm Loyalist, has separated from her husband since the commencement of the present troubles, and lives very much respected in the city of New York." And this when, at the moment, she was actively engaged in every form of kindness and relief to his suffering army.

The tone of some letters, in the correspondence of civil and military officials a century ago, seems to us, accustomed to the courtesies of such documents at the present time, incredible. Not long after the battle of Bunker Hill, Washington wrote to General Gage on his treatment of our officers who were in the Boston jail. His letter was in very mild terms, carefully avoiding any expressions that might be regarded as indecorous. The answer was in an entirely different strain; it was directed to " George Washington, Esq.," and called our people Rebels, Usurpers, and the like, affecting great clemency in having " forborne to hang our prisoners."

But, amid all this misjudgment and maltreatment, Washington, dishonored by British officials, and slightly esteemed even by the Loyalists of his own country, had abundant evidence of the almost idolatrous regard in which he was held by every true patriot in the land. How touching are such tributes as this, taken from the old Essex Gazette, January 7, 1776. " This morning the sixth daughter of Captain Bancroft of Dunstable, Massachusetts, was baptized by the name of Martha Dandridge, the maiden name of his Excellency, General Washington's, lady. The child was dressed in buff and blue, with a sprig of evergreen on its head, emblematic of his Excellency's glory and provincial affection."

And not by personal homage alone, but by the spirit of multitudes of both sexes, Washington was cheered and sustained in many a trying moment. Notice the devotedness that permeated his native State. Says the Pennsylvania Journal, July 16, 1777: —

We hear that the young ladies of Amelia County in Virginia, considering the situation of their county in particular, and that of the United States in general, have entered into a resolution not to permit the addresses of any person, be his circumstances or situation in life what they will, unless he has served in the American armies long enough to prove by his valor that he is deserving of their love.

A writer in the British army at Charleston, South Carolina, in a letter to a friend in London, December, 1781, says: —

The assemblies which the officers have opened, in hopes to give an air of gayety and cheerfulness to themselves and the inhabitants, are but dull and gloomy, — the men play at cards, indeed, to avoid talking, but the women are seldom or never to be persuaded to dance. Even in their dresses the females seem to bid us defiance; the gay toys which are imported here they despise; they wear their own homespun manufactures, and take care to have in their breastknots, and even on their shoes, something from the flag of the thirteen stripes. An officer told Lord Cornwallis, not long ago, that he believed if we had destroyed all the men in North America, we should have enough to do to conquer the women.

History shows few instances in either sex of a heroism equal to the following. In 1779 Congress passed this resolve, honorable to them, and still more so to the heroine this body thus appreciated: —

Resolved, That Margaret Corbine, who was wounded and disabled at the attack of Fort Washington, while she heroically filled the post of her husband who was killed by her side, serving a piece of artillery, do receive during her natural life, or the continuance of the said disability, one half of the monthly pay drawn by a soldier in the service of these States; and that she now receive, out of the public stores, one complete suit of clothes, or the value thereof in money.

The confidence of those who knew Washington best, in his transcendent abilities and final success, is most touching. Surgeon Thacher speaks of a visit of the Commander-in-Chief at the hospital in his charge, and his deep interest in the sick and wounded, and particular inquiries as to their treatment and comfortable accommodations: —

His personal appearance is that of the perfect gentleman and accomplished warrior. He is remarkably tall, — full six feet, — erect and well proportioned. The serenity of his countenance and majestic gracefulness of his deportment impart a strong impression of that dignity and grandeur which are his peculiar characteristics; and no one can stand in his presence without feeling the ascendancy of his mind, and associating with his countenance the idea of wisdom, philanthropy, magnanimity, and patriotism. His nose is straight, and his eyes inclined to blue. He displays a native gravity, but devoid of all appearance of ostentation. No man could have more at command the veneration and regard of the officers and soldiers of our army, even after defeat and misfortune. This is the illustrious chief a kind Providence has decreed as the instrument to conduct our country to peace and independence.

This was said, we are to recollect, amid the last gloomy days of October, 1778, after a time of depression, and on the eve of that dreary season to be spent largely under canvas tents, and amid exposures to cold and storms.

Often those of the British who spoke well of Washington personally, regarded his army and the people in this country generally as too wicked to prosper. So good a man in the main as young Aubury, an English letter-writer in America at the time, says: "As to redress from the Americans, little is to be expected. Though their Commander-in-Chief possesses a humanity that reflects the highest honors upon him, he has not been able, notwithstanding so much love and esteem, to diffuse that benevolence and godlike virtue among others." He speaks of the many "horrid barbarities and persecutions which arise in consequence of this unnatural war, and which have branded the name of America with an odium that no time can obliterate, no merit expunge." Speaking of Burgoyne's army, then prisoners of war, he says: "For ten days the officers subsisted upon salt pork and Indian corn made into cakes," and adds, "they had not a drop of any kind of spirit. . . . Many officers to comfort themselves, put red pepper into water to drink, by way of cordial."

It is refreshing, amid the misstatements of many British accounts during the war, to find a better element occasionally appearing in their writers. An officer says, speaking of Andre's doom as a spy: "General Washington shed tears when the rigorous sentence" was passed, denying Andre the privilege of a soldier and sending him to the gallows, "and when it was put in execution," "he would have granted his request to die a military death." But the writer adds, to his credit: "He [Washington] felt certain the effect would be disastrous; and the board of general officers, at the same time evincing the sincerest grief, could not deviate from the established custom in such cases."

For all he had endured from evil tongues and the treason of trusted men, downward to the humblest of his disloyal opponents, he received afterward abundant compensation. We can imagine no reward for his military toils and sufferings greater than that he must have seen and felt at the moment when he parted from his companions in arms at the evacuation by the British in New York. He said to them, trembling with emotion as he stood, "I cannot come to each of you to take leave, but I shall be obliged if each of you will come and take me by the hand." General Knox, his bosom friend, stepped forward and received the first embrace. The other officers silently followed in succession, and every one was in tears. What a compensation to him was that scene in which Washington read the touching proclamation of peace to the army, April 19, 1783, precisely eight years from the day of the first bloodshedding at Lexington.

And amid all the anxiety of the hour, the contrast with much of the past must have cheered his heart in a subsequent year when he was borne by acclamation into the Presidential chair. What rewards for his faithfulness, toils, and sacrifices on the field were his, as he passed in the autumn of 1789, during his first year's civil service, through the towns of New England in that better than regal progress! See him in an open carriage, drawn by four white horses, his private secretary near him, riding in advance, and a single servant, his ever true attendant. A volunteer courier who precedes Washington announcing his approach, rides bareheaded as they enter some town. With one hand he guides his careering steed; in the other he bears a trumpet, whose blast arouses the people, followed by his shout, "Washington is coming! Washington is coming!" The parish bell is rung; the schoolmaster ejaculates "school's dismissed," and away rush the delighted children to see the hero and his train. An escort of horsemen are at once in line, and the first men of the town proceed to welcome the idol of the people. Sometimes, as when he visited the large town of Haverhill, Massachusetts, Washington, in a drab surtout and wearing a military hat, is mounted on an elegant horse; his tall, erect form and majestic bearing give him an air of unsurpassed dignity, as he moves onward in what he calls "the pleasantest village I have passed through." This ride is made immortal by the pen of Whittier: —

> And he stood up in his stirrups,
> Looking up and looking down
> On the hills of gold and silver,
> Rimming round the little town.
>
> And he said, the landscape sweeping
> Slowly with his ungloved hand:
> "I have seen no prospect fairer
> In this goodly eastern land."
>
> Then the bugles of his escort
> Stirred to life the cavalcade;
> And that head, so bare and stately,
> Vanished down the depths of shade.

KNOX FAMILY.

HENRY KNOX deserves a prominent place in any mention of the Society of the Cincinnati. He was, by his early suggestion of it and his earnest labors for its organization, essentially its founder. Born July 25, 1750, he died October 25, 1806. From his boyhood he took an interest in the affairs of his country, and at every stage of his life was devoted to the cause of freedom, and dedicated all his powers of body and mind to its advancement. He was fond of reading, and at the age of twenty-one he opened a bookstore opposite Williams's Court in Cornhill, Boston, which became a great resort in 1771 for the British officers and Tory ladies, who were the *ton* of that period. This store was, not many years afterward, while Knox was engaged with the besieging army, robbed and pillaged; but still the occupant, with characteristic honor, paid his London creditors, before his decease, a large portion of his dues to them. He was invited to join the royal standard, but rejected promptly the proposal, and embarked, heart and hand, in the Patriot cause.

August 9, 1775, we find him at Cambridge, dining with Washington. He soon proposed to go to Fort Ticonderoga, and, with the approval of his General, transported from that place some fifty cannon, and stores in boats and sleds, which rendered great service in the siege of Boston. The furious cannonade from Knox's batteries, March 4, 1776, obliged the British finally, on the 17th of that month, to evacuate Boston. His eminent military skill at Trenton, Monmouth, White Plains, Yorktown, and elsewhere, entitles him to a very high rank among those who achieved our independence.

After the close of the war General Knox held important civil offices. Made Secretary of War by Washington in 1785, he was in his cabinet until he resigned in 1794. He was a commissioner to settle the eastern boundary on the River St. Croix, a member of the General Court of Massachusetts in 1801, and June 2, 1804, was appointed one of the Council of Governor Strong, by whom he was consulted on many important questions. His literary and scientific attainments induced Dartmouth College in 1793 to confer upon him the honorary degree of Master of Arts; and December 16, 1805, he was chosen a Fellow of the American Academy of Arts and Sciences. General Knox stood probably first, although Lafayette was very near him, in the esteem, affection, and confidence of Washington. Entering the army in his youth as a volunteer, he rose by the force of his character and by his services to the rank of major-general, the highest position below that of the commander-in-chief.

HENRY KNOX THATCHER, eldest grandson of General Knox, succeeded him in the society of the Cincinnati, in 1843. He was born in Thomaston, Maine, May 26, 1806, and died April 5, 1880. I knew him personally, as a member of the New England Historic Genealogical Society, to which he presented, with very interesting remarks, the invaluable collection of his grandfather's manuscript letters, elegantly bound in fifty-six folio volumes. He entered the United States Navy, March 4, 1823, as a midshipman, and was commissioned lieutenant in 1833. He was made commander in September, 1856, and captain in 1861; commissioned commodore in 1862, and during the late Civil War took part in the capture of Mobile, April 12, 1865. He was promoted to rear-admiral in 1866. He was retired May 26, 1868, and was post-admiral of Portsmouth, New Hampshire, until 1870. In that year he became vice-president of the Society of the Cincinnati, and in 1871 was chosen president. His last residence was at Winchester, Massachusetts. He married Susan

C., daughter of Dr. Croswell, of Plymouth, Massachusetts. They had no children.

BARON VON STEUBEN, after General Knox, should be named next in this connection. The first general meeting, after the disbanding of the army, to consider the formation of the Society of the Cincinnati, took place at the City Tavern, in Philadelphia, May, 1784. The Baron called the meeting to order. Washington took the chair and was, May 15, unanimously chosen president, Major-General Gates being vice-president, and Major-General Knox, secretary.

Frederick William Augustus von Steuben, born in Prussia, November 15, 1730, died near Utica, New York, November 28, 1794. He offered his services to Washington, December 1, 1777, and was directed to join the army at Valley Forge in midwinter, and acted an important part, in connection with Lafayette, at the siege of Yorktown and in the battle of Monmouth. He was appointed inspector-general, with the rank of major-general, and did much to improve the condition of the troops in our army. He afterward wrote a manual, which was of great value to the discipline of the army, and contributed very largely to the success of the Revolution. He had served under Frederick the Great of Prussia, and was one of his aides-de-camp. With all his distinction he is reported, however, as quite irascible, and not very reverent. Knowing little of our language, in a moment of excitement, when drilling an awkward squad, he exclaimed to a subordinate, "Come and swear for me in English; these fellows will not do what I bid them."

His generosity in furnishing supplies, equipments, and comforts, at his own expense, for our soldiers — so great that he frequently shared his last dollar with a suffering soldier — impoverishing himself; yet it was not until 1790 that Congress relieved him by an annuity of $2,500. See his portrait! Here is a robust and athletic frame, surmounted by a head firmly fixed on the body, and a face expressive of a rare union of energy of character with sweetness and kindliness. We are not surprised to learn that he had a great gift of conversation, had warm personal friends, and was very popular in general society. He was a man to be trusted; power and decision were written in his eye and on his lips; and he was no less loved for all that is generous and attractive. The following letter, brought to light at a dinner given to our German guests at Washington, October 22, 1881, six of whom descended from the Baron, being the very last written before the author of it resigned his office as commander-in-chief of the American Army, is an eloquent testimonial to the worth of its subject: —

ANNAPOLIS, Dec. 23, 1783.

MY DEAR BARON, — Although I have taken frequent opportunities in public and private of acknowledging your great zeal, attention, and abilities in performing the duties of your office, yet I wish to make use of this last moment of my public life to signify in the strongest terms my entire approbation of your conduct, and to express my sense of the obligations the public is under to you for your faithful and meritorious services. I beg you will be convinced, my dear sir, that I should rejoice if it could ever be in my power to serve you more essentially than by expressions of regard and affection, but in the mean time I am persuaded you will not be displeased with this farewell token of my sincere friendship and esteem for you. This is the last letter which I shall write while I continue in the service of my country. The hour of my resignation is fixed at 12 o'clock to-day, after which I shall become a private citizen on the banks of the Potomac, where I shall be glad to embrace you, and to testify the great esteem and consideration with which I am, my dear Baron, etc.,

GEORGE WASHINGTON.

The place won and retained in the heart of Washington by Baron von Steuben will be his perpetual commendation.

JOHN BROOKS was born in Medford, Massachusetts, and baptized May 31, 1752. I recollect him well when he was governor of Massachusetts. A classmate of mine, his nephew, told me much of his systematic habits of life,—and, among his peculiarities, that he always omitted one dinner every week. At the age of twenty-one he commenced practice as a physician in Reading; and in 1774 he married a celebrated beauty, Lucy Smith. On the 19th of April, 1775, he marched at the head of a company of minute-men, and met the British near Concord, on their return.

To him, as to many others, the battle of Lexington sounded the death-knell of all hope of a reconciliation between this and the mother country. That spark struck fire in his as in every true American bosom, and no wonder the chronicles of the day are filled with accounts of the people rising " as one man, taking their firelocks, and rushing toward the opening scene of blood." East, west, north, and south we read of companies formed to march toward that spot, and our history is filled with the names of one and another reported as " present at the battle of Lexington." Haffield White dies at Danvers, and the fairest line of his record is that he was at the battle of Lexington. Thomas Nixon dies at Framingham in 1800, Samuel Bowman at Lexington in 1818, Joseph Balcom at Templeton in 1825, two men named Jackson at Newton, Thomas Hunt in Cincinnati, — time would fail me to write out the whole list. This one event of their lives — their presence at the battle of Lexington — is their crowning glory; even the rumor that they were there is sometimes sufficient for their fame. Captain John Brooks, it has often been said, was in this battle; but the truth was he did not reach Lexington until the British forces were on their return from Concord, when his men posted themselves, as did others, behind the barns and fences, and fired thence on the enemy.

He was, June 16, ordered to Cambridge, but could take no part in the noble work of the 17th at Bunker Hill. He was in the battle of White Plains, and his corps received the acknowledgment of Washington for its brave conduct. A skilful disciplinarian, at Valley Forge he was appointed by Washington to aid Baron von Steuben in his new system of military tactics. He was adjutant-general in the battle of Monmouth. When the Newbury letters appeared, suggesting an insurrection, Washington rode up to Brooks, to learn how the officers stood affected, and to counsel them against the treasonable step. "Sir," replied Brooks, "I have anticipated your wishes, and my orders are given." With tears in his eyes Washington took him by the hand and said: "Colonel Brooks, this is just what I expected from you."

After the war he retired in poverty, and resumed the practice of his profession. He was made major-general of the militia, and often elected to civil offices. From 1816 to 1823 he was governor of Massachusetts. After declining a re-election, in his retirement he was chosen to preside over several societies. From 1783 to 1785, he was the first secretary of the Cincinnati of Massachusetts, gave the first of its orations, July 4. 1787, and was its president from 1810 to his death, March 1, 1825, and vice-president of the General Society from 1811 to 1825. He received from Harvard College, in 1781, the honorary degree of A. M.; in 1810 that of M. D.; and in 1817 that of LL. D.

THE BATTLE OF BUNKER HILL.

He had, I recollect, a fine portly figure, and a Roman countenance, expressing firmness and courage; his bright eye and his mouth, somewhat compressed, showed a strong character, united with a pleasant disposition. He had a soldierly bearing, a graceful deportment; dignified, and of the Old School in manners, his whole appearance was an index of his generous and noble heart.

JOSEPH FISKE was born in Lexington, Massachusetts, December 24, 1752. He died September 25, 1837. Having studied medicine and begun its practice, he was led by his patriotic spirit to accept the commission of surgeon's mate in Vose's Regiment, in 1777. He was made surgeon, April 17, 1779, and served in the army seven years. He was present at the surrender of Burgoyne in 1777, and of Cornwallis in 1781. He was frequently at my father's house, and was very agreeable. I drank in greedily his accounts, given to my grandfather, — who was with him in the company of Captain Parker, April 19, 1775, — of his own experiences as a surgeon in the War of the Revolution. It was a time when all shared in common privations. General Washington would sit down with his highest officers to a small piece of beef, with a few potatoes and some hard bread. The veteran told us of sitting with officers at a plank table in the camp, where a single dish of wood or pewter sufficed for a mess; a horn spoon, and a horn tumbler were passed round, and the knife was carried in the pocket; sugar, tea, and coffee were unknown luxuries, and if perchance a ration of rum was given out — this was in the dead of winter — the question would be raised, "Shall we drink it, or shall we put it in our shoes to keep our feet from freezing?"

During the pursuit of Cornwallis the soldiers had not decent clothing; and an old cloak of one of the generals, they having not a blanket left, was nearly the whole winter shared with two other officers. Dr. Fiske would corroborate, in my hearing, accounts of the need of medicine and comforts for the wounded. Wine, spirits, and even the ordinary medicines could not be procured; and after searching miles upon miles nothing of the kind could be found but small portions of snakeroot. And as for bandages, the case was still worse, if possible; nothing could be done for their supply but to cut up a tent found on the field.

He related mirthful, no less than sad reminiscences of the war, and used to tell anecdotes of this kind of one Captain Houdin. This French officer lived to see the National Government established, and asked an office of General Knox, then Secretary of War. "Captain," said the Secretary, "you have abused the new government, and how can you ask office under it?" "Oh," said the Captain, "I only did it because that was popular; I did n't mean anything by it." When Washington was told this anecdote he gave a hearty laugh, a very rare thing for him. The Captain succeeded at last, it seems, in getting an office.

Dr. Fiske was a member of the Society of the Cincinnati, and of the Massachusetts Medical Society. He married, July 31, 1794, Elizabeth Stone, born November 13, 1770, who died March 6, 1849, aged 78. They had six children, of whom the oldest son, Joseph, born in Lexington, Massachusetts, February 9, 1797, succeeded his father in the Cincinnati Society in 1839. He was a member of the Massachusetts Medical Society. He died in his native place, May 4, 1860.

CAPTAIN BENJAMIN GOULD was born in Topsfield, Massachusetts, in 1751; He died in Newburyport in 1841, at the age of ninety. At this place I met and conversed with him in 1839. His military spirit and his decided patriotism were shown throughout the war. He was an ensign in Little's Regiment, and wounded April 19, 1775. He was in the Continental army, took part in the battles of Bennington, Stillwater, and Saratoga, and served under Lafayette in Rhode Island; was at West Point at the time of Arnold's treason, and was one of the first to detect that dark crime. What joy it must have given this veteran of fourscore and three years to meet the nation's guest on his visit to Newburyport in 1825. Here, too, it was that Daniel Foster, who served in Lafayette's corps of light infantry, met, on that occasion, sword in hand, his old commander. "I am proud to see you," said the old hero, " once more on American soil." Lafayette embraced him and replied, "I look upon you as one of my own family."

The son of the Captain, Benjamin Apthorp Gould, was born in Lancaster, Massachusetts, June 15, 1787, and died October 24, 1859, in Boston. He taught the Latin School in that city with eminent success, and became afterward a distinguished merchant. He was editor of the first American editions of Virgil, Ovid, and Horace. Personal intercourse with Mr. Gould impressed me with his intelligence and courtesy. He graduated at Harvard College in 1814. He was an illustration of the advantages of a liberal education and high scholarship, not only in the "professions," but in commercial life. His broad views and naturally correct judgment of men and affairs had been improved by mental culture. This impression was strengthened by many testimonials from one who was a partner in business with him. His unchallenged integrity equalled and adorned his high mental qualities and attainments. Having known Captain Gould, the father, and enjoyed the friendship of his daughter, Miss Hannah F. Gould, — a writer of distinction for her graphic and original poetry, especially her patriotic ode at the re-interment of the martyred soldiers at Lexington, April 19, 1835, — it is a pleasure to speak of them with confidence.

Benjamin Apthorp, the grandson of Captain Gould, was born in Boston, September 27, 1824. He was admitted to the Society of the Cincinnati in 1864, by the rule adopted by the General Society in May 1854. His intellectual ability has been shown in many positions.

Professor Gould graduated at Harvard College in 1844; received a degree from Göttingen in 1848; edited, for twelve years, the "Astronomical Journal;" was on the United States Coast Survey from 1852 to 1867, when I knew him well; organized the Dudley Observatory in Albany, of which he was director, 1856–59; was in the Sanitary Commission, Statistical Department of the Civil War, and published the "Military and Anthropological Statistics of American Soldiers." He worked in the Washington Observatory twelve years, and since 1873 has been director of the National Argentine Observatory in Cordova. He was, in 1868, president of the American Association for the Advancement of Science, and is a member of various scientific societies and academies in Europe.

EDWARD STRONG MOSELEY, born June 22, 1813, was admitted, in May 1867, a member of the Society of the Cincinnati, under the rule of May 1854. His family have shown military tastes, and have claims connected with the Revolutionary War. Ebenezer, grandfather of Edward Strong Moseley, graduated at Yale College in 1763; was a missionary among the Western Indians several years, from 1767; and in April 1775, was commissioned captain in Putnam's Connecticut Regiment, which he accompanied to Cambridge; and he was in the battle of Bunker Hill. In 1777, the governor of Massachusetts authorized him to raise ten hundred and ninety-two men to join the army at Providence under General Spencer, and he was appointed one of the captains. He was colonel of the Connecticut Regiment of militia in 1789-91. During the latter part of the Revolution, and for some subsequent years, he was representative of Windham, Connecticut. He died March 20, 1825, aged 84 years. His son, Hon. Ebenezer Moseley, born November 21, 1781, graduated at Yale College in 1802, and settled in Newburyport. He was colonel of a regiment of the Massachusetts Militia, 1813 –14; representative and senator of Massachusetts, and master in chancery; president of the Essex County Agricultural Society; and filled many other positions of public trust and honor. His son, Edward Strong, was a successful merchant many years in the East India trade, is president of the Mechanics National Bank and of the Institution for Savings in Newburyport. In 1870 he received the honorary degree of A. M. from Yale College, of which, from 1829, he was nearly three years a member.

It is fitting that the native town of Mr. Moseley should be represented in the Society of the Cincinnati. We are astonished and pained by the sufferings endured by our soldiers; but we seldom realize what must have been the sufferings of those who saw their husbands and brothers, on all sides, summoned to go forth and encounter dangers and death in the most trying forms. I happen to know a striking illustration of hardships not unusual in other towns at that time. The town of Newburyport — where I spent nearly eight years among the descendants of those who endured privations of this kind — was, in August 1777, required to raise for the Continental Army one sixth of all her men capable of bearing arms. Added to this, those who remained at home were taxed to the highest point, and obliged to deprive themselves of not a few of the comforts and sometimes of what we should think the necessaries of life. " The whole town," says her historian, " was so early turned into a military camp, and the troops kept in such a state of preparation, that when on the day of the battle of Lexington, the news of it was brought to town, before eleven o'clock that night reinforcements from Newburyport were on their way to join their brothers in the bloody struggle."

The public spirit of Newburyport was shown in another form, when Washington, in the autumn of 1789, on his tour through the North, visited that town. He was received with great enthusiasm; a committee met him at Ipswich; two companies of cavalry escorted him to the town; a procession, including all classes of people — the largest body that of the school-children — greeted his entrance. There were four hundred and twenty scholars, each with a quill in hand, headed by their teachers, the motto on their banner: " We are the freeborn subjects of the United States." An elegantly dressed vessel in the harbor, from Teneriffe, fired the salute of her nation, twenty-one guns. This was gracefully noticed by Washington, of which the "Essex Journal" of November 4, 1789 says: "We cannot but admire, among the admirable traits in the President's character, that of his politeness to foreigners." As the procession moved on, the drums beat and a salute was fired; afterward a meeting was held at which an ode was sung, and an address delivered by John Quincy Adams, then a law student with Chief Justice Parsons in Newburyport, and destined himself to be one of Washington's successors. In the evening, guns were fired; a display of fireworks took place, and every demonstration of joy was manifested. An aged lady, one of my parishioners, told me she was among the school-children on that day, and Washington gave her a kiss.

TIMOTHY PICKERING was born in Salem, Massachusetts, July 17, 1745, and died there January 29, 1829, aged 84 years. He was an original member of the Pennsylvania Society of the Cincinnati. He joined Washington in New Jersey with his regiment in 1776; was made adjutant-general of the army in May, 1777; a member of the Board of War in November, and quartermaster-general August 5, 1780. He was postmaster-general of the United States, November 7, 1791 – January 2, 1795; secretary of war, January 10, 1795 – December 10, same year; secretary of state, December 10, 1795 – May 12, 1800; United States Senator, 1803–11; member of the Massachusetts Board of War, 1812–15; and member of Congress 1815–17. Active in the cause of education, he was an able writer, a brave and patriotic soldier, and, as a public officer, energetic and disinterested. Of the Old School of manners, he was highly gifted in conversation.

JOHN PICKERING, son of Timothy Pickering, born in Salem, Massachusetts, February 17, 1777, died May 5, 1846. He was admitted a member of the Massachusetts Society of the Cincinnati in 1843. He had a large practice as a lawyer, and still, by his rare industry, became one of the first scholars in the country. He was chosen professor of Hebrew in Harvard College in 1806, and invited to the chair of Greek literature; he was president of the American Academy of Arts and Sciences, and of the Oriental Society of Boston. He was a member of many scientific and literary bodies in Europe. Familiar with twenty-two languages, he wrote several treatises upon philology, and produced a Greek and English Lexicon, on which he was engaged 1814-26. He was also a very able lecturer. In the winter of 1829-30 I had the pleasure of hearing from him an able lecture, in Boston, before the Young Men's Association, and was impressed by his massive brow and scholarly appearance.

JOHN PICKERING, eldest son of the former, born November 8, 1808, succeeded him in 1867 in the Society of the Cincinnati. He was for many years a successful stock-broker in Boston, and resided in the old family house at Salem, built in 1651. A pleasant personal aquaintance with him, and the privilege of having heard learned words from his distinguished father, and known, as a neighbor, his brother, Octavius Pickering, eminent as a reporter in the Massachusetts Supreme Court, and occupied, at the age of seventy-five, on the Life and Writings of his father, Timothy Pickering, have given me special satisfaction in paying this tribute to their honored family. Mr. John Pickering died in Salem, January 20, 1882. His son John, born May 24, 1857, was admitted to the Society, July 4, 1882.

Louis Baury (de Bellerive), born in St. Domingo, September 16, 1753, died in Middletown, Connecticut, September 20, 1807. He was admitted to the Society of the Cincinnati in 1789. He was educated at the same school as Napoleon, in Brienne, France, and became a planter at St. Domingo. He took part at the siege of Savannah, as captain in a volunteer corps, and remained in the service until the close of the war. In 1787 he was aide-de-camp to General Lincoln in suppressing the Shays Rebellion. He was of a military family, his father having been a captain of cavalry, and his eldest son, Francis, was killed at the age of 17, while acting as aide to General Rochambeau at St. Domingo in March, 1802. Frederic, son of Louis Baury, succeeded him in the Society of the Cincinnati in 1813; was a midshipman at 17, in 1809; served in the ship "Constitution" at the capture of the "Guerriere" and the "Java;" was on the

"Wasp" when she captured the "Reindeer," in 1814, and at the time she was lost in September of that year.

ALFRED LOUIS BAURY, D.D., born September 14, 1794, succeeded his brother in the Society of the Cincinnati in 1823. Although occupied in business for a time, he left it in early life, and after the study of theology, was admitted to Deacon's Orders, September, 1820. In July 1822 he was chosen rector of St. Mary's, Newton Lower Falls, Massachusetts. I often had the pleasure — while teaching school a winter during my college life, not far from his church — of hearing some of his able sermons, delivered with uncommon dignity and force. His reading of the service was very impressive. In personal appearance he was marked by much of that combination of dignity with sweetness which we see in the portrait of his father, although the mouth is more compressed and his gravity more observable. There is much in his figure and face that reminds me of those of the English preacher, Robertson. Both had a union of military decision with benevolence and spirituality. Dr. Baury wrote a clear, firm, and upright hand. It corresponded with his personal air and bearing. He was tall, erect, and graceful, with fine classical features. When I first saw him he was yet young; but throughout his life, he is said to have been a most agreeable companion, honored for his professional ability, and loved by all who enjoyed the privilege of his society and knew his high moral worth. He was chosen vice-president of the Massachusetts Society of the Cincinnati, July 4, 1857, and president in 1865. He died in Boston, December 26, 1865.

JOHN HASTINGS was born in Cambridge, Massachusetts, March 23, 1754; and died there February 16, 1839. He graduated at Harvard College in 1772, entered the army in 1775; was commissioned captain in Jackson's Regiment, May 25, 1777, and in Brooks's Regiment in 1783. He was the son of Jonathan and Elizabeth (Cotton) Hastings. He married, December 7, 1783, Lydia, daughter of Richard and Lydia (Trowbridge) Dana, the parents of Chief-Justice Francis Dana. She died in Woburn, May 8, 1808. They had seven children, of whom the only son was Edmund Trowbridge. John Hastings lived to the age of eighty-five. I knew him for some six years of the last of his life, and at the remarkable age of eighty-two, he had, I recollect, the whooping cough. He was a brave man, and testified his patriotism by serving through nearly the whole Revolutionary War.

EDMUND TROWBRIDGE HASTINGS, the only son of John, succeeded him in the Society of the Cincinnati in 1839. He was born in Woburn, Massachusetts, May 15, 1789; and died in Medford, Massachusetts, May 13, 1861. His wife Elizabeth died November 30, 1880, aged 85 years. I was once a member of his family, and knew well his high moral excellence, the integrity which marked him as a merchant, and the kind traits of himself and family. He had two sons, Edmund Trowbridge and John Walter, born November 27, 1819, who married Sarah E. Gannett, September 4, 1850, and one daughter, Harriet Elizabeth, born August 3, 1818, who married, October 5, 1841, John Bryant Hatch.

EDMUND TROWBRIDGE HASTINGS, eldest son of Edmund T. Hastings, whom he succeeded in the Society of the Cincinnati in 1863, was born in Cambridge, Massachusetts, March 3, 1816. He resides in Medford, Massachusetts, on his father's estate, unmarried.

AFRICA HAMLIN was born in Pembroke, Massachusetts, in 1756, and died in Waterford, Maine, in 1808. He was one of the original members of the Society of the Cincinnati. He entered the army in the humble capacity of a waiter at the beginning of the Revolutionary War; was commissioned ensign, January 1, 1781, and served to the close of the war. In 1788 he removed to Waterford, Maine, then a wilderness. He spent his winters in teaching school, and, having unusual abilities, held many responsible offices in the town. On one occasion he showed his versatility and readiness, when — the Fourth-of-July orator failing to appear—at the request of his townsmen he took his place, and gave great satisfaction by his address.

His father had a large family and named four of

his sons, Europe, Asia, Africa, and America. Another of his sons, Dr. Cyrus Hamlin, was the father of Vice-President Hannibal Hamlin. Africa Hamlin married, in 1785, Susanna Stone of Groton, Massachusetts. They had six children, all daughters. Asia Hamlin lived many years in Westford, Massachusetts. I boarded in his family while fitting for college in the academy of that town. Mr. Hamlin was a man strong in body and mind, social, facetious, and, as might be expected of one born and trained as he was, he used very plain speech. He was somewhat eccentric, although, like his excellent companion, a lady of culture, he was kindhearted and friendly to us boys. He lived, I think, to nearly the age of ninety.

JOB SUMNER, an original member of the society of the Cincinnati, was born in Milton, Massachusetts, April 23, 1754. He entered college in 1774; but when the students were dispersed after the battle of Lexington, he immediately joined the army, and continued in it until its final disbandment in 1784. He was a lieutenant in Moses Draper's Company, of Gardner's Regiment, at Bunker Hill; in Bond's Twenty-fifth Regiment at the siege of Boston and in the invasion of Canada; commissioned captain in Greaton's Third Regiment, January 1, 1777, and made major in 1783. He had "the reputation of an attentive and intelligent officer," and was commissioned, after the war, to settle the accounts of the United States with Georgia.

He died of poison in New York City, September 16, 1789.

CHARLES PINCKNEY SUMNER, only son of Major Job, succeeded him in the Society of the Cincinnati, in 1803. He was born in Milton, January 20, 1776, and died in Boston, April 24, 1839. He graduated at Harvard College in 1796, studied law, was several years clerk of the Massachusetts House of Representatives, and was sheriff of Suffolk County from 1825 until his death. He was a man of literary culture, and delivered several orations, addresses, and poems on public occasions. I recollect him well through many years, and observed his uniformly courteous and gentlemanly deportment.

CHARLES SUMNER, the eldest son of Charles P. Sumner, succeeded him in the Society of the Cincinnati in 1840. He was born in Boston, January 6, 1811, and died March 11, 1874; graduated at Harvard College in 1830, and at the Dane Law School in 1834. He was a great favorite of Judge Story, who was then professor in the Law School. I recollect him well, his fine figure and marked face, at that early age. I heard his oration on "The True Grandeur of Nations," beside other addresses. Becoming afterward personally acquainted with him, I enjoyed highly his remarkable conversational powers. His extraordinary reading, memory, and general culture, his graceful manner and rare eloquence, from the beginning of his career, impressed me deeply. He was a strict censor of himself, and said once to me that he feared he was falling into a "beat" in his style of speaking.

I watched earnestly the long struggle in the Massachusetts Legislature, in the session of 1851, over his candidacy for the United States senatorship. He was anxious, at one time, to withdraw from the arena, but his friends urged him to let his name still be used in the balloting. When, after many ballots, April 24, 1851, he was declared elected, the excitement was intense. I was among the first to reach his house on Hancock Street, to congratulate him on the result. He seemed quite sober, and said: "It is a very responsible position. I am by no means sure this result is best, either for the country or for me." His course in the United States Senate enhanced the admiration of antislavery men. A thrill of horror filled our hearts when, after the delivery of his great speech, "The Crime against Kansas," May 19-20, 1856, he was brutally assaulted in his seat by Preston S. Brooks, a representative in Congress from South Carolina. After being disabled for about three years, on resuming his seat in the Senate he made, June 4, 1860, his famous speech on "The Barbarism of Slavery." He was among the first to propose emancipation as the best means of ending the Rebellion; and he afterward originated and aided the enactment of those Constitutional Amendments by which the Freedmen obtained political rights. In 1862 I visited him at Washington, when he seemed to have recovered much of his original health and spirits. Amid his grave and earnest labors he had moments of wit and humor. He read one day, out of a mass of daily newspapers, an amusing anecdote of a French milkwoman, who one day left her milkcan with only water in it. "Oh," said she, when rebuked for it, "I forgot to put the milk to it."

His decided course against slavery made him many political enemies; but since his death, March 11, 1874, he has stood — and in the ordeal of the future will more confessedly stand — on the summit of national honor, as a scholar and statesman, distinguished in history for his legal and civil attainments, his eloquent writings and speech, his devotedness to the cause of human freedom, the purity of his principles, and his incorruptible integrity.

WILLIAM EUSTIS, an original member of the Society of the Cincinnati, was born at Cambridge, June 10, 1753; was in the Boston Latin School in 1761; graduated at Harvard College in 1772; studied medicine under Dr. Joseph Warren, and, on the day of the Lexington battle, was at the scene of action, and aided in dressing the wounds of the soldiers. He was commissioned surgeon of Gridley's Artillery Regiment, April 19, 1775, and, January 1, 1777, was commissioned surgeon and physician at the hospital opposite West Point. He remained on the medical staff until the close of the war. He was a volunteer surgeon in the Shays Rebellion; a member of the General Court, from 1788, for six or seven years; a member of Congress in 1800-05, and again in 1821-23; was appointed by President Madison, secretary of war in 1809, and resigned in 1812. He was minister to Holland, 1815-18, and was governor of Massachusetts, 1823-25, dying in Boston while in office, February 6, 1825, at the age of seventy-one. He was vice-president of the Cincinnati Society, 1786-1810, and again in 1820. He delivered the annual oration before that Society, July 4, 1791. He received the honorary degree of LL. D. from Harvard University in 1823, and received honors from other colleges. He was a member, and for some time a counsellor, of the Massachusetts Medical Society.

While in the army he was humane, faithful, and indefatigable in his office. His urbane manner and social feelings made him everywhere a popular companion. His house — the Governor Shirley mansion in Roxbury — was a hospitable and pleasant resort to friends and strangers. His father, Benjamin Eustis, married in Cambridge, May 11, 1749, Elizabeth Hill, who died May 30, 1775. I find on a roll of Captain Parker's Company of men who were called to Cambridge, June 17, 18, 1775. the name of William Eustis. Governor Eustis was then twenty-two years old. At a celebration of July 4. 1814, at Lexington. among the guests was Hon. William Eustis. It is certain that, although not born there, he felt a strong interest in Lexington. In the old cemetery of that place — where according to his wish he was buried by his mother's side, is a handsome monument over the remains of Governor Eustis and his wife, who was Caroline, daughter of Hon. Woodbury Langdon of New Hampshire, and survived him many years.

I recollect well the form and face of Governor Eustis, whom I saw frequently while he was in office. He was quite tall and graceful, — his eyes a dark blue, and his complexion florid. Like very many of the Revolutionary officers he returned from the war poor. He once said : "With but a single coat, four shirts, and one pair of woollen stockings, in the hard winter of 1780, I was one of the happiest men on earth."

ISAAC PARKER succeeded his brother Elias — who was in the battle of Bunker Hill and served through the war — in the Society of the Cincinnati in 1830. He was Royal Professor of Law in Harvard University while I was in college, and his lectures excited great interest in my class. He was pleasant, and sometimes facetious, in his intercourse with us. I recollect, on one occasion, when, having driven out of Boston, he came to the door of Harvard Hall, where he gave his lectures. We students had gathered around the door, and, not withdrawing, as was proper at his approach, and he being a stout man requiring wide space, he said jocosely to us, " Open to the right and left ; " and suiting the action to the word, he wielded his whip to part us.

Isaac Parker was born in Boston, June 17, 1768, and was the eighth son of Daniel and Margaret (Jarvis) Parker. He graduated at Harvard College in 1786 ; studied law with Judge Tudor ; settled as a lawyer in Portland in 1801, and in Boston in 1806 ; was a member of Congress from the Maine District of Massachusetts, 1797-99 ; president of the Massachusetts Constitutional Convention in 1820 ; professor of law, in Harvard University, 1816-27 ; associate judge of the Supreme Court of Massachusetts, 1806-14, and chief-justice from 1814 until his death, July 26, 1830. He was a member of the American Academy of Arts and Sciences, the Bible Society, and many others, and always active in his place. He received the degree of LL. D. from Harvard College in 1814. "For more than a quarter of a century he was one of the most influential men in the Commonwealth of Massachusetts. This influence was noiseless and constant ; it was found in the temples of justice and the halls of legislation, in the seminaries of learning, at the ballot-box, on change, in the social circle, — everywhere. He had genius without eccentricity, and learning without pedantry. In him firmness was united to flexibility, and delicacy with decision."

John Popkin was of a Welsh family ; born in

Boston in 1743, and died in Malden, Massachusetts, May 8, 1827. Before the Revolutionary War he was a member of Paddock's Artillery Company. In the army he was a captain of artillery in Gridley's Regiment, and was in the battle of Bunker Hill, and at the siege of Boston. He was commissioned captain in Knox's Artillery, and was in the battle of White Plains; was made major in Greaton's Regiment, January 1, 1777; was aide to General Lincoln at Saratoga, and commissioned lieutenant-colonel of Crane's Artillery Regiment, July 15, 1777, in which he continued until the disbanding of the army in 1783. After the war he resided in Bolton and in Malden, Massachusetts. He was an inspector of customs in Boston, and walked to and from Malden, four miles, every day, from 1789 until he was more than eighty-four years old.

JOHN S. POPKIN was the eldest son of Colonel John Popkin, whom he succeeded in the Society of the Cincinnati in 1827. I knew him well, from my entrance in college to the close of his life. He was born in Boston, June 19, 1771, and died in Cambridge, Massachusetts, March 2, 1852. He graduated at Harvard College in 1792; was Greek tutor there from 1795 to 1798; professor of the Greek language, 1815–26; Eliot Professor of Greek literature, 1826–33. He received the honorary degree of D. D. from Harvard College in 1815. He had been pastor of the Federal Street Church in Boston (Dr. Channing's) from 1799 to 1802, and of the First Church in Newbury from 1804 to 1815.

When I entered college he examined me in Græca Minora, and my class recited to him for three years. He was a model of thorough instruction, and kindly, gentle, and impartial in his manner. He would assist a student in such a way as to call out his ability, without making him indolent or in danger of leaning too much on his teacher. His hearing was not perfect, and roguish youth would sometimes take advantage of this infirmity. A student in a class after mine, was once " taken up" by him on a lesson in history, of which branch the Professor was for a long time the teacher. "A —, who was the third king of France?" The student replied promptly, as if certain of being right. "What did you say?" asked the unsuspecting Professor. The answer was very quick, and might sound like several short names. On a repetition of the confusing word, — "I am a little deaf," said the Doctor, "but I believe you are right." "Very far," whispered a fellow-student, "from the truth."

In important business transactions with Dr. Popkin I found him very exact, as accurate as he was in his college offices. Few men excelled him in a knowledge of practical affairs, and his integrity, honesty, and reliability were eminent; the man was a counterpart of the scholar and instructor.

CONSTANT FREEMAN, an original member of the Society of the Cincinnati, was baptized at Charlestown, Massachusetts, February 27, 1757, and entered the Boston Latin School in 1766. He was commissioned lieutenant in Knox's Artillery in 1776; was lieutenant and was acting captain in Crane's Artillery, October 1, 1778; appointed captain in the United States Infantry, March, 1791, but declined; afterward commissioned major in the regular army, lieutenant-colonel, brevet-colonel (July 10, 1812), and on the reduction of the army in 1815, was mustered out of service. He held offices in the navy department at Washington from 1816 until his death. Constant Freeman, his father, married, September 23, 1754, Lois Cobb, and had two children, Constant and Rev. James Freeman, D. D. Major Freeman died February 27, 1824.

CHARLES HENRY DAVIS was a son of Hon. Daniel Davis — whom I well recollect as a dignified and efficient public officer — and Lois Freeman, sister of Constant. Through her Admiral Davis succeeded, as nephew, Major Constant in the Society of the Cincinnati, in 1843. He was born in Boston, January 16, 1807; made A. M. by Harvard College in 1841, and LL. D. in 1868.

It was toward the close of his life, while spending a season in company with him and Mrs. Davis, whom he married in 1842, that he deeply impressed me with those marked and commanding qualities which had led to his advancement, and honorable career through life. At the age of sixteen, August 12, 1823, he was appointed a midshipman in the United States Navy. He was made lieutenant March 3, 1834; commander, June 13, 1854; captain, November 15, 1861; and rear-admiral, February 7, 1863. He was fleet-captain in Dupont's expedition against Port Royal, in the War of the Rebellion, and distinguished himself in operations on the Mississippi River at Memphis and Vicksburg. He was also eminent as a mathematician and physicist, and contributed various papers to scientific journals upon "Tidal Currents," the "Law of Deposit," etc. He wrote a paper on the "United States Coast Survey," in 1849; was founder of the "Nautical Almanac," and superintended it 1849-56; was chief of the bureau of navigation, Washington, in 1862; commander of the South Atlantic Squadron, 1867-69; and commandant of the navy-yard, at Norfolk, Virginia, from 1873 to his death, February 18, 1877.

Admiral Davis possessed large native abilities, which were highly cultivated. By his earnest spirit and rare industry he made most valuable contributions to science, while his practical skill and executive talent made him successful in whatever he undertook. The country owes him a large debt for his patriotic and successful devotion in serving the Union in the late Civil War. His gentlemanly manners and extended information rendered him as agreeable in private as he was honored in public.

JOHN COLLINS WARREN was the eldest son of Dr. John and Abigail (Collins) Warren. His father was professor of anatomy and surgery in Harvard College from 1783 until his death, which occurred in 1815. His son, Dr. John C. Warren, studied medicine, anatomy, and surgery with him, he being a distinguished practitioner. The son had also the advantage of studying in the celebrated hospitals of London and Paris.

Dr. John Collins Warren was a nephew of General Joseph Warren, and as such was admitted to the Society of the Cincinnati in 1854, under the rule adopted that year, having been elected previously, in 1847, an honorary member. He was assistant professor of anatomy and surgery in Harvard College, 1805–15; full professor, 1815–47; and afterward professor *emeritus*. As he occupied the professor's chair while I was in college, I had an opportunity, in my senior year, to hear his admirable course of lectures, and to know a good deal of him. I have before me an engraving of his portrait painted by Stuart, when he was but twenty-nine years old. The face is striking in its combination of strength and sweetness. The ruffled-bosomed shirt, high collar, and "choker" cravat give a good idea of the style of that period. His bright eye, Grecian nose, and finely formed mouth and chin show the great personal beauty, of which much remained when we saw him in his place as a lecturer. His manner might be called dry by one not interested in his subject, but with the details of anatomy he mingled much of his native facetiousness. Holding up before us one day part of a skeleton, he said : " You notice here a process — or rather you do *not* notice it, for it is wanting in this subject." He was recommending, at another time, moderation in diet. "If," said he, " you will set a plate by the side of that from which you take your dinner, and place upon it, for each article, another portion of the same size as you eat, you will probably be astonished at the mass left before you. I see nothing but the weight of this accumulation that could carry such amounts through all the processes of digestion."

Dr. Warren's long life — he was born August 1, 1778, in Boston, and died there May 4, 1856 — was filled with activity, and he received its deserved honors. He began practice in Boston in 1802, and became specially distinguished as a surgeon. He was, in 1846, the first to use ether in surgical operations. He was one of the founders of the Massachusetts General Hospital in 1820, and principal surgeon in daily attendance there until his death. He was also a founder of the McLean Asylum for the insane ; was president of the Massachusetts Medical Society 1832-36, and of the Boston Society of Natural History at his death ; and was a member of the principal scientific bodies in America and Europe. He devoted much of his later life to the natural sciences; and his collections in comparative anatomy, osteology, and paleontology, one of the best private collections in the world, included the most perfect skeleton of a mastodon known to exist. He was an earnest friend of temperance, and for many years president of the Massachusetts Temperance Society. He was mainly instrumental in establishing the "Boston Medical and Surgical Journal," and from 1828, for some years, was its associate editor. He also wrote and published numerous treatises upon medical and other subjects.

DANIEL WEBSTER was unanimously admitted an honorary member of the Massachusetts Society of the Cincinnati, at the annual meeting July 4, 1851. His father, Hon. Ebenezer Webster, although not a member of the Cincinnati, was in the military service of the Revolutionary War. He was a captain in the New Hampshire line, and fought in the memorable battle of Bennington.

For his surpassing intellectual ability, his eminence as a lawyer and his distinguished services as a statesman, for his patriotism and his deep interest in our Revolution, in all its civil as well as military aspects and relations, the name of Daniel Webster should appear in this book.

Keeping the main purpose of this volume in view, I shall only bring forward a few personal reminiscences of him and his work. I first heard him in the year 1822, when he was in the prime of manhood. He was then arguing, in the Supreme Court of Massachusetts, a case where the validity of a will was in controversy. The contest was between the heirs of the deceased and a certain church, to which, it was contended, unduly influenced by its clergyman, the testator in his last hours had devised most of his property. Mr. Webster claimed that the deceased was then too feeble in mind to make a true will. His whole argument was a masterly production; but one anecdote, related in his impressive manner, I particularly recollect. It was an incident which occurred in Spain. A rich Catholic on his death-bed was visited by a certain friar, and in solemn form was thus interrogated: " Is it your last will and testament that your estate in Andalusia shall be given to Holy Mother Church?" The dying man replied, " Yes." The friar proceeded: " Is it your last will and testament that your estate in Castile be given to Holy Mother Church?" The answer was, " Yes." And thus the eager ecclesiastic went on until the son of the testator who stood near, anxious lest his dying parent would will away his entire property, angrily interposed: " Father, is it your last will and testament that I should take your gold-headed cane and drive this friar out of the chamber?" "Yes," was the still affirmative reply. The dramatic power with which this thrilling story was told produced an electric effect on every one present. The intellectual force and moral enthusiasm, the majestic form, leonine voice, and fire-winged eye of the speaker, and the apparently consecrated absorption of his inmost nature in the matter at issue, gave a measureless power to his condensed and commanding language.

After hearing Mr. Webster in his memorable eulogy on the death of Adams and Jefferson, which occurred July 4, 1826, and on other public occasions, in the year 1840 I became personally acquainted with him. It was at a dinner given, during the heat of the Harrison campaign, to the Hon. W. J. Graves of Kentucky, then a member of Congress. I recall the circle that gathered there. It was at Porter's Hall in Cambridge. The eye and ear of every individual were directed to one and another, as they came in with fresh news of some State announced as for the hero of North Bend. No one listened more eagerly to these tidings than Mr. Webster. Who could ever forget that grand figure, the broad shoulders and capacious chest, the blue coat and bright buttons, the buff vest, that broad and massive forehead beetling above his powerful features, his thick glossy hair of a jet blackness, those large, dark and beaming eyes, that exquisitely carved mouth, those versatile, fascinating lips, that radiant smile, the childlike glee, his irrepressible humor, and the merry ring of his contagious laugh? At the head of the table sat our noble Webster; on his right, Mr. Graves, the guest from Kentucky; next the accomplished and dignified Everett, then governor of the Commonwealth, and second only in attractiveness to the master of the feast. On his left sat Robert C. Winthrop, the orator and statesman, whose offices in Congress, as representative and speaker of the house, and member of the senate, covering a period of many eventful years, were a deserved tribute to his own merits, no less than to one in the illustrious line of the Winthrops.

I shall refer to but one other of the many occasions on which Mr. Webster showed his power at the bar. When at the height of his fame he argued a case in the District Court of Boston, with William Wirt as opposing counsel. Wirt then stood at the summit of his reputation as a leader of the bar, combining native genius with liberal culture. That was one of the red-letter days in the legal calendar; it was as if Demosthenes and Cicero should stand up as opponents in the same forum. Wirt represented the classic orator of Rome. He presented a figure large and imposing, like his antagonist, — a face of winning sweetness, a smile to charm, a rich, almost perfectly modulated voice —, and his gestures, replete with grace, took captive the mass of earnest listeners who crowded the court room. Many ladies, as well as gentlemen, were present. Mr. Wirt, in his exordium, casting a glance on the multitude, alluded felicitously to the dryness of the law, and regretted that, instead of bringing graces which might entertain the imagination, he was to lead those present " through the arid paths and over the barren plains of the law." But such was the magnetism of the man himself that, quite independently of his argument, we were enchained by the spell of his manner.

Mr. Webster by his crystal clearness of thought, his compressed sentences, and deliberate and ponderous utterance, — and by those pauses, hardly less impressive than the words that preceded and followed them, — carried bench, bar, ladies, and even the sternest of the men to the last step of his honored and triumphant march.

HAMILTON FISH was born in New York City, August 3, 1808. His father, Nicholas Fish, was an officer in the Revolution, and an original member of the Society of the Cincinnati. He led heroically at Yorktown, was an excellent disciplinarian, and enjoyed the confidence of Washington. In 1797 he was chosen president of the New York Society of the Cincinnati. He was a man of elegant scholarship, and of great refinement and cultivated manners. His portrait expresses bravery and strength, joined with attractive and winning qualities of character. Hamilton Fish succeeded his father in the Society of the Cincinnati. He graduated at Columbia College in 1827; he was admitted to the bar in 1830; was in the legislature of New York in 1837; representative in Congress, 1843–45; lieutenant-governor of New York, 1847–49; governor of New York, 1849–51; United States Senator, 1851–57. In 1862 he was a member of the commission to visit the soldiers confined in Confederate prisons; in March, 1869, he was appointed secretary of state by President Grant, which office he held eight years. He was president of the New York Historical Society in 1880, and president of the Union League Club.

In 1854 he was elected president of the National Society of the Cincinnati, and still holds that office. I received valuable information by letter from him in regard to members of that Society, and prize highly his autograph. He was present at the dinner of the Phi Beta Kappa Society of Harvard University, in 1871, when he received from that institution the degree of LL. D.; which honor he had previously received from Columbia and Union colleges in New York. I occupied a seat near him, and was impressed by his classic face, which expresses intellectual power with moral eminence. His dignified and eloquent speech on that occasion was worthy the high position and character of the man.

The wife of Hamilton Fish was great-great-granddaughter of Governor Stuyvesant of New York.

COBB FAMILY.

DAVID COBB, an original member of the Society of the Cincinnati, was born in Attleborough, Massachusetts, September 14, 1748, and died April 17, 1830. His record is highly honorable. He graduated at Harvard College in 1766. In 1777 he was lieutenant-colonel of Henry Jackson's Regiment, and was distinguished by Revolutionary services in New Jersey and Rhode Island. He was aide-de-camp to Washington from June 15, 1781, to 1783; and took part in the capture of Cornwallis; he was made lieutenant-colonel, commanding the Fifth Regiment, January 7, 1783, and afterward brigadier-general by brevet. He was in the Massachusetts House of Representatives, 1789–93; and a member of Congress, 1793–95; member of the Executive Council in 1808; president of the Massachusetts Senate, 1801–04; lieutenant-governor of Massachusetts in 1809; resident of Maine, 1799–1820; chief-justice of the Court of Common Pleas, 1803–09; major-general of the Fifth Division of Massachusetts Militia; vice-president of the Massachusetts Society of the Cincinnati, 1810–11. He was a member of the Academy of Arts and Sciences, and of the Massachusetts Medical Society. His portrait was, on February 23, 1882, presented by Hon. S. C. Cobb to the State; and — a richly deserved honor — it was that day placed in the Massachusetts Senate chamber, with addresses by the president of the senate and other members of that body.

SAMUEL CROCKER COBB is a grandson of General David Cobb, and was born in Taunton, Massachusetts, May 22, 1826. He was admitted to the Society of the Cincinnati in 1856; was its secretary 1865–71, its vice-president in 1871, and president in 1880. Mr. Cobb was an alderman of the city of Roxbury in 1861 and 1862; he was president of the Roxbury Charitable Society, and held other important public trusts in that city. He was mayor of the city of Boston, 1874-76, in which office he manifested an energy, courage, and firm non-partisanship which, with his inbred courtesy, good judgment, and experience, made his administration very popular. He was elected actuary of the Massachusetts General Hospital in 1880. He married Aurelia L. Beattie in 1848. They have no children.

Mr. Cobb has been eminent in business, an honorable and successful merchant; and his intelligence, high moral standing, and engaging manners have won for him confidence and respect both in private and public.

I am indebted to him personally for valuable aid in relation to the General and State Societies of the Cincinnati, and for suggestions derived from other quarters through his courteous assistance.

THE LIBERTY TREE.

CHAPTER XIII.

REVOLUTIONARY MEN IN THE WAR OF 1812.

AMONG the families who retained personally or received by inheritance the military or naval spirit of the Revolution, are several too prominent to be overlooked. Passing by, of necessity, many to whom I would gladly do justice in this connection, I can speak of a few only whose friendship I have enjoyed, and others whose acquaintance has been a privilege.

HENRY DEARBORN was born in Hampton, New Hampshire, in March, 1751, and died at Roxbury, Massachusetts, June 6, 1829. He was an original member, in New Hampshire, of the Society of the Cincinnati. In 1814, July 4, at a public dinner in Lexington, Massachusetts, I first saw General Dearborn. He was received with great enthusiasm, and I looked upon him with intense interest. His large and commanding figure, his rich military dress, his brave air, his martial face, and urbane manners attracted universal attention.

Henry Dearborn was practising medicine in Portsmouth, New Hampshire, when, on the 20th of April, 1775, hearing of the battle of Lexington, he immediately marched, with a company of sixty volunteers, and reached Cambridge, distant sixty-five miles, the next day. He was made a captain under General Stark; was at the battle of Bunker Hill, June 17; and accompanied Arnold on the expedition to Quebec. At that place he was taken prisoner, December 31, 1776, and was exchanged in March, 1777. He served as major at the capture of Burgoyne, September 19, the same year, and distinguished himself and his regiment by a brave charge at the battle of Monmouth, in April, 1778. He was in Sullivan's expedition against the Indians in 1779; was with the army of Washington at Yorktown in 1781, as colonel of the First New Hampshire Regiment; in garrison duty in 1782 at Saratoga; and in the main army until the peace of 1783.

He was appointed, by President Washington, marshal of the district of Maine; was twice a member of Congress; and for eight years, under Jefferson, was secretary of war. In 1812 he became senior major-general in the United States Army. In 1813 he captured York in Upper Canada, and Fort George at the mouth of the Niagara, and afterward was placed in command of the military district of New York. In 1815 he resigned his commission in the army, and, after holding for some years the office of collector of the port of Boston, May 7, 1822, was appointed Minister to Portugal. At the end of ten years he left that position, at his own request.

General Dearborn in his prime, and, as seen in his portrait painted by Stuart, was tall, well proportioned, and appeared very vigorous, fitted for the great toils and fatigues of his life. His countenance and whole figure were dignified and commanding; although in later years when I saw him, he seemed somewhat encumbered with flesh. He was well fitted for the various offices, military and civil, which he held. His mind was solid and comprehensive, and improved constantly by culture. He had a native loftiness of character which forbade intrigue and duplicity, and was above envy and the low art of disparaging others to exalt himself. In his domestic and private life he was singularly happy; and of his two children one, who was the honored son of an honored father, appreciated his character and manifestly aimed to follow his precepts and copy his example.

The connection of General Henry Dearborn with the War of 1812 leads me to speak of that contest, and of the fears and superstitions it awakened. I was but a small boy when war between the United States and Great Britain was declared by Congress, through James Madison, then President. The country was intensely excited at that time by the animosities of the two great political parties, Federal and Democratic. My father was a warm Federalist, and of course I was a sage follower in his path. I heard constantly of the wickedness of our rulers, called Jacobins, who had plunged us needlessly into the war, with all its atrocities and sufferings. The Indians were employed by our foe as allies, and when the scalps of our people were brought in, the British officers congratulated the savages for their bravery, and gold was paid them for these trophies. Again and again no quarter was given to prisoners, and the helpless and fallen were put to death. My young blood was chilled when I read in the papers such language as that of Admiral Cockburn — referring to the conduct of the Russians in their contest with Napoleon — "The Cossacks spared Paris, but we did not spare the capital of America." I noticed many years since, when the Admiral died, the "London Times" lauded that act — although the capital was then entirely unprotected — as "a splendid achievement." I was shocked to hear of a British officer who went to a quiet house on Chesapeake Bay, and, finding three young ladies there at tea, gave them only ten minutes to clear their house, and at the expiration of that time, set fire to the building. It seemed hardly consistent in the organ of the British government, in our recent struggle to save the life of the nation, after having justified such acts, to lecture us, as it did, for our lust of power and our barbarity in warfare, and to call England the guardian of civilization. Let us rejoice that a better spirit now prevails in our mother country.

I recall many brave men whom I saw at that period, and among them the noble figure of General Miller, the hero of Fort Erie. How he towered up, as I looked on him afterward at my father's house, and thought of his glorious words when ordered to storm that fort: "I'll try, sir."

My pulse was stirred when an uncle returned from a privateering expedition — a good Christian man he was, too, and his course was thought no sin — and told us of his conflicts on the seas, and made us children presents from the trophies of his adventures. Among these things I remember a pair of nice gloves, enclosed in an English-walnut shell.

My father, though opposed to the war, joined a company of "Lexington Exempts," and his gun and knapsack, marked with the initial of our town, stood in sight, ready for the call to the battle-field. We boys, too, formed our little company, of which I was proud to rank as ensign, with my redoubtable tin sword and plush belt and cockade. Did not my heart swell with patriotism as we paraded through the streets? Sometimes we had an evening drill, which was specially enjoyed when some generous friend would invite us to halt in front of his window, and would bring forth a liberal entertainment.

The privations we suffered during the War of 1812 were only second to those of our fathers in the Revolution. I can never forget the straits to which it brought us in the family. Nearly all imported articles were beyond our means; our garments were of cheap fabrics. A blue broadcloth cloak of American manufacture, presented to my father, was made for long years to do service, until its threads could be almost counted. Not only foreign coffees and all the best teas were denied us, but at last the miserable bohea tea and rye coffee were cut off from constant use; and we would sit around our board, confined, one and all, to the oft-recurring baked apples and milk.

Not only did the whole country feel the indirect pressure of want, but a fearful direct taxation consumed their very substance. The race of children then learned one virtue, to which many in the present day are strangers; we acquired no taste for luxuries. Simple food, and moderate indulgence at the table, left us, in after life, with no cravings for the ten thousand superfluities which now so often injure both health and character.

It was the custom throughout the war to follow each great victory with some national song. Mrs. Margaret Sanderson, widow of Colonel Henry S. Sanderson, who died in New York in 1882 at the age of eighty-five years, was only fifteen years old at the time of the bombardment of Fort McHenry in 1812; but she made with her own hands, out of costly silk, the flag which inspired Francis Scott Key to write the "Star-spangled Banner." She presented it to Colonel George Armstead, the commandant of the fort, just before the British appeared in the bay. During the subsequent engagement the flag floated over the fort, and was seen by Key while he was confined in a British man-of-war. After the war the flag was returned to its maker, and the original Star-spangled Banner is one of the treasures of the Sanderson family. My youthful heart thrilled with fresh delight, as the noble Perry's achievement on Lake Erie, or the heroism of Hull in the old "Constitution," or some other like success, was set forth in quickening verse.

Nor was it our own country alone which called forth these poetic effusions. The fortunes of France were then watched with eager eyes; and the little Federalists rejoiced with the older ones when the great Napoleon had at last been conquered and captured; and when, as the song of the day ran, he was "cooped up in the Island of Elba." When, after his ninety days' exile, his return, and renewed battles, tidings came of his Waterloo defeat, and I saw Boston illuminated for the victory of the "Holy Alliance," I joined, with my father and all the fathers of Federalism, in shouting the loud pæan of the hour.

After a struggle of nearly three years' duration the war terminated. Although this was more than sixty years ago, I recollect the very spot where I stood, by the stove in the old, one-story schoolhouse, when, February 13, 1815, a companion whispered to me as he came in, "There is peace." A jubilee at once filled our young hearts, and precious little study was there through that long afternoon. In the evening the two field-pieces of our artillery company were dragged through the deep snow to the venerated Common of Revolutionary fame, and a salvo was fired to which all hearts responded. Erelong I joined with the older boys of our party in the *jeu d'esprit* of the hour: "Peace ratified; Federalists gratified; Democrats mortified."

My paternal grandfather, full of personal memories of the great contest of 1775, designated this short and comparatively unimportant conflict as "the Sixpenny War of 1812." But it was claimed by many, at the time, that our glorious victories, especially those by sea and on the lakes, vindicated our national honor on the water as on the land, and made Great Britain pay us a more just respect.

Many thought the fearful events of that period were the frowns of Providence on our wicked war. As I look back to those years, they seem to me full of thrilling experiences. Soon after the war, in September, 1815, occurred that memorable gale which sent terror throughout our community. It began between eight and nine o'clock in the forenoon, coming from the southeast, and continued about four hours. Houses and barns were blown down, chimneys were overthrown, and windows dashed in; the tides in Boston and Cambridge, we heard, were fearfully high; and in the latter place a vessel was washed up from the shore and driven into the main street of the town. I saw, during the morning, trees of the larger size uprooted in every direction. A new shed one hundred feet long, which my father had built for his hotel, was taken up, carried high in the air as if by a giant's hand, and dropped a long way from its foundation. I followed my father to one of his houses, where he saw the roof at one end beginning to rise, and rushed with him to the attic, where, axe in hand, he dashed out the windows at the other end, and thus saved the unroofing of the house. The air, at the distance of thirteen miles from the ocean, was so saturated with salt water that it was difficult to breathe. This was Saturday; and the next day the church was not opened, for the roads were all so covered with trees uprooted and blown into them, that, as was said, " the people could not ride to meeting."

Still another calamity. The very next year the weather was fearfully cold. The first of May, 1816, there was talk about " spots on the sun ; " and, as we looked through smoked glass, we could see them very plainly. They continued on through June, and in July the same or similar spots were clearly to be seen. Some evenings we had to make fires in order to be comfortable. There were heavy frosts, and many vegetables were cut down. Several mornings ice was to be seen nearly half an inch thick. There was, in the month of June, snow enough to nearly cover the ground. In July and August it was less cold, although there were, in some places, slight frosts; but in September snow fell several hours in succession. The crop of corn was nearly all destroyed on my father's land. We stripped the ears, but they turned black, and we could not even use the corn for our cattle. The next spring, seeds of many kinds were sold, not by measure, but by number.

This loss of the crops, with the frightful debt brought on our country by the war, was the constant talk in every place. We were obliged to straiten ourselves in clothing, in every kind of indulgence, and even in our food. The hungry boy was only too happy, some times, in having his appetite satisfied with what was too meagre for his elders.

The superstitions of that period led us to look with terror on what we, in 1882, call beautiful. The fiery comet of 1811 was thought to have been sent as a harbinger of the dread war of the next year. It was said " the beetles had a *W* on their backs, predicting war." It had been forgotten that this same prophetic letter is always there. Some said, " The end of the world is near." Many a day, in the autumn of that same year, as I looked up and saw the smoke in the air, caused in reality by forest fires, I trembled, as did older spectators, at the idea that the burning up of the earth had begun, and the Judgment Day must be coming.

An incident of this conflict illustrates the romantic fortunes of war, and shows that, like peace, it has, in its history, truths stranger than fiction. Abram Johnson, recently (1881) died at Salem, Pennsylvania, having attained the great age of one hundred and eight years. He was born in Vermont in 1773. Mr. Johnson enlisted in the army in the War of 1812. He was made captain of a company of Oneida Indians, under the command of General Macomb. He was at the battle of Plattsburg, and received several wounds in that engagement. One of these was made by a bayonet-thrust in the knee, and another was a sabre-cut in the neck. He was left as dead. He was taken from the field after the battle by his Indian soldiers. Oneida, the sixteen-year-old daughter of a chief, nursed him until he was able to go out again. They loved each other and, when peace was restored, were married. Johnson and his Indian bride went to Sussex County, New Jersey. There they settled down and had a daughter. When this girl was twelve years old her mother's health had failed so that her life was despaired of. She longed to go back to her people. Her husband took her to her old home among the Oneidas. There she soon afterward died, and was buried with all the ceremonies of her tribe. The daughter found a home in a family in Sussex County. When she grew up she joined the Oneida Indians, and married the son of a chief. Her father gained a competency at farming. He lost his money through unlucky speculation, and finally became a town charge and died a pauper. His mind was sound up to the time of his death.

One of the anticipated signs of the end of the world was thought to be the earthquake of 1814. I well remember the terror of the night on which it occurred. One of my sisters said to me: "I hope this is not for our warning only; I shall ask our neighbors in the morning if they felt it too." And when we learned that it extended to other places, and perhaps over the whole country, we joined in the prevailing opinion that it was "a judgment upon the people."

An Association of Veterans of the War of 1812 was formed in 1853, and continued until October, 1879. At the time of its dissolution, the surviving members met in Boston for that purpose. There were sixteen veterans present; the youngest was seventy-nine and the oldest ninety-two years of age. The sum of their ages was thirteen hundred and fifty-one years. The venerable president, Hon. Charles Hudson of Lexington, at the age of eighty-four, made a patriotic and affecting address. With happy recollections of the past, he said: "On the whole we have reason to rejoice in the part we took in the war which supplemented and perfected the treaty of 1783, and secured to our commerce the freedom of the seas and gave us the rights and prerogatives of a sovereign nation." In the closing portion of his address he said: " And now, fellow-soldiers and comrades, as we are about to part to meet no more on earth, let us extend the hand of brotherhood, and say, as none but soldiers can in the same spirit, Farewell!"

HENRY ALEXANDER SCAMMELL DEARBORN was born in Exeter, New Hampshire, March 3, 1783, and died in Portland, Maine, July 29, 1851. He became a member of the Massachusetts Society of the Cincinnati in 1832, and was president of the General Society, 1848-51. I saw him often in public offices and situations, especially in military capacities, and was struck with his finely proportioned figure, his manly and intelligent face, his martial bearing when on parade, and his dignified and courteous manner in society. I was for several years associated with him as a member of the Massachusetts Horticultural Society, of which he was at one time president. We have a fine portrait of him, taken while in that office, hanging on the walls of our Horticultural Hall.

He was active among the original founders of the Mount Auburn Cemetery, with which the Massachusetts Horticultural Society is closely connected.

He graduated at William & Mary College in 1803; studied law with William Wirt and afterward with Judge Story. He was collector of the port of Boston 1813-29; commanded the troops in Boston Harbor in 1812, and was brigadier-general of the Massachusetts Militia in 1814. He was a member of the Massachusetts Constitutional Convention in 1820; representative in the legislature from Roxbury in 1830; member of Congress 1831-33; adjutant-general of Massachusetts 1834-43, and mayor of Roxbury 1847-51. He was active in originating and founding the Bunker Hill Monument Association; in completing the Hoosac Tunnel, and inaugurating the Forest Hills Cemetery. He wrote many books: "Commerce and Navigation of the Black Sea" in 1819; "Letters on the Internal Improvement and Commerce of the West" in 1839, and the "Life of the Apostle Eliot." He left unpublished materials for several volumes, among them a "History of Bunker Hill Battle," lives of Colonel William Raymond Lee, Commodore Bainbridge, and his father, General Henry Dearborn.

He was very popular in society. His house was the abode of hospitality. Every important enterprise, public or private, received his encouragement and aid. He was a member of the American Academy of Arts and Sciences, the American Antiquarian Society, Massachusetts Historical Society, New England Historic Genealogical Society, and the American Association for the Advancement of Science. His surpassing industry is shown in the fact that, in addition to the above-named works, he left unpublished a Diary, in forty-five volumes; " Grecian Architecture," two volumes folio; a volume on Flowers, with drawings, and a " Harmony of the Life of Christ," eight volumes.

WILLIAM HULL was born in Derby, Connecticut, June 24, 1753. He was an original member of the Society of the Cincinnati. He graduated at Yale College, with honor in 1772, and was admitted to the bar in 1775. In April of that year he was made captain of a company, and marched with Colonel Webb's Regiment to Cambridge. This regiment was in the battles of Brooklyn and White Plains. In December, 1776, at the engagement of Trenton, Captain Hull acted as field-officer of his regiment. July 1, 1777, he was made major in the Eighth Massachusetts Regiment; and before the battle of Princeton he rendered important service to Washington. In April, 1777, he marched with three hundred men to Ticonderoga; and on the retreat to the Hudson River, Major Hull received the thanks of General Schuyler. He took part in the capture of Burgoyne, October, 1777, and at the battle of Monmouth in 1778. After valuable services he was promoted to be lieutenant-colonel, August 12, 1779. About this time the appointment of aide to General Washington was offered to Colonel Hull, but circumstances prevented its acceptance. In January 1781, for his gallant conduct of a force against the British at Morrisania, he received the thanks of Washington and of Congress. He was complimented by the Commander-in-chief, when he escorted him with his troops into New York on the evacuation of that place by the British. When, December 4, 1783, Washington took leave of his officers in New York and disbanded the army, excepting one regiment, Colonel Hull was selected by him for lieutenant-colonel of that regiment.

When General Hull returned to Boston he was

made successively judge of the court of common pleas, major-general of the Third Division of Massachusetts Militia, and senator in the State Legislature. In 1805 he was appointed by President Jefferson, governor of Michigan Territory. In 1812 he reluctantly accepted the command of a military force to protect the northern frontier against the Indians. Subsequently he had command as major-general in defending that region against the British troops, who were under the lead of General Brock; and, apprehending an assault from him on Detroit,—where General Hull then was with his forces,—the latter, fearing the total destruction of his own army, as well as of that town, which contained, as a fort, a large gathering of helpless women and children, surrendered it to the enemy.

On account of this surrender General Hull was charged, by a court-martial, in 1814, with neglect of duty, cowardice, and other offences, and was tried and condemned to death. But after sentence had been passed on him, President Madison declined to execute it. Public opinion, at first strongly against General Hull, was, on investigation, greatly changed; and in 1825 a public dinner was given him, at which the leading men of Boston expressed their sympathy and respect for him. I believe posterity will render that justice to him which a train of unhappy circumstances had led many to deny him. We should be slow to give credence to charges of cowardice and treason against a man who during his Revolutionary services received the thanks of Washington and of Congress, and had the approbation of his superior officers, and whose courage and patriotism at that time were never doubted. Although, when deprived of the auxiliary forces he had just reason to expect, he surrendered his military position at Detroit, it is by no means certain that this was not a wiser and more humane course, than to incur the risk of sacrificing his army and the town in those desperate circumstances. He avowed to the last his sense of right-doing in that act, and he was sustained also by many testimonials, both public and private, in his declining years.

From 1786 his home was on his farm in Newton, Massachusetts, where he died peacefully, November 29, 1825, at the age of seventy-two years.

THE WASHINGTON ELM.

CHAPTER XIV.

OLIVER HAZARD PERRY.

CHRISTOPHER RAYMOND PERRY was born at South Kingston, Rhode Island, in 1761, and died June 1, 1818. He was in the service, both military and naval, during the Revolutionary War. While in the navy his frigate was captured by the British, and he suffered for three months untold horrors in the famous Jersey prison-ship. In 1783, after peace was declared, he was appointed collector in a district of Rhode Island.

In October, 1784, he married Sarah Alexander, a reputed descendant of Wallace of Scotland. They had a son, OLIVER HAZARD PERRY, born in Newport, Rhode Island, August 25, 1785. After his victory in the battle of Lake Erie, he was chosen an honorary member of the New York Cincinnati Society, October 21, 1813.

He inherited from his mother an amiable disposition, joined with courage and commanding qualities of character. Like her he possessed a warm temper, but kept it under admirable control. While at school he manifested a strong mind, which he earnestly cultivated. He gave early promise of his future distinction. In 1799, when only fourteen years of age, he entered the navy as a midshipman, and was in active service under his father in the frigate " General Greene," in her cruise on the West India station in 1799 and 1800. In 1807 he was promoted to the rank of lieutenant, and in 1809 was in command of the schooner " Revenge," and cruised on the coast of the United States until January 1811, when his vessel, without his fault, was wrecked. When the War of 1812 opened he, at his own request, was placed on the lakes, under the command of Commodore Isaac Chauncey. He was soon called to aid an attack on Fort George, in which he acquired great credit. In August, 1813, in the momentary absence of a British squadron then watching him, he employed the force, which he had equipped, to lift his larger vessels on " camels," and took them out of port; and although deficient in officers and men, and poorly prepared, he brought the British squadron to an engagement, with complete success on his side. After co-operating with General Harrison in regaining possession of Detroit and transporting troops, and taking part in another battle, at the close of the campaign of 1813 he resigned his command. Congress voted him a gold medal, and he was, dating from September 10, 1813, appointed to the " Java," and promoted in the service. In 1814 he was employed in annoying the British squadron which sailed up the Potomac to destroy the public buildings at Washington, and was stationed in the defence of Baltimore. March, 1819, he sailed, in command of a squadron, for the coast of Columbia.

On the 1st of February, 1813, he received from Commodore Chauncey the following compliment: "You are the very person that I want for a particular service, in which you may gain reputation for yourself and honor for your country." This service was the command of a naval force to be created on Lake Erie. Secretary Rogers wrote to him: "You will doubtless command in chief. Mr. Hamilton mentioned this to me two months past; you may expect some warm fighting and, of course, a portion of honor."

The world knows the result of this appointment. The battle on Lake Erie reads, in its details, like a romance. The prospect of a conflict between the American squadron with only fifty-four guns, and the British squadron under Commodore Barclay, with sixty-three guns, might have intimidated a man of less bravery than Perry; but he was of that stern purpose that, conscious of the right, does not quail before numbers. The battle on Lake Erie, September 10, 1813, opened at fifteen minutes before noon, and after two hours and three quarters the order was given to "close action." Perry, having quitted his ship, the "Lawrence," in an open boat, for another ship, the "Niagara," after a desperate struggle, at three o'clock compelled Commodore Barclay to strike his flag; and at four o'clock the American hero wrote to General Harrison, then in command of our forces at the North: —

DEAR GENERAL: — We have met the enemy, and they are ours.
Yours with great respect and esteem,
O. H. PERRY.

At the same hour he wrote in a spirit of religious humility to the Secretary of the Navy: —

SIR: — It has pleased the Almighty to give to the arms of the United States a signal victory over their enemies on this lake. The British squadron, consisting of two ships, two brigs, one schooner, and one sloop, have this moment surrendered to the force under my command, after a sharp conflict.
I have the honor to be, sir,
Your obedient servant,
O. H. PERRY.

The effects of this victory were instant and far-reaching. It created an unbounded enthusiasm, which found expression in many forms, and among all classes of people. Who that lived in those days can forget that when, in the spring of 1814, Commodore Perry visited the theatre in Boston, the stage exhibited the inspiring motto: "The Hero of the Lake, on the glorious 10th of September, 1813." The man who had seen but twenty-eight years, on the day of this world-renowned victory, was greeted with the applause seldom won except by veterans on seas or fields. American poetry celebrated its triumph in strains which stirred the hearts of old and young. I recall a few lines of one of these effusions, which we boys of the day repeated through the streets with the utmost glee. Its wit turns upon the fact that *perry* was the name of a beverage then in common use, made from pears, as cider is from apples.

Before the Battle.

Bold Barclay one day
To Proctor did say:
" I'm tired of Jamaica and Sherry,
So let us go down
To that new floating town,
And get some American Perry.
Pleasant American Perry, —
Sparkling American Perry."

After the Battle.

" O cursèd American Perry."

This splendid achievement gave courage to a desponding people, and led to the overthrow of British power in the great Northwestern territory of the United States. It animated the whole country until the close of the war.

The name of the youthful hero, then but twenty-eight years old, was on all lips. It was emblazoned in the journals of the day, repeated with enthusiasm in the streets, placed on the signs of taverns, and given to halls and other buildings, public and private. It was worn as a badge by both sexes, and placed on articles of household use. I have before me a snuffbox, probably some seventy years old, bearing on one side a well executed representation of the battle, with its ships, and the Commodore passing, in the heat of the contest, in an open boat, from one vessel to another. Underneath is the inscription, not elegant but expressing the spirit of the times: —

VICTORY OF THE LAKE ERIE.

Reported by the American over the English the 10th of September 1813. The Commodore Perry fights alone with his ship all the Enemy's squadron commanded by the English Commodore Barclay, all to be reduced to be nothing more than carcasses — then he goes on board the Niagara, continues the battle, ended by the total destruction of the English division.

Nota The English General Barclay, was tried on account of the defeat.

On the other side of the snuffbox is a likeness of Commodore Perry. I have seen many pictures of the Commodore, but this, I think, not excepting the portrait of him by Stuart, is perhaps the most striking of them all. It corresponds to his youthful age. The head is large and well proportioned; the eyes full and expressing intellect and energy; the nose inclined to a Roman shape; the mouth with a clear Cupid's bow, firm, yet amiable; and the chin marked by decision and self-control. The family speak of him as a handsome man. His face has nothing, however, feminine in its form or expression; it is manly, determined, remarkable for its intelligence, and indicates a man as great in action as he was noble in thought and pure in heart.

The Commodore had a son named Oliver H. Perry, Jr., who, a boy at the time of his father's death, himself afterward entered the navy. He eventually left it for mercantile pursuits. Commodore Perry had five children, one of whom married Rev. Dr. Francis Vinton of New York City.

It was my good fortune to be present, July 4, 1838, at a celebration on Lake Erie, on the very scene, it was said, of the battle. A bright day and a fine oration, with stirring music, filled all present with patriotic memories of the great victory achieved on that spot.

In 1860, September 10, the inauguration of a marble statue by William Walcutt, to the memory of Commodore Oliver H. Perry, took place at Cleveland, Ohio, when Hon. George Bancroft gave an oration. An address was given by Usher Parsons, M. D., surgeon at the battle of Lake Erie; and others followed, among whom was Oliver Hazard Perry of Andover, Massachusetts, the only surviving son of Commodore Perry. Hosea Sargent, who helped fire the last gun of the battle, and bore the flag of the "Lawrence" to the Commodore in his boat as he took command of the "Niagara," was present. Thomas Brownell, pilot of the "Ariel" on that day, was also present.

It will be remembered that the town of Newport, Rhode Island, the native place of Commodore Perry, presented him with a vase eighteen inches high, of solid silver; it has on its sides two sketches of the battle, finely engraved. This is in the possession of his grandson, Oliver Hazard Perry, who has also a sextant which the British commander, Commodore Barclay, presented to Commodore Perry, "as a memento of his regard," on taking leave of him soon after the day of the battle. In return Commodore Perry forwarded to Barclay, some months after, a highly finished American rifle, made expressly for him by a celebrated gunsmith of Albany.

The following testimonial of Surgeon Parsons, on the character of Commodore Perry, is invaluable: "Possessed of high-toned moral feeling, he was above the low dissipation and sensuality that many officers of his day were prone to indulge in. His conversation was remarkably free from profanity and indelicacy, and in his domestic character he was a model of every domestic virtue and grace. Every germ of merit in his officers was sure to be discovered and encouraged by him. . . . Generous to the full extent of his means, his elegant hospitality reflected great honor on our navy." He commends also his mental culture and habits of "patient thought," and the perfect order and discipline on his ships and among his officers and men.

Unhappily the invaluable life of Commodore Perry was cut short in its prime. He died at Port Spain, Island of Trinidad, on his birthday, August 25, 1819, at the age of thirty-four years, of a painful disease, surrounded with every discomfort, yet with a calmness and resignation honorable to his character and worthy of his renown.

MATTHEW CALBRAITH PERRY, brother of the preceding, was born in South Kingston in 1795, and died in New York City, March 4, 1858. He was chosen an honorary member of the Society of the Cincinnati on the same day with his brother. This was an honor well merited by his distinction in the United States Navy, from the day when he entered the service as midshipman, and served under Commodores Rodgers and Decatur, to his crowning work, beginning March 2, 1852, when he was appointed to the command of the Japan expedition, which opened the way to our present commerce with that country. His skill and indomitable energy and perseverance gave him a signal position in our naval history.

THE HOLMES HOUSE.

CHAPTER XV.

PERSONAL APPEARANCE OF REVOLUTIONARY OFFICERS.

ALTHOUGH it is not always safe to judge of character by personal appearance and impression, there is often a striking correspondence between the two. This is to be noticed both in the military and naval history of our country. In turning over a volume prepared to exhibit the names, characters, and achievements of several of our American military officers, I was impressed by the remarkable personal appearance of many of these men.

The frontispiece of that volume gives us the picture of Washington so often presented, yet a subject which can never cease to interest. Who ever tires of looking at the portrait of this man? See his tall and well-proportioned figure, so manly and commanding in its every part. Those features — grave, dignified, expressing inward vigor (although in complete repose), courage, steadiness of purpose, and perseverance united with caution — indicate the good soldier and the equally good statesman, wise, calm, but replete with earnestness. They bring before us an individual, in some moods all thoughtfulness, in others a hero, the embodiment of decision and intense activity. They express candor, sincerity, and simplicity, joined with kindness, and a humanity which was pained to see a man even justly punished, and was intent on relieving the sick and suffering. They show also an intellect guided by the highest moral principle, and a religious faith ever looking toward and leaning upon the divine Providence. The commander-in-chief of the Revolutionary army carried with him a personal air and manner that supplemented the influence of that rare wisdom which gave him power and ascendancy at the head of the nation, alike in military and civil affairs. To see him while he lived was much more than to hear of his deeds or to read the truest description of his life and actions. In looking on that noble figure, and resting one's eyes on that grand face, there is nothing to detract from his fame, but everything to enhance it.

Many scenes occurred, both in the military and civil experiences of Washington, any one of which furnishes a vivid picture of his personal appearance, — as when he took command of the army at Cambridge; or when, with three thousand men around him, crying from their huts, "No pay, no clothes, no provisions," he was overheard in his tent at Valley Forge, as he knelt in prayer for divine aid. A soldier, knowing this, said: "If the Lord will listen to any one, it is George Washington, and our independence is certain."

In 1792 Trumbull painted a portrait of Washington, in which he represented his appearance the night before the battle of Princeton. "We talked," says Trumbull, "of the scene, its dangers, its almost desperation. He *looked* the scene again, and I transferred to the canvas the lofty expression of his animated countenance, the high resolve to conquer or to perish." This was a picture of him "in his heroic, military character," and it exhibits a fire and resolution in his face quite in contrast with his usual placidity, and especially with his calm dignity during his subsequent presidency.

But nothing of this character has impressed me like the following vivid portraiture of Washington, drawn by one who heard his address to Congress after he was elected President for a second term. We are indebted to Mrs. Kirkland for a graphic description of this scene, which she quotes, in the words of one living when she wrote it: —

I was but a schoolboy at the time, and had followed one of the many groups of people who, from all quarters, were making their way to the hall in Chestnut Street, corner of Fifth, Philadelphia, where the two houses of Congress then held their sittings, and where they were that day to be addressed by the President, on the opening of his second term of office. Boys can often manage to work their way through a crowd better than men can. At all events, it so happened that I succeeded in reaching the steps of the hall, from which elevation, looking in every direction, I could see nothing but human heads — a vast fluctuating sea, swaying to and fro, and filling every accessible place which commanded even a distant view of the building. They had congregated, not with the hope of getting into the hall, for that was physically impossible, but that they might see Washington. Many an anxious look was cast in the direction in which he was expected to come; till at length, true to the appointed hour (he was the most punctual of men), an agitation was observable on the outskirts of the crowd, which gradually opened, and gave space for an elegant coach, drawn by six superb white horses, having on its four sides beautiful designs of the four seasons. . . . It slowly made its way till it drew up immediately in front of the hall.

The rush was now tremendous; but, as the coach door opened, there issued from it two gentlemen, with long white wands, who with some difficulty parted the people, so as to open a passage from the carriage to the steps, on which the fortunate schoolboy had achieved a footing, and whence the whole proceeding could be distinctly seen. As the President emerged from the carriage, a univeral shout rent the air, and continued, as he very deliberately ascended the steps. On reaching the platform he paused, looking back on the carriage, thus affording to the anxiety of the people the indulgence they desired, of feasting their eyes upon his person.

Never did a more majestic personage present himself to the public gaze. He was within two feet of me; I could have touched his clothes, but I should as soon have thought of touching an electric battery. Boy as I was, I felt as in the presence of a divinity. As he turned to enter the hall the gentlemen with the white wands preceded him and, with still greater difficulty than before, repressed the people and cleared a way to the great staircase. As he ascended I ascended with him, step by step, creeping close to the wall, and almost hidden by the skirts of his coat. Nobody looked at me, everybody was looking at him; and thus I was permitted, unnoticed, to glide along, and happily to make my way (where so many were vainly longing and struggling to enter) into the lobby of the chamber of the House of Representatives. Once in, I was safe; for had I even been seen by the officers in attendance, it would have been impossible to get me out again. I saw near me a large pyramidal stove which, fortunately, had but little fire in it; and on which I forthwith clambered, until I had attained a secure perch from which every part of the hall could be deliberately and distinctly surveyed. Depend upon it, I made use of my eyes.

On either side of the broad aisle that was left vacant in the centre were assembled the two houses of Congress. As the President entered, all rose, and remained standing till he had ascended the steps at the upper end of the chamber, and taken his seat in the Speaker's chair. It was an impressive moment. Notwithstanding that the spacious apartment, floor, lobby, and gallery, were full, not a sound was heard; the silence of expectation was unbroken and profound; every breath seemed suspended. He was dressed in a full suit of the richest black velvet; his lower limbs in short clothes, with black silk stockings. His shoes, which were brightly japanned, were surmounted with large square silver buckles. His hair, carefully displayed in the manner of the day, was richly powdered, and gathered behind into a black silk bag, on which was a bow of black ribbon. In his hand he carried a plain cocked hat, decorated with the American cockade. He wore by his side a light, slender dress-sword, in a green scabbard, with a highly ornamented hilt. His gait was deliberate, his manners solemn but self-possessed; and he presented, altogether, the most august human figure I had then, or have since, beheld.

At the head of the Senate stood Thomas Jefferson, in a blue coat, single-breasted, with large bright basket buttons, his vest and small clothes of crimson. I remember being struck with his bright eye and foxy hair, as well as by his tall form and square shoulders. A perfect contrast was presented by the pale, reflective face and delicate figure of James Madison. In the semicircle which was formed behind the chair, and on either hand of the President, my boyish gaze was attracted by the splendid attire of the Chevalier D'Ynigo, the Spanish ambassador, then the only foreign minister near our infant government. His glittering star, his silk *chapeau bras*, edged with ostrich feathers, his foreign air and courtly bearing, contrasted strongly with those nobility of nature's forming who stood around him. It was a very fair representation of the Old World and the New.

Having retained his seat for a few moments, while the members resumed their seats, the President rose and, taking from his breast a roll of paper, proceeded to read his address. His voice was full and sonorous, deep and rich in tones, free from that trumpet ring which it could assume amid the tumult of battle (and which is said to have been distinctly heard above all its roar), but sufficiently loud and clear to fill the chamber and be heard with perfect ease in its most remote recesses. The address was of considerable length; its topics, of course, I forget, for I was too young to understand them. I only remember, in its latter part, some reference to claims or disputes on the part of the Indian tribes. He read everything with a singular serenity and composure, with manly ease and dignity, but without the smallest attempt at display.

Having concluded, he laid the manuscript on the

table before him and resumed his seat; when, after a slight pause, he rose and withdrew, the members rising and remaining on their feet until he had left the chamber.

Most impressive must have been that scene when, in November 18, 1783, the British army retired at one point in New York City, and the American army entered it at another. Washington is on horseback at the head of the American procession. Through these streets he has often ridden in his state carriage, drawn by six horses, in which he journeyed afterward through New England. And here too, when the long agony is at last over, a few days later, he takes a final leave of his officers, and, from the barge in which he is crossing the water on his way homeward, turns to his countless friends, as they stand on the shore, and waves his military hat and bids them a silent farewell.

The personal power of their leader is seen as we look upon the delineated forms and features of the distinguished circle of heroes on the field, or of sages in the cabinet, which Washington gathered around him. No one who had seen the men whom he received to his confidence in the army — such as Henry Knox, for example, of so commanding a figure, and whose every feature bespoke the brave, the generous, the patriotic, the faithful, and true man — could question their being entitled to their position. Look at the early portrait of Lafayette, — second only, if not first, in the esteem of Washington,— how full it is of the noble expression seen on that day when, at less than twenty years of age, he presented himself to his chief, to be ever after a bosom friend. When I saw him on his visit to this country in 1824 — after the weight of age had come upon him, and marks were manifest of the untold sufferings he had experienced in the dreary prisons of Olmutz and Magdeburg, in the hardships of war in our own country, and amid the anxieties and reponsibilities of that terrible Revolution in his own — I recalled vividly what a price he had paid that we might be free, and none the less when I saw that his bowed form still carried much of its pristine dignity, and the massive face, especially the eye, lighted up with its "wonted fires" as he spoke. We who then saw him thought of his sacrifices wellnigh to death for our sakes, and when we heard from his own lips words of love to his old companions in arms, our hearts burned within us, and we felt a warmth toward him which the cold page of history had never kindled.

And so it is, in a lower degree, as we to-day look on the portraits of those men who braved such dangers and suffered such pains, that our country might be born into freedom and independence. Baron von Steuben's portrait — by that strongly marked face and head, both of the Roman stamp, with eyes large, bright, and attractive, a nose firm, and a mouth combining great beauty with a frank and noble energy of purpose — reinforces our previous estimate of the great work he did for us, more especially in maturing and perfecting the discipline of our ill arranged troops. John Brooks, who more than once received the personal commendation of Washington for his courage and good judgment in the field, bore in his personal appearance tokens of that manly power he everywhere exhibited. General Marion shows in his face a combination of Northern energy with Southern— I might almost say—fascination; and we see united in his picture, with manly beauty and sweetness of character, a strength of purpose, good judgment, and perseverance in action, that make us believe he richly deserved the testimony of the commander-in-chief that, at Eutaw Springs he " conducted his troops with great gallantry and good conduct," and, with two others to co-operate, achieved a renowned victory.

I have spoken of Eustis at the time he held the office of governor. He was then about seventy years old, but there were still left traces of his early personal appearance. On looking at his portrait, painted in his prime, by Stuart, I am struck with its remarkable attractiveness. A large expansion of brow, indicating strong intellect, a bright eye, Grecian nose, and a mouth uniting firmness with benevolence, all form a head and a face, that bespeak a man genial, social, refined, yet not wanting in self-reliance and energy. We see this latter trait manifested by the confidence he inspired in the officers of the army, being offered at one time by General Knox a commission as lieutenant of artillery, although his desire to be perfected in medicine led him to decline it, and adhere to his work as surgeon in the army.

The name of John Lillie should have a place here. An excellent engraving of him, by F. T. Stuart, gives us a face in which Roman dignity and firmness are united with a prepossessing smile. The arch expression of the eyes, the pleasant yet intelligent mouth, the well-set chin, all give evidence of a frankness and force of character that one does not easily forget. Born in Boston, July 18, 1753, he died September 22, 1801. Yet this short life was filled with services to his country. He was commissioned second lieutenant, May 1, 1775; first lieutenant in Knox's Regiment of artillery, in 1776; acting captain in Crane's Regiment, in 1777; captain in 1778; aide-de-camp to General Knox, May 1, 1782; captain of the United States Artillery, February 16, 1801, and commandant at West Point at the time of his death. An unsought certificate was given him by Washington, December 1, 1783, in these words: "Whereas Captain John Lillie has behaved with great propriety during his military services, I have therefore thought proper to grant this certificate." After enumerating his rapid promotions and many offices, Washington adds: "In all which several stations and capacities Captain Lillie has conducted himself, on all occasions, with dignity, bravery, and intelligence." He was presented with a sword by Washington, and also with one by Lafayette, which was in 1873, and at this time doubtless is, in the possession of his grandson, Hon. Henry L. Pierce of Boston.

I select another Revolutionary officer who secured the marked favor of Washington, Captain Henry Lee. One would observe the face of this man in a gallery, among hundreds of others, as singularly attractive. The features are all nearly perfect,— a high and well proportioned forehead, surmounted by well adjusted hair, clubbed into a queue; the eyes clear and bright, with finely shaped eyebrows, a classic nose, with a mouth of the rarest benevolence, and a chin of corresponding effect,—the whole figure compact, a military coat, the lappels at least a hundred years old in style, the ruffled shirt-bosom, the official epaulettes, every part and the whole together, bespeak no ordinary man. The record of this man comes up to what we anticipate. "Captain Lee," says a contemporary writer, "who has for some time past been posted at Valley Forge with his troops, has added another cubit to his fame." We have then an account of his great skill and courage at a point where he was surprised in a house occupied only by himself and seven other persons, by a party of two hundred men, whom he compelled "disgracefully to retire," with a loss of two killed and four wounded, while only one of his little band was injured. For this exploit he received the following testimonial: "The Commander-in-chief returns his earnest thanks to Captain Lee, and the officers and men in his troop, for the victory which their superior bravery and address gained over a party of the enemy's dragoons." With the same adroitness, August 20, 1779, Captain, now Major Lee made an attack on the British garrison at Poule's Hook. The preponderance of his opponent's force was such that, in a letter to Washington, Lee calls his men " the forlorn hope." Yet his success was complete. He speaks of the " patience of his troops under their sufferings," and their " resolution which reflects the highest honor on them." After gaining the fort, his soldiers refrained from plunder, although in the midst of temptations. "American humanity," he says, " has been again signally manifested. Self-preservation strongly dictated, in the retreat, the putting the prisoners to death, and British cruelty fully justified it; notwithstanding which, not a man was wantonly hurt." This noble conduct was what one would have anticipated who had ever looked on a likeness of Major Lee. His high character was transfused into his men; his honor became an inspiration to theirs.

I might easily fill pages with records of this kind which would confirm the claims of physiognomy in the brave and generous men of the Revolutionary War.

These remarks apply equally, I may add, to the impression made upon one's mind by the personal appearance of many of our great civilians in later no less than Revolutionary periods. I once saw in the United States Senate a cluster of men who produced this effect. Among them were Henry Clay, whose tall figure, courageous, unique, and expressive face and manner, the essence of courtesy, attracted one as those of no ordinary person; Thomas H. Benton, compact in frame,— a Western air of freedom united with a gait and movement as solid as " the hard money " which in his pet measure he advocated; John C. Calhoun, slender, stern, with an intellectual face, and an eye one did not care to meet, — so determined, so like many a master's as he gazes on his slave.

What I have remarked of the faces of such men as I have spoken of is true, in a degree, of other personal indications of their characters. We can see something of this even in their handwriting. We can trace indications of remarkable traits in many men of distinction even in their penmanship. I have in this volume repeatedly spoken of the rare eloquence of Edward Everett. As one saw and heard him in his great orations, the feeling was strong that such power as this can belong only to a man whose genius is concentrated, if not confined in these masterly productions. And yet look at the man in any of the ordinary, commonplace marks of character, and you see the very same care for completeness and perfection. A letter of his, when president of Harvard College, calling us to a committee meeting, would be written, even to the punctuation, as exactly as if he were only secretary of the board instead of its head. He had system and method in a business letter as in a finished oration. Look at a little note of his, its signature, its whole contents. It equals, in these respects, the exactness of Washington.

In looking over twenty pages of the autographs of members of the Society of the Cincinnati, I was struck with them as illustrations of character. Begin with Washington; his clear and firm autograph shows what the man was—upright, judicious, calm, self-possessed. Here is a person whose portrait announces, what I heard a neighbor of our family often say of some wise man, that " he is one who understands himself;" when the hour calls for action, how steadily and smoothly, yet how determinately he will move forward. See the signature of Henry Knox, fair, like his face, yet downright, and ponderous, like his massive frame. Benjamin Lincoln's hand is firm, honest, uniform. John Brooks's is plain, upright. William Eustis has a bad pen, but here is perseverance. Samuel Adams writes a hand firm, upright, and clear. See the signature of John Hancock on the Declaration of Independence,—bold, decided; here is a name to be read by all men. Franklin's handwriting, in mid-life, was clear, firm, even, and not ungraceful. Jefferson's signature was widespread and decided; although in a letter his handwriting was often different, and in the latter part of his life, quite narrow, compact, and very legible. The signature of John Adams was broad, plain, and emphatic, like

the man. His son, John Quincy, in 1832, wrote a
set hand, quite in character, very readable, but by
no means graceful. Andrew Jackson penned his
name with the energy of a hero and the decision
of an autocrat. Henry Clay writes with a delicacy
and fine penmanship that exhibit courtesy and
great powers of persuasion. Reading one of the
letters of Josiah Quincy now before me, I find it
marked, as everything from his head or heart was,
by tokens of a man strong both in intellect and
sensibilities. Uprightness, decision, energy, are
in this autograph. And so with those of his father,
grandfather, and back to the earliest members of
this family. Here is a noble race, who write down
in their signatures, as they do by their lives and
actions, the record of their honored and imperishable work. Note the penmanship of John Parker,
as he testifies of his part in the battle of Lexington; it is bold, emphatic, steadfast, like the man.
Israel Putnam's hand is uncultured, uneven,
but firm and strong. Henry Dearborn writes out
in every letter his energy and persistence. Stuart
gave life to those who sat for their portraits. So
do such men as James Otis, Daniel Webster, Henry
Knox, utter the living word by the stroke of their
pen. See the autograph of Baron Von Steuben,
not graceful, but marked, showing a man of action.
Look at our allies in the War of the Revolution:
the Count de Grasse writes his name with the energy of a commander; and the Count de Rochambeau leaves a signature expressing modesty, and

yet a decision that in a good cause will not flinch or falter to the end. Here is the name of William Prescott, commander at Bunker Hill, June 17, 1775, — written with a purpose, a plain hand, yet saying in action as well as plan, " I will do my best." John Stark signs his name as if he held an iron sceptre, — his deed as sure as his word.

And so of men whose qualities we dislike or question. Edmund Andros writes his name as if saying inwardly, " I fear nothing that comes in my way." These penmarks show impatience, imperiousness, one equal to whatever injustice may tempt his action. Benjamin Church, Jr., has a signature varying with the times, smooth and plausible to-day, bending to treason to-morrow.

I might fill pages with these tokens of character. The growing custom is good, to present in books, not only the picture of the face, but also the signature of the hand. In a volume of history or biography, as the printed page and illustration should show us the fully illuminated face of the man, so his method of writing his own name is needed to supplement our knowledge of his character, by the lights and shades it will often furnish to help our discoveries.

CHAPTER XVI.

ANDREW JACKSON.

ANDREW JACKSON deserves notice in this connection. He was the last president of the United States whose birthday preceded the opening of the Revolutionary War. He was born at Wexham Settlement, South Carolina, March 15, 1767, and died June 8, 1845, aged seventy-eight years. His ancestors were Irish, and removed to Scotland. They emigrated to this country in 1765, and were a patriotic and disinterested family.

The military spirit of Jackson displayed itself in his early boyhood. At less than fourteen years of age he joined a military corps to defend his native State; and August 6, 1780, he was in the battle of Hanging Rock, South Carolina. In 1781 he was taken prisoner by the British; and when an officer ordered him to clean his boots he refused, for which offence he received from the officer a deep wound, that remained on him through life.

At various periods he took part in our wars, against the Indians in Georgia and Alabama, also against the Creoles, and, still later, against the

Seminoles. His victory in the War of 1812, at the battle against British troops in New Orleans, January 8, 1815, brought him prominently before the country, and opened the way for his elevation to the presidency in 1829.

To find the germ of the democratic principle which led to Jackson's success we must go back to Jefferson. It may be traced through his spirit to the close of the administration of John Adams. We owe much to the high tone and honorable character of the old Federal party; but, after all, that party lacked the breadth of the one represented by Jefferson. With all his errors of conduct, his main idea was correct, and he expressed the will of the people at large better than his immediate predecessor. But in Jackson came a distinct announcement from the presidential chair that ours is fundamentally a government of the popular will. He boldly advanced the idea, since embodied by Abraham Lincoln, that ours is " a government of the people, by the people, and for the people." In other words, that in every office, and on every occasion, the will of the people is ultimately " the test of law, equity, and right." The party which elected Andrew Jackson wrote this doctrine on their banners, making the phrase " the will of the people" their rallying-cry; and by it his administration secured popularity, ascendency and a stable power. Much of this result was due both to the nature and qualities, and the experience and training, of the man at the head of the government.

Born of Scotch-Irish parents, Andrew Jackson combined in his character the warlike spirit of the one race with the impulsiveness of the other. These traits were illustrated by him when, in a military capacity, he caused two British soldiers to be hung, — hastily and rashly, it was charged; but, after a long trial for what was alleged in this act to be criminal, Jackson was finally acquitted. Known as a brave and enduring soldier, he passed through life under the title of Old Hickory. In public his manner was often brusque, and his language decided and sometimes rough; yet in private he was usually courteous, and was said to be tender in his domestic relations.

While on a visit at Washington in 1830, during his presidency, I had an interview with him in his special room at the White House. He was tall in person, erect and slender, weighing, as I judged, about one hundred and forty-five pounds; his head was long and covered with bristling hair; he had a brow well arched, projecting, and deeply furrowed by wrinkles; his eyes were dark blue, clear and commanding, the nose prominent, the chin firm, the lips compressed, and the whole face signifying decision and force, with an expression, like his language, rapid in its changes. I could easily believe that, with his excitable temperament, he would use words not always reverent, yet probably not exceeding, as a habit, his somewhat frequent phrase, " By the Eternal."

In his conversation at my visit he spoke on

several topics, — among the rest, in regard to the kindness of his friends in presenting him a variety of pens, some of which he exhibited. "I have tried this and that one, and others," he continued, "but have not yet found just what I want. I have so many grants to sign" — alluding probably to grants for the sale of public lands — "that I use a great many pens, and need one of a peculiar kind." He became, as he went on, so earnest that the fate of the nation almost seemed to depend on his procuring the right pen. Meantime his very long pipe sent forth ever-increasing volumes of smoke as he grew more eloquent.

I saw him again early in the summer of 1833, when he made a tour north and east, as far as Portsmouth, New Hampshire. He was received with great respect at all points, and nowhere with more marked attention than in Boston, although a city most decidedly opposed to him and his policy. The corporation of Harvard College at this visit held a special meeting to confer on him the degree of Doctor of Laws; and, to witness the deferential manner of all classes of the people toward him, and his own courtesy and serenity joined with official dignity, one could hardly believe him the same man about whom such intense party indignation had been within a short period expressed, and who had himself, when aroused, uttered language not specially measured or mild.

Jackson — you could not look on him without

feeling it — was a marked man. He had an indomitable will, a clear insight into human motives and character, a rare moral and physical courage, and his decisions were apt to be irreversible. To those whom he regarded as his personal or political enemies, he was open in opposition, contradiction, censure, and combativeness; but to his known friends his gentleness, kindness, and frank and affable manner were unfailing. His faults lay largely on the surface of his character. Prejudice and passion were strong in him, but time showed him at heart a true patriot and an honest man.

Whatever there may be to pardon in the personal character or public administration of Andrew Jackson, we are to remember that he had the confidence of Washington, who appointed him to the office of United States District Attorney in the year 1791; and however some of us may say he was addicted to certain faults, errors, and perversities, he deserves credit for many good acts in his public conduct; and we may never forget that on the 28th of February, 1815, the legislature of Massachusetts, a State opposed to the war in which he had achieved his victory at New Orleans the previous month, passed a vote of thanks for his heroism on that occasion.

The country owes Jackson much for the stand he took in 1832, when South Carolina seemed on the brink of secession on account of the tariff question. When told in private, that affairs appeared very threatening in South Carolina, he replied, "But, by the Eternal, things shall go right there." Although in his proclamation to those deluded people he used language, firm and decided, yet parts of it were tender and even parental. We are indebted to him also for that victory in the battle at New Orleans, in which, with only three thousand militia, he vanquished fourteen thousand picked British troops.

His courage never faltered in the path of danger or duty. And let his judgment err, as it sometimes did, he was always honest, upright, outspoken, and clear in conduct and motive. "He was ambitious," do you say? Passing at the period referred to, in review, as I did daily, an array of remarkable men in and out of Congress, Clay, Calhoun, Benton, Webster, Van Buren, and others, it was difficult to select one in the whole catalogue whom I could judge less personally ambitious or more sincerely patriotic than Andrew Jackson. It is to the credit of Daniel Webster that in those exciting days that great statesman, — amid his opposition to President Jackson in the contest on the United States Bank, although he believed the President had transcended his constitutional powers, — and so voted, as a Senator, — through all the contest never spoke of the President but with respect. He never forgot the moral courage and the patriotism of Jackson in his noble appeal to South Carolina, when by his proclamation in 1832, he stayed the impending disloyalty and menacing secession spirit of that misled people.

I remember the fearful excitement at the North when Jackson ordered the removal of the national deposits from the banks in Boston; and, looking back, I could name grave, sober men of that orderly city, and some of them of high social and moral standing, who talked, in the frenzy of the time, of " muskets being shouldered, and a march to Washington."

And yet, after the old hero had retired from the presidency, most of us were ready to say, " to err is human, to forgive divine." And, when he had passed up to his final award, the fires of party spirit went down, and of whatever was honest and pure, patriotic and self-sacrificing, in this man — and it was no small sum — we agreed in saying, " That will endure throughout our nation's history." He had a resolute wellnigh irresistible will, but it was usually put forth on the side of right, freedom, and the Constitution. It was in no selfish spirit that he uttered that great sentence, the spirit of which is the palladium of our institutions, " The Union must and shall be preserved." If he ever seemed to stretch his authority, it was commonly an excess of what began in the true direction.

CHAPTER XVII.

THE ANTISLAVERY MOVEMENT.

THE whole American people, including the Northern States, not excepting Massachusetts, where the Revolution began its great work, was involved in the custom of slaveholding. An ancestor on my own father's side was implicated in this practice, abhorrent at it now seems to us all.

Down to the opening scene of blood at Lexington, we find evidences of the unblushing traffic in human flesh. Slaves were sold and bought openly like cattle and horses. Witness the following:—

BILLERICA, May 2, 1761.

Know all men by these presents, that I, Hannah Bowers, of Billerica, widow, have sold unto Lot Colby, of Rumford, in the province of New Hampshire, a mulatto Negro boy, named *Salem*, and have received forty-five shillings sterling, in full consideration for the said boy, witness my hand,

HANNAH BOWERS.

Test: { JOSEPH WALKER,
JOSIAH BOWERS.

Put with this the following from the "Essex Journal" (Newburyport) March 2, 1774: —

To be sold,

A HEALTHY NEGRO GIRL,

ABOUT TWENTY-THREE YEARS OLD, BORN IN THIS COUNTRY.

Likewise

A SERVICEABLE MARE,

WHICH GOES WELL IN A CARRIAGE. ENQUIRE OF THE PRINTER.

But, in men then living, a new view of human rights was soon to prevail.

HENRY WARE, — born April 1, 1764, at a time when the American colonies were deeply agitated for the advance of national freedom, and in the twelfth year of his age when the battle of Lexington woke a continent to take up arms for liberty and independence, — as a boy, must have felt, what the man afterward so clearly exhibited, a strong interest in the dawn of that Revolution, which was destined to place this nation in the front rank of free countries.

Filled with the spirit of liberty, Henry Ware was, early and late, a decided advocate of equal rights and a firm emancipationist. Wise, calm, judicious in all his conduct, he carried these noble qualities into every measure he favored, and every step he took toward the abolition of American slavery. In 1834, being a professor in Harvard College, he joined a local association originated for this purpose. At that time the Cambridge Antislavery Society was formed, and a preamble and constitution were adopted, among the signatures to which Henry Ware's name stands first. Its object, purposes, and plans — which afford a fair illustration of the spirit then prevalent in a large section of the North on the antislavery movement — will be best understood by the following extracts from its records : —

Preamble.

We, the undersigned, regard the system of Domestic Slavery which now prevails over a large portion of the United States, as, not in the abstract merely, but in practice, an evil of the greatest magnitude, and a source of incalculable mischief.

We consider slaveholding, in itself, morally wrong ; though we would not impute it as a crime to those who conscientiously believe themselves not justified in immediate emancipation.

We believe that the emancipation of all who are in bondage is the requisition, not less of sound policy than of justice and humanity ; and that it is the duty of those with whom the power lies at once to remove the sanction of the law from the principle that man can be the property of man, — a principle inconsistent with the spirit of our free institutions, subversive of the purposes for which man was made, and utterly at variance with the plainest dictates of reason and Christianity.

Whereas it has been said that slavery is a subject with which citizens of the Non-slaveholding States have no concern, we feel that we are, equally with the citizens of the Slaveholding States, responsible for its existence in the District of Columbia, and in some of the Territories of the United States, and that it is our duty to exercise our constitutional right in promoting its abolition in the said District and Territories.

We think that we are also called upon by our relations to the citizens of the Slaveholding States, as fellow-men and citizens of this federal republic, to endeavor, by appealing to their reason and conscience, and by extending to them every aid in our power, to induce them to abolish slavery in their respective commonwealths; and no longer to withhold from the colored population the fair protection of the laws, and the inestimable blessings of religious and mental education.

There appearing to us to be no means by which public opinion can be so easily influenced upon this subject as by the formation of associations for that purpose, we agree to unite in one, which shall be governed by the following

CONSTITUTION.

ARTICLE I. The objects of this society shall be, by all means sanctioned by law, humanity, and religion, to promote the abolition of slavery throughout the United States, and improve the character and condition of the free people of color.

ARTICLE II. The society shall seek to obtain and to diffuse accurate information as to the real character of slavery in our country, as to the character and condition of the people of color, bond and free, and as to the best modes of emancipation, as taught by reason and experience; to promote the establishment of better schools for the free people of color than those to which they now find access, and to aid their efforts at self-instruction and improvement.

Henry Ware,	Artemas B. Muzzey,
Sidney Willard,	Barzillai Frost,
Charles Follen,	Charles T. Brooks,
H. Ware, Jr.,	Frederick H. Hedge,
Jona. Aldrich,	John Owen,
Francis J. Higginson,	John M. Smith,
John Q. Day,	John Livermore,
Thomas F. Norris,	Nathl. P. Hunt,
Stephen Lovell,	John N. Barbour,
Wm. H. Channing,	Edward Brown, Jr.,
Levi Farwell,	William Farwell.
Henry M. Chamberlain,	

In this list of twenty-three names are found not only young men, full of the earnestness and impulsiveness of their age, but men like Henry Ware, Sidney Willard, Levi Farwell, Henry Ware, Jr., Charles Follen, and others in the meridian of life, or past it. These, and several who possessed in early life the wisdom of age, while they sympathized with the object and the aims of the Massachusetts Antislavery Society, questioned some of the proposed measures, and the spirit and language of prominent members in its ranks.

Charles Follen, LL. D., born in Hesse Darmstadt, Germany, September 4, 1795 — prominent abroad and in this, his adopted country, as a champion of human freedom — took a lively interest in our movement. Being secretary of the Cambridge association, I became intimate with him, and knew well how thorough and pronounced were his antislavery principles; and that, although not in full accord with William Loyd Garrison, he honored his character, and, in common with every member of our society, was no less than that man, a decided abolitionist. "I remained long" said Dr. Follen, "in the same society with Garrison, earnestly hoping and striving to induce him, without abating his antislavery zeal, to tone down some of his expressions, and especially to moderate some of the language he applied to slaveholders." Dr. Follen thought this course would give Mr. Garrison an influence over that class of men, abate their personal hostility to himself, and thus lead them to accept, and eventually take steps toward carrying out, the great doctrine of human rights, a final emancipation of the slave. Instead of denouncing the church, like Garrison, as in league with the slaveholder, Dr. Follen would labor to reform it, and to infuse into it the spirit of Christian liberty; and instead of blazing forth against the Consitution, like some others, as a bond of slavery and death, and a "covenant with hell," and therefore to be broken down, he would uphold it, and keep all the States, north and south, in the Union; and by an earnest moral influence, encourage them all to work together for the full and final emancipation of the slaves.

In these views the Cambridge Antislavery Society agreed. It seemed to them that for the existence of slavery in some parts of our country, especially at the seat of government, we of the North were indirectly, if not directly, responsible. Accordingly the following vote was passed by the society: —

At a meeting of the Cambridge Antislavery Society on the evening of July 4, 1834, it was voted that

    Rev. Charles Follen,
    Rev. T. F. Norris,
    Rev. J. Aldrich,
    Mr. H. M. Chamberlain,
    Mr. F. J. Higginson,

be a committee to draft a petition to the Congress of the United States, praying them to take immediate measures for the abolition of slavery in the District of Columbia; and that the same persons be a committee to procure signatures thereto in the town of Cambridge and the vicinity.

We had all hoped by this, and other similar quiet means and methods, to help accomplish the great end which every true friend of his country must desire. But Providence had decreed otherwise; and though our humble endeavors must have contributed their share toward moulding the needed public opinion on this subject, and though the noble work of Garrison — whom we honored for his moral courage — did then, as we all know, lay the foundation stones of this mighty achievement, yet, where the olive branch proved ineffectual, the sword was at last the direct instrument of success.

At the North, prejudice against the colored race was a barrier in many hearts to an interest in emancipation. I rejoiced in being free from it. Among the pleasant memories of my early boyhood I recall that of a colored family which lived not far from my father's house. The head of the household, a thoroughbred negro, was good-natured and as faithful as the sunshine ; and how gentle and motherly the wife was. Shall I ever forget the kind tone with which she always spoke to me ? And the two daughters — I loved them as if they had been my own relations. One of them, long years after, walked several miles to see me, and told me, with a beaming face, that she had lately joined the church. Her pleasant smile and kind manner carried me back almost to infancy. That dear old circle, in their small unpainted cottage, still shines on memory's page. And I believe a lifelong interest in their race dates back to that spot. It made me yearn to see them receive their God-intended liberty and equal rights ; and it made my heart leap for joy when I read at last the noble proclamation for their emancipation, penned by the immortal Lincoln and confirmed by our National Congress.

THE STOCKS.

CHAPTER XVIII.

BOUTELLE FAMILY.

TIMOTHY BOUTELLE, born January 1, 1739, was distinguished for his patriotism and his military service in the Revolution. Immediately upon the receipt at Leominster of news of the battle of Lexington, a company was enlisted in that town into the Continental service for eight months, in the "23d Regiment of Foot," under the command of Colonel Asa Whitcomb, to be stationed on Prospect Hill in Cambridge. This company was under the command of Captain David Wilder, and numbered sixty-seven men, of whom fifty-nine enlisted on the 19th of April, 1775. My grandfather Boutelle was that day commissioned as lieutenant of the company, which was in Colonel Whitcomb's regiment while it was at Roxbury, and marched from there to Dorchester Heights on the evening of March 4, 1776. It was afterward in the Northern army, and took part in the battle of Saratoga and was present at the surrender of Burgoyne.

In 1786 Daniel Shays, who had been a captain in the Continental army, headed an insurrection against the government of Massachusetts, which was created under the pressure of heavy taxation and pecuniary embarrassments caused by the late war, and by a prejudice against the courts. It resulted in an organized resistance to the laws of the State. Governor Bowdoin ordered out a detachment of the militia to suppress the rebellion, under the command of Major-General Lincoln. Leominster furnished its quota of men; and two of the officers were taken from that town. One was Major Timothy Boutelle, who subsequently was promoted to the rank of colonel. The insurgents had encamped at Petersham. On an intensely cold night, February 4, 1786, in which many of the soldiers were frozen on the march, Colonel Boutelle, to the great anxiety and distress of his wife, my grandmother, left alone at her home, led the advanced guard, and arrived in Petersham so early as to surprise the insurgents in their beds. They all surrendered, and this terminated the rebellion, without a shot or any resistance. "Colonel Boutelle," says the historian of Leominster, "acquired great credit for the tact and skill which he exhibited on that trying occasion, and for many years afterwards continued to be the commander of the regiment."

Ensign John Buss, a brother-in-law of Colonel Boutelle, also took part in the same service. He was soon promoted, and for some time was captain of a company in Leominster.

Colonel Boutelle was highly respected in town, and was chosen representative to the General

Court in 1786 and 1793. He owned and occupied a fine farm in Leominster, Massachusetts, a mile northwest of Leominster Centre, which, after being familiar with it in childhood as the home of my maternal grandparents, I visited in 1867, and found the old house, the outbuildings, workshop, barn, &c., almost identical with those of former days. On Boutelle Hill, one of the most elevated and commanding sites of that richly landed and beautiful town, my grandfather spent most of his life. Timothy Boutelle married Rachel, daughter of Luke Lincoln of Leicester. He died May 1810, aged seventy years. His wife died January 1, 1828, aged eighty-six years.

My grandfather was a strict Sabbatarian, very constant at meeting. The old family chaise was used every Sunday and for every service, morning and afternoon. The young men, and sometimes the young women of the family, would add to the number one or more persons on horseback, while the children would walk the long mile to reach the meeting-house. To descend the hill to the church was easy; but to climb its steeps homeward, especially in the heat of a midsummer day, was a test of the little boy's love and obedience to his grandparents. When Sunday came, however, no questions were asked, but one and all must either put on their garments and go to meeting, or, if sickness was suggested, it was proposed to send for the doctor. The thought of his big potions and bitter pills made me quite willing to endure the pains of hard walking.

Think of the contrast between those times and the present in this regard. Go back to the old meeting-house where I saw, in my early days, the stocks in the vestibule and the tything-man with his rod in the gallery. Go back to the ages of the forefathers. We children were wearied by the sermon of an hour's length; but good pastor Shepard of Cambridge habitually turned his hour-glass up twice before he ended his discourse; and on the planting of a church at Woburn, Massachusetts, and dedication of the meeting-house, "Rev. Mr. Syms," as we read, "continued preaching and prayer about the space of five hours."

The contrast in Boston and its vicinity, between the present mode of spending Sunday and that of the year 1677 is most striking. Look at the ideas and practices of those early days in this respect; in that year we read: —

The Court order and enact that the Sabbath laws be twice read annually, in March and September, by the minister, and the selectmen are ordered to see to it that there be one man appointed *to inspect every ten families of his neighbors;* which tything-men are empowered to do in the absence of the constable, to apprehend all Sabbath breakers, &c., and carry them before the Magistrate or other authority, or commit them to prison, as any Constable may do, to be proceeded with according to law.

This system of the espionage of neighbors,

seems to us so intolerable that we should think it an outrage on our natural rights.

Read another of these statutes: —

> For the better putting in restraint and securing the offenders who transgress against the Sabbath laws in the meeting-house, or by misbehavior, by making any noise or otherwise during the daytime, they shall be laid hold of by any of the inhabitants near the said person and carried and put into the cage, by those authorized to execute this law, to be forthwith erected in Boston, which is appointed by the Selectmen to be set up in the market-place, and in such other towns as the County Court shall appoint, there to remain till the authorities shall examine the person of the offender, and order his punishment, as the matter may require, according to the laws relating to the Sabbath.

This cage was a contrivance to secure each foot and each hand, and the head also, by thrusting them into an upright machine with holes in it for this purpose. And this machine was set in the market-place, not as we confine criminals, in a secluded room.

What would those good people say if they could know our present notions about the observance of Sunday: a large proportion of the community never even entering the door of a church, but riding, walking, going where they please for any enjoyment on the Lord's Day; many in the same old Boston, frequenting places for questionable indulgences — concerts, hardly bearing a trace of anything "sacred," and lectures on many subjects wide from texts of Scripture; and even some of the best people of the day visiting museums of Art and libraries of all kinds, under the sanction of the civil authorities. Would they as readily excuse all our ideas and practices on the Sabbath, as most of us excuse, and rightly, I think, the errors in thought and practice, of the Puritans?

The children of Timothy and Rachel Boutelle were Lydia, born April 1, 1769, who married Amos Muzzey, Jr., of Lexington, October 10, 1795. He died May 20, 1829, aged sixty-three years; and she died December 24, 1838, aged sixty-nine years and nine months.

Timothy, born in 1779, died November 12, 1855, aged seventy-seven years. He graduated with honors at Harvard College in 1800, and received the degree of A. M. in 1804; he was in the same class with Rev. Joseph Stevens Buckminster, Washington Allston, and Chief Justice Shaw of Massachusetts, who was Mr. Boutelle's college room-mate and lifelong friend. After leaving college Mr. Boutelle was for one year assistant in Leicester Academy. He then studied law with Abijah Bigelow in Leominster, and finished his studies with Edwin Gray in Boston. He began the practice of law in Waterville, Maine, in 1804, where he was highly successful. His legal knowledge was extensive and accurate, and his judgment sound. In January, 1811, he married Helen, daughter of Judge Rogers of Exeter, New Hampshire, who was born April 19, 1788, and died in

1880, aged ninety-two years. He took an active interest in political affairs, was six years in the House of Representatives of Maine, and for the same time in the Senate. In 1816 he was chosen a presidential elector; in 1839 he received the degree of L L. D. from Waterville College, now Colby University, in Maine, of which he was a trustee and the treasurer for many years. For twenty years he was president of a bank in Waterville, and the first president of the Androscoggin and Kennebec Railroad. He kept up his interest in classical studies, and was a wide reader. He was devoted to the interests, educational, moral, and religious, of his town and community; and served in various relations, public and private, with ability. His memory is held in respectful and affectionate regard by his numerous friends and acquaintances. His disposition was social, and he was a warm friend. With strong sense and a native wit he was an instructive and agreeable companion.

Enoch, son of Colonel Timothy Boutelle, had the military spirit of his father, and was an officer in the militia. I remember seeing his *spontoon* at my grandfather's old house. This weapon sometimes called a *half-pike*, was used in France during the Revolution of 1789, and was introduced later into this country.

Enoch Boutelle occupied the old homestead in Leominster until 1817, when he died, from a sudden disease, known as the "melting of the caul," occasioned by overheating himself while pursuing a stray animal.

Caleb Boutelle graduated at Harvard College in 1806, and studied medicine; he was a member of Massachusetts Medical Society. He established himself first at Belfast, Maine, in 1810, with his classmate, Joseph Green Coggswell, who at the same time began there the practice of law. Dr. Boutelle remained in Belfast some two years, and then removed to Lexington, Massachusetts. In 1812 he was a surgeon in the navy during the war with Great Britain, and was taken prisoner and carried to Gibraltar. He subsequently removed to Plymouth, Massachusetts, and died there in 1819. Trusted as a faithful and skilled physician, he was greatly respected, by all who knew him, as a man of high integrity, and beloved and lamented by his kindred and friends. He married Anne, daughter of General Goodwin of Plymouth, where she died at an advanced age. They had children, among whom was Charles Otis, of the U. S. Coast Survey. His son, James Thacher, graduated at Harvard College in 1867, and received the degree of M. D. 1871, and was a member of Massachusetts Medical Society.

CHAPTER XIX.

LAFAYETTE.

THESE biographical reminiscences have thus far been confined almost exclusively to native-born men and their families. But there was one man of foreign birth, who took a part in our great Revolutionary struggle, so nobly disinterested, that he ought to hold in our memories and affections the place of an adopted son of America.

LAFAYETTE, born September 6, 1757, belonged to an ancient and noble stock. The original family name was Motier. Some of his male ancestors were remarkable for military ability, and some of the women for literary talents. His property and influence were increased by his marriage, at the age of eighteen, to a lady of the illustrious line of Noailles. His full name, incorporating several of his ancestors, was Marie-Paul-Joseph-Roch-Yves-Gilbert-Motier de la Fayette. The rank and affluence of his family gave him the fullest education, not only in classical and general literature, but in military tactics.

LAFAYETTE.

His mind, both by nature and cultivation, was imbued with a strong love of liberty. He learned early the situation of our country, and its purpose of revolution and independence. Writing subsequently to the president of the Continental Congress he says: "The moment I heard of America, I loved her; the moment I knew she was fighting for liberty, I burnt with a desire to bleed for her."

In the month of January, 1777, he reached our shores in a vessel purchased at his own expense, entered the American army, bought clothing and arms for the troops under General Moultrie of South Carolina, and advanced to Washington 60,000 francs for the public service. In July of the same year, although less than twenty years of age, he was commissioned by Congress a major-general. At Brandywine, Valley Forge, Monmouth, and onward to his valiant and successful attack of the British redoubts at Yorktown, his deeds and his sacrifices were as noble as his generous promise in the outset.

Washington wrote of him to the president of Congress, October 13, 1778, as "an officer who unites to all the military fire of youth an uncommon maturity of judgment." He was honored and loved by his companions in arms, and lauded and sustained by Congress, that body on the 21st of October, 1778, passing a resolve, to cause "an elegant sword, with proper devices, to be presented in the name of the United States, to the

Marquis La Fayette." He soon became the pride of the nation, and was taken to the bosoms of a grateful people. Grave and judicious men gave him their testimonials. Franklin writes to him from France: "I find it easy to express everything but the sense we have of your worth and our obligations to you." Samuel Adams says to him, June, 1780: "My particular friendship for you would be a prevailing inducement with me," &c. And Chief Justice Marshall speaks of "the joy and affection with which Washington received him," and "the distinction and regard of Congress" for him, "to which his constant and indefatigable zeal in support of the American cause," and "his signal services, gave him such just pretensions."

After the war had closed there was one heart in which the old love never waxed cold. In 1784 Lafayette revisited Washington, and when they parted at Annapolis it was never to meet again. But Washington, writing afterward to Lafayette, said: "Every hour since, I have felt all that love, respect, and attachment for you, with which length of years, close connection, and your merits have inspired me." And the letters of Lafayette to him show what affection he could awaken in a bosom friend.

It was my good fortune to see Lafayette under circumstances of special interest, very soon after, having accepted the invitation of Congress to revisit this country, he had landed at New York City, August 15, 1824.

When, a few days later, he entered the city of Boston, the enthusiasm of the people was unbounded. As he passed out of Washington Street into State Street, a multitude of every age and description poured forth their demonstrations. Not the young or middle-aged alone, but hoary heads were carried away by the excitement of that occasion. In their midst, to my surprise, I saw the great Dr. Bowditch moving along in the crowd, waving his hat in the air; and, as he approached the barouche in which Lafayette was riding, he joined in the shouts of the throng like a youth. Who else could have so stirred this grave man, the mathematician renowned the world over; and whom, not many months after this event, I saw, on commencement day, seated among the Corporation of Harvard College, — so staid, so dignified, one might have asked, " Does that man ever smile ?"

But, after all, the order of that day was perfect. If we had been in France, the chance is that such an event would have been accompanied by very different scenes. I am not surprised that Lafayette asked at that time, as he looked on the thousands upon thousands that followed in his train, — so orderly in their deportment, and so well dressed, — " Where are the common people ?"

On the 26th of August, 1824, the Harvard Phi Beta Kappa Society held its annual meeting for public services in the old meeting-house of the First Parish in Cambridge, which stood on the spot now (1882) occupied by the Law School. The fame of the orator, Edward Everett, and the expectation of seeing the illustrious Lafayette on that occasion, drew together an eager and crowded assembly. This, we all felt, was a proud day for Harvard. Lafayette had already been welcomed by thousands, but new lustre was shed upon his name when he came to the Commencement of our ancient college. Our hearts beat with rapture as we saw him enter our precincts. A magnificent arch had been erected and handsomely decorated in Cambridgeport. On either side of the street were our school-children, the girls in white frocks and the boys in blue jackets. Through the thronged line Lafayette rode to Cambridge. Cheer upon cheer burst from the multitude as he moved forward. When the distinguished stranger entered the church, the delighted audience rose in a mass and greeted him with unstinted demonstrations. But when the orator, toward the close of his address, turned toward Lafayette and commenced his allusions to him, all eyes were fixed on that noble figure, and the enthusiasm of the multitude broke forth in still louder applause. The personal address to him kindled a yet more fervent expression of the joy of all hearts. After speaking in a touching strain of his old companions in arms — Lincoln, Greene, Knox, and Hamilton — Mr. Everett added, "But they are gone;" and, rising to the climax of the scene, he proceeded : —

Above all, the first of heroes and of men, the friend of your youth, the more than friend of his country, rests in the bosom of the soil he redeemed. On the banks of the Potomac he lies in glory and peace. You will revisit the hospitable shades of Mount Vernon, but him whom you venerated, as we did, you will not meet at its door. His voice of consolation, which reached you in the Austrian dungeons, cannot now break its silence to bid you welcome to his own roof; but the grateful children of America will bid you welcome in his name. Welcome, thrice welcome to our shores; and withersoever, throughout the limits of the continent, your course shall take you, the ear that hears you shall bless you, the eye that sees you shall bear witness to you, and every tongue exclaim, with heartfelt joy, " Welcome, welcome, Lafayette."

For a moment the enraptured listeners paused to recover their breath, and then, with tears on their faces, burst into prolonged and reiterated applause. Lafayette shared in these thrilling emotions, sensibly affected by the allusion to his own services and sufferings, and especially at the name of Washington. At the dinner of the Society we enjoyed, under the presiding genius of Judge Story, a feast of wit and hilarity, heightened by a long line of distinguished speakers,— Everett, Josiah Quincy, Governor Eustis, ex-Governor Brooks, and others — not the least of whom was our world-renowned guest, whose native accent was almost overcome by his cordial appreciation of the scene, making us all, as one, feel that such a fellowship as this band of brothers now awakened we might never again enjoy. And when he read the sentiment he there gave, he called up a picture of scenes in the old world, part of which he himself had been: "The *Holy Alliance* of virtue, literature, and patriotism,— it will prove too powerful for any *coalition* against the rights of man."

A few days after his arrival, on September 2, Lafayette accepted an invitation of the town of Lexington to visit that place. This gave me an opportunity for a personal introduction to him in my native place, and on the very spot hallowed as the birthplace of American liberty. At the line of the town he was met by a body of horse and a procession of citizens, who escorted him to the Common. An arch of evergreen and beautiful flowers had been erected, with the motto: "Welcome, Friend of America, to the birthplace of American liberty." Among the large concourse assembled to honor the guest of the nation were the children of the schools, and fourteen of the brave men who took part in the battle of the 19th of April, 1775. The procession, under salutes from an artillery corps, moved to the Monument, where an eloquent address of welcome was given by Major Elias Phinney of Lexington. To this cordial tribute Lafayette, with great emotion, replied, thanking the people of Lexington for their kind attention, and expressing his happiness in standing upon ground "consecrated by the blood of the first martyrs to American freedom, a cause whose influence had been felt the world over."

He spoke of his joy in looking upon the survivors of that heroic band of "venerated men" who here inaugurated that resistance to tyrants which is obedience to God.

When these exercises were completed Lafayette was introduced to the revered fourteen of that gallant company who, nearly a half-century before, had stood on that spot and defended the rights of our people in presence of a defiant enemy. After warm greetings from the large company around him they sat down to a collation, and it was an occasion never to be forgotten by those present. I was impressed by the personal appearance of our guest. He was tall and well proportioned. His head was large; his face oval and regular, and marked by an unmistakable benevolence. His forehead was lofty and open; his eyes were of a grayish blue, large and prominent, and surmounted by light and well-arched eyebrows. His nose was aquiline, and, like his ears, large, both indicating longevity. His mouth wore an evidently natural smile. His complexion was light, and his cheeks were slightly colored. When he spoke his voice was the organ of his soul, indicating a sincerity and frankness that fascinated those who talked with him. The French accent of his conversation added to the impression and interest produced by the whole man. I noticed he seemed a little lame; and the marks left by his long and dreary imprisonment of two years in the dungeon of Olmutz and three years at Magdeburg,— in which imprisonments he was emaciated by fevers and lost all his hair, — and the effect of wounds, received both in our Revolution and that of France, were so evident in his form and figure as to draw tears, as one reflected on the sacrifices and sufferings he had passed through in his noble devotion to human freedom.

The last opportunity I had to see Lafayette was when he was present, June 17, 1825, at the laying of the corner-stone of Bunker Hill Monument. The procession, including a vast array of civil and military bodies with banners of every variety marched through the streets of Boston amid the rapturous applause of spectators looking eagerly for the barouche in which rode the cynosure of all eyes. He was followed by forty survivors of the battle of Bunker Hill; the school-children, clad in their neatest apparel, were arranged in the streets; the ladies waved their handkerchiefs, and the men clapped their hands and uncovered their heads, as the hero of the day passed by. How our hearts rushed back to that day of terror and bloodshed, as we looked on those old men, their silver locks, their bending forms, and their venerated faces. Among them was the brave old chaplain, the Rev. Joseph Thaxter of Edgartown who was chaplain of Colonel Prescott's Regiment June 17, 1775, and survived, after fifty years had elapsed, to raise his voice in prayer to the God of armies, who, out of the perils, struggles, and death-groans of that fearful strife, brought a united nation to liberty and independence.

When the procession halted on Bunker Hill, it was a long time before, not the "uncounted" but seemingly countless "multitude" could be brought to order. I found myself forced on by the crowd until I was at last in the seats assigned to the United States Senate. Mr. Webster at length rose and attempted to produce order. "Every one," said he, "rises to bid his neighbor sit down. Let all who have seats now, keep them." In this way quiet was at last secured. The ceremony first performed was the laying of the corner-stone, under the direction of King Solomon's Lodge. The plate, containing a very long inscription, was deposited in its proper place. The Masonic services were conducted by John Abbot, Lafayette assisting; and it added to one's interest in this service to recollect that there stood a man who had shared with Washington, nearly a half-century before, the labors and pleasures of this ancient order. Then came the literary exercises. A grand hymn, written by the Rev. John Pierpont, was sung to the tune of Old Hundred. Then followed the address by Mr. Webster, president of the Bunker Hill Monument Association. He was then in his prime, about forty years of age. His majestic figure, commanding face, and powerful voice arrested every eye and ear; and we felt, here is a man, an orator, a patriot, who, by a single hour of seeing and hearing him, takes us back to the best days of Grecian eloquence. An inspiring hymn by the Rev. Dr. Flint of Salem, a solemn and fervent prayer by the Rev. James Walker of Charlestown, a touching ode, and the benediction by the revered Joseph Thaxter, completed the services.

Although forty survivors of the battle were then present,— eighteen years afterward, June 17, 1843, when Mr. Webster gave the oration on the completion of the Monument, only fourteen of that honored band remained. And meantime the venerated Lafayette had passed away, May 19, 1834, at the advanced age of seventy-seven years.

Lafayette's name and presence, during his journeys in our land, awakened an extraordinary enthusiasm.

We may adduce one example as an illustration of the reception given him throughout the whole country. August 31, 1824, he visited Newburyport. At Ipswich, 9 o'clock P. M., he was met, under the escort of a battalion of cavalry from that place, by the Newburyport Artillery and the Washington Light Infantry. The houses along the road, as well as in the streets of Newburyport, were illuminated; and his approach was announced by the ringing of bells, the firing of cannon, and the display of rockets, as he was conducted under an arch — thrown across the head of State Street, with the motto, "The Hero of Two Continents" — to the residence of James Prince, on State Street. Mr. Prince's elegant mansion was put in readiness to receive him. He occupied at night the apartment in which Washington had slept on his visit to this town in 1789, and the furniture had never been changed. On his arrival he was addressed by Hon. Ebenezer Moseley as follows: —

GENERAL LAFAYETTE, — The citizens of Newburyport are happy in this opportunity of greeting, with the warmest welcome, a distinguished benefactor of their country.

The important services you rendered this people in the day of their distress, the devotedness which you manifested in their perilous cause, and the dangers which you sought for their relief are incorporated in our history and firmly engraven on our hearts.

We would lead you to our institutions of learning, charity, and religion, we would point you to our hills and valleys covered with flocks and smiling in abundance, that you may behold the happy effect of those principles of liberty which you were so instrumental in establishing. Our children cluster about you to receive a patriot's blessing. Our citizens press forward to show their gratitude. Our nation pays you a tribute which must remove the reproach that republics are ungrateful.

As the zealous advocate of civil liberty, we give you welcome ; as the brave defender of an oppressed people we make you welcome ; as the friend and companion of our immortal Washington, we bid you welcome.

To this address the General made a brief and appropriate reply, in which he modestly said the great attention paid him was far beyond his expectations or deserts,— that his feelings of attachment toward this country could not be expressed, but only felt by a heart glowing with the most ardent affection.

At an early hour the next morning a levee was held, at which the veteran hero was introduced to many of the citizens of Newburyport. The children were not forgotten on the occasion; and a near friend of mine says she well remembers, when the tall man was about leaving, she, a girl only a few years old, received from him a kiss, with the adieu, "Good-by, dear little girl." Her father told her she must never forget the notice that great and good man took of her; and she has kept his injunction to this day.

The bond between Lafayette and his old comrades in arms was very strong. He was an original member of the Society of the Cincinnati, and soon after he reached America, August, 1824, an address was made to him by General John Brooks in the name of that society. To this Lafayette replied in the following touching words: —

Amidst the inexpressible enjoyments which press upon my heart, I could not but feel particularly eager and happy to meet my beloved brothers-in-arms. Many, many I call in vain; and, at their head, our matchless paternal chief, whose love to an adopted son, I am proud to say, you have long witnessed.

But, while we mourn together for those we have lost, while I find a consolation in the sight of their relations and friends, it is to me a delightful gratification to recognize my surviving companions of our Revolutionary army. — that army so brave, so virtuous, so united by mutual confidence and affection. That we have been the faithful soldiers of independence, freedom, and equality, those three essential requisites of national and personal dignity and happiness, — that we have lived to see these sacred principles secured to this vast Republic, and cherished elsewhere by all generous minds, — shall be the pride of our life, the boast of our children, the comfort of our last moments. Receive, my dear brother soldiers, the grateful thanks and constant love of your old companion and friend.

And elsewhere many an old soldier of the Revolution took him by the hand with tears of joy at the privilege. One of these met him at Albany, and, as he looked in his face, said: —

General, I owe my life to you! I was wounded at the battle of Monmouth. You visited me in the hospital. You gave me two guineas, and one to a person to nurse me. To this I owe my recovery, and may the blessing of Heaven rest upon you.

But nothing could have tried Lafayette like that affecting scene when, one Sunday morning, he visited the tomb of his dearest American friend at Mount Vernon. He is accompanied by the stepson of Washington. There rest the mortal remains of one whom he loved as he did no other beyond his own family, and whose memory fills him with a fresh veneration. He stands by the grave of his leader and exemplar in youth, his model through life, and one whom he hopes to meet again at his own not distant departure. On this spot Mr. Custis, adding another precious bond to his sacred recollections, presents him with a ring containing hair once on the head of the immortal Washington.

But let us now go back to the first appearance of Lafayette on our shores in the Revolution. His reception in the army was most enthusiastic. "The confidence and attachment of the troops," says an eye-witness, who wrote only a year afterward, "are for him invaluable possessions, but what is still more flattering for a young man, [he was then, we must recollect, only twenty years old] is the influence and consideration he has acquired among the political, as well as the military order; private letters from him have frequently produced more effect on some States than the strongest exhortations of the Congress. On seeing him, one is at a loss which most to admire — that so young a man as he should have given such eminent proof of talents, or that a man so tried should give hopes of so long a career of glory."

One could hardly exaggerate the esteem and affection this French nobleman inspired in our countrymen; it was surpassed only by their love of their illustrious chief. He had the secret of winning all hearts. Gentle, courteous, frank, dignified without pride, full of zeal and activity in our cause, entirely independent of the court of France, he secured at once and uniformly the admiration and confidence of our greatest and best man, the head of the army.

His example was powerful on the young men of

the whole country. When Lafayette lay wounded at Bethlehem he was visited, among others, by Charles Pinckney, a member of the First Provincial Congress from South Carolina at the age of twenty-six, from whose pen came at that period productions which would have done honor to the head, no less than the heart of the most experienced statesman and purest politician of the day.

What was true of Washington at that crisis might, in some respects, have been said of Lafayette. The remark of Rochefoucauld, that "no man is a hero to his valet," would not apply to either of these men. Those nearest to Washington loved and respected him most. His clear head and disinterested heart, the energy of his mind and his wise action, were all but a type of the same high qualities in Lafayette. Both were equal to great emergencies. The ardor of the Frenchman never blinded his understanding, never diminished his calm and clear good sense.

There was a certain resemblance in the exterior of the two men. The fine figure of our great commander had its counterpart in the early days of our noble French ally. The physiognomy of Washington, mild and agreeable, made his face attractive. Neither grave nor familiar, he inspired respect and secured confidence; if his smile was rare, it was never cynical or sarcastic, but the smile of benevolence. All this might be said, from his earliest to his latest day, of the heroic, the gentle, and the generous Lafayette.

It is evident that Washington gained and secured his vast influence largely through his caution; this amounted in many cases to the strictest secrecy. Very few of the men nearest in person to him enjoyed his perfect confidence. His plans and operations were kept largely to himself. But Lafayette from the first secured the confidence of his chief. That, in his extreme youthfulness as a major-general, he did this, shows the rare penetration of Washington into character. He seldom erred in his judgment of men; and in this case he seems to have found a man, who, to the ardor of the Frenchman, joined a sagacity and wisdom worthy of other and the gravest nations. He gave Lafayette, for instance, at the most critical moment, before the engagement at Monmouth, the honor and responsibility of confronting the attack of the enemy until his own army was perfectly formed; and the result justified his reliance upon him.

This confidence was justified by the power Lafayette afterward showed, when he calmed that fearful mob in the Faubourg St. Antoine, at the commencement of the French Revolution. His message to Washington, sent through Colonel Trumbull at that period, startles us by its masterly prediction of scenes that actually followed in the sequel of that bloody drama. The tender regard and gratitude of Washington for Lafayette were shown in one of his subsequent letters to him, congratulating his country on the King's accept-

ance of the constitution offered to him by the
National Assembly. After referring in terms of
sympathy and hope to the condition of France at
that moment, he closes in this grand spirit toward
Lafayette personally: —

No one will rejoice in your felicity, and for the noble and disinterested part you have acted, more than your sincere friend and truly affectionate servant,

GEO. WASHINGTON.

This reliance and trust were seen throughout
their military relations, not in the field alone, but
in the camp, where Washington and his friend,
in their social hours, would sit together, enjoying
their wine, then the universal beverage, in moderation; the nuts, hard hickory, would fill up the
evening, a dish of apples being the supplement.
This simple repast, taken with unbent brow and
liberated speech, illustrated and cemented the peculiar and lifelong friendship of those two men.

No sketch of Lafayette is complete which does
not present him in his near and special relations
to Washington. All personal reminiscences of
the two men by cotemporary writers should be
supplemented by records of these close interviews.
It is said that Washington took at once to Lafayette when introduced to him, a youth of nineteen
who had left his home, his newly connected wife,
his country, his all, in the dark hour of our early
struggles with one of the mightiest powers on
the globe for freedom and national independ-

ence. The act itself must have prepossessed our noble commander-in-chief; and Lafayette's personal appearance added to this attraction. His cultivated bearing, ingenuous manner, the self-devotion and sacrifice written on every feature of the portraits we have of him at that period of his life, no less than his subsequent deportment, confirmed the love and respect of Washington; and their friendship was strengthened by the gallant conduct and the faithful services of Lafayette to the last.

We are fortunate in having descriptions of their intercourse written both by American and foreign witnesses. One especially by the Marquis de Chastellux, a French traveller, brings before us vividly an interview at which Lafayette was present with that visitor at the quarters of Washington. We here see the latter in his military family and at his usual dinner table. His guest is presented to Generals Knox, Wayne. etc., and to his family, then composed of Colonels Hamilton and Tighlman, his secretaries, and his aides-de-camp, and of Major Gibbs, commander of his guards. "I soon felt myself," writes the Marquis de Chastellux, "at ease near the greatest and the best of men. The goodness and benevolence which characterize him are evident from everything about him; but the confidence he gives birth to never occasions improper familiarity." The next day Washington puts his army in motion, including the light infantry, " which were detached with the Marquis de Lafaytte." After a review of the troops, the General proposes a visit to the camp of Lafayette, which is accepted, and the guest enjoys the hospitality of the latter. The party soon rejoin the quarters of General Washington, where are "about twenty guests, among them General Saint Clair. The repast was in the English fashion, consisting of eight or ten large dishes of butcher's meat and poultry, with vegetables of several sorts, followed by a second course of pastry, comprised under the two denominations of pies and puddings." The cloth is removed, and apples and a great quantity of nuts are served, which General Washington usually continues eating for about two hours. "These nuts are small and dry, and have so hard a shell [hickory nuts] that they can only be broken by the hammer; they are served half-open, and the company are never done picking and eating them. The conversation was calm and agreeable. His Excellency was pleased to enter with me into the particulars of some of the principal operations of the war, but always with a modesty and conciseness which proved that it was from pure complaisance he mentioned it." The drinking of wine, the prolonged toasting, I omit, adding — what is a more pleasant circumstance to us, with our present social customs and habits — the testimony of a foreigner: "But to do justice to the Americans, they themselves feel the ridicule of these customs, borrowed from Old England, and since laid aside by her."

It was not unusual for the British to speak with contempt of Lafayette when he joined our army, on account of his youth. When Lord Cornwallis took command of the British forces in Virginia he felt himself so superior to the Americans that he triumphed in his prospect of success. Despising the youth of his opponent, Lafayette, he unguardedly wrote to Great Britain, *The boy cannot escape me.* This boy, in the sequel, sent General Wayne, with about three hundred Pennsylvania riflemen, to watch the British army in Virginia; and soon we read that, "with a handful of Pennsylvanians, he frightened into a retreat the whole of Cornwallis's army of undaunted Britons."

One who saw Lafayette at the age of twenty-one says: "He is nearly six feet high, large but not corpulent. He is not very elegant in form, his shoulders being broad and high, nor is there a perfect symmetry in his features; his forehead is remarkably high, his nose large and long, eyebrows prominent and projecting over a fine, animated, hazel eye. His countenance is interesting and impressive. He converses in broken English, and displays the manners and address of an accomplished gentleman."

An eye-witness, who saw Lafayette after he was brought on a litter from the Brandywine battle, contrasts his appearance at that time and at the period of his visit to this country by invitation from Congress. "He was then tall and slender, and of a rather light complexion. After a lapse of forty-seven years I again met him, a few days after his landing at New York, in August, 1824. It was with difficulty I could realize him to be the same man I had seen almost a half-century before at Bethlehem. I could scarcely discover the slightest resemblance. Age, wounds, and care had completely metamorphosed him in person and features."

There are, or have been, those who, infected by the old English prejudices, which, I regret to say, have not yet wholly died out, call Lafayette " a weak man." Even Washington had enemies in his lifetime, who on certain occasions charged him with indecision and a want of energy. Men of great wisdom, calmness, and deliberation are often subject to this reproach. But time rebuts such groundless accusations. Looking in the worn face of Lafayette, and recalling his noble past, one could not but repeat the fitting tribute,

"E'en in their ashes live their wonted fires."

What a history gathered about that failing form. Looking recently at his portrait, painted, I think, by order of Washington, which represents him as he appeared when he volunteered, at the age of nineteen, to serve without pay in the cause of the American Revolution, I could not conceive of him as a " weak " man. It is a face which, although gentle and instinct with kindness, is full of fire, energy, and resolution.

If you doubt his force and decision of character, see him in the great struggle at Yorktown. This is the account we have "from the narrative of an old soldier of the American army, who was met by M. Levaseur in the neighborhood of Yorktown in 1824," and was himself an eye-witness of and took part in the engagement which he describes.

October 1781, after five days' contest, in which Washington put the match to the first gun himself, the British were left masters of no external works except two large redoubts; these Washington determined to take. Lafayette, at the head of the American light infantry, was ordered to attack the redoubt on the left of the besieged troops. He thought nothing but a bold and rapid onset would enable young soldiers, like his, to carry entrenchments defended by disciplined troops. He formed his men in solid column, ordered the whole of his division at the word of command to fire; he then headed them himself, and, supported by the proffered aid of the noble and intrepid Alexander Hamilton, charged, sword in hand, through the mounds in the face of the enemy's fire, forced his way into the redoubt and in a few minutes carried it, with the loss of only a handful of men.

Cornwallis, on the 17th, demanded a parley, and on the 19th surrendered his army; in the presence of Generals Rochambeau and Lafayette, his sword was delivered, through the gallant O'Hara, to Washington. It is a singular coincidence that, in 1824, forty-three years after this battle, Lafayette was in Yorktown, and stopped at the very house then occupied by Cornwallis, and the rooms were lighted by a remnant of the same wax candles once used by Cornwallis.

Nothing is more touching, as a proof of the heroism of Lafayette, and the attachment and bravery of his soldiers at that siege, than his meeting on that spot, in 1824, one of the veteran survivors of that battle, who, seizing the General by the hand, exclaimed: "I was with you at Yorktown; I entered yonder redoubt at your side. I too, was at the side of the gallant De Kalb, your associate in arms, when he fell in the field." The tears poured from his eyes as Lafayette, showing his emotion, said, "Yes, my brave soldier, I am happy to have lived to meet you once more."

Indeed the single fact that Washington took Lafayette, almost from the first, to his bosom confidence, speaks volumes for the force, as well as sweetness of his character.

His heroism never shone forth on the battle-field more brightly than it did at one moment in the Reign of Terror in his own country. He has braved the excited mob in his place with the National Guard. The hour has come when the King is to be murdered. Lafayette stands by him, never more calm than at this fearful moment; but even the mad populace are awe-struck when they see him step forward, take the Queen's hand, and kiss it. Truly this is the "hero of two worlds!"

The whole connection of Lafayette with our country seems, as we review it, like a romance. He no sooner learns the character of the war in

America than he resolves to offer his services in our cause; he asks Franklin, one of our commissioners in Paris, to secure him a passage in the first public ship sent to our shores. He replies, " we have not the means or the credit to procure a vessel in all the ports of France." "Then," says the youthful hero, "I will provide my own." And when our country was too poor to offer him a passage to America, he left all the wealth and honors before him, and hastened to our aid, offering generously to serve without pay. He left a home of plenty and peace, and plunged into our scenes of poverty and blood. From the camp at Valley Forge he writes his wife: "We are in small barracks which are scarcely more cheerful than dungeons." The men had made these huts of logs and mud, and there this noble man, with Greene, Steuben, and other officers of high rank, passed one of the dreariest winters of the whole war.

Contrast that day of small things, and of the darkest prospects, with the period, when, after forty years, he revisits our country. He lands at New York amid shouts and national salutes; he visits the east; Boston sends her greeting in the form of an immense military array, and twelve hundred horsemen as an escort. He is borne five thousand miles in triumph from Maine to Florida, in relays of vehicles — it is before the day of railways — until he again reaches Boston to join in the magnificent celebration of the fiftieth anniversary of the battle of Bunker Hill. Soon every one of us puts on his badge inscribed " Welcome, Lafayette." Our theatres cannot go on with their ordinary performances unless they sing odes in his praise. The following verse was inscribed on a banner hung across Washington Street, at the corner of Dover Street, when Lafayette entered Boston : —

> The fathers in glory shall sleep,
> That gathered with thee to the fight;
> But the sons will eternally keep
> The tablet of gratitude bright.
> We bow not the neck ; we bend not the knee :
> But our hearts, Lafayette, we surrender to thee!

This was a selection from the now historic ode by Charles Sprague, which was that day sung for the first time, and which roused my heart as I listened to its stirring strains.

When Lafayette had completed his more than regal progress over our borders, he returned again to his home. At length, full of years and honors, " his silver temples were laid in their last repose." Memorable was the scene of his burial at Paris in the cemetery of Picpus, where, by his request his body was placed by the side of Madame de Lafayette's. No words were uttered, the tears and sobs of his friends bearing sufficient testimony to his worth. After the customary prayers the earth sent from America was mingled with that of his loved nation ; muskets were discharged in honor of his military rank, and the throng, not the rich and titled alone, but the humble poor whom he had blest, turned a last sad look to the spot where he rested, while a few of his kindred paused, loath to quit that garden of death, the gateway of immortality.

After the tidings of his departure had reached us we gathered in Faneuil Hall to listen to the eulogy of Everett which thrilled all hearts, as he alone could, on such occasions. I remember well the moment when he turned to that grand picture of Washington by Stuart and exclaimed, "Speak, glorious Washington, break the long silence of that votive canvas;" and then, apostrophizing the bust of Lafayette that stood on the platform before him, he pressed on with these electric words: "Speak, speak, marble lips, teach us the love of liberty protected by law." A chastened rapture, accompanied by tears, ran through every heart; and the vast audience, as we gazed on the features of Washington, almost felt that those lips would respond to the orator's appeal, and bid us be sons worthy our sires.

We may never forget, that while we owe it to many others in France, who united with him, that our independence was at last secured, — to the valiant Rochambeau, whose arrival in America gave Washington a joy second only to that he felt at the coming of Lafayette, and who with his six thousand men had a large share in forcing Cornwallis to capitulate at Yorktown, October 19, 1781, and to De Grasse for his most timely naval assistance, — there was one other to whom our debt is inferior only to our unmeasured obligations to Washington himself. No ordinary memorials should satisfy the hearts of the American people, when they turn to the sacrifices of this man in our cause. It was a touching tribute that a few of our citizens offered to the memory of our great benefactor a few years ago. Being at Paris on the return of our autumnal Thanksgiving, they went out of the thronged city, and, taking a wreath of immortelles, laid it tenderly and reverently on the simple tomb of Lafayette, which is in the burying-ground of the convent of the Sisters of the Sacred Heart.

One debt still remains to be paid to our illustrious friend and ally. We have sought to honor him and perpetuate his fame in many ways, by naming our children for him, by calling streets and towns after him, by blending his history closely with our own at very many points. But while others have had this distinction shown them, not more entitled to it than he, not a single statue worthy of him has yet been erected in his honor. The University of Vermont proposes (1882), and is the first to propose, paying him this long-delayed tribute. These centennial years should not all pass without some testimonial of this kind being at least initiated in the Capital of our country. Let this be done promptly and unitedly by this widespread nation. In this way — and when our cities and the people at large pour out their gifts in this offering to our foremost friend and helper in the day of our extreme need — we shall demonstrate to the world that a republic can be and is grateful to one of its noblest benefactors.

MOUNT VERNON.

CHAPTER XX.

EMERSON THE PATRIOT.

RALPH WALDO EMERSON, born May 25, 1803, whose death, April 27, 1882, was so recently recorded, demands a prominent notice in these pages, partly for his Revolutionary family. Within a half-century the most varying epithets have been applied to him. In his early life admired as a preacher, denounced ere long as a heretic, to-day his numerous eulogists give him diverse designations. Men of all denominations unite in calling him a prophet, and — if not altogether yet almost — a Christian. Thinker, genius, philosopher, poet, essayist, leader, and king in how many realms, there is one more name which I think he richly deserves. He was, by eminence, a Patriot.

He stood in the eighth generation, on both father's and mother's side, in the clerical line. He bore marks of this lineage so clear that all who knew or saw him perceived, in his air and manner, traces, never to be eliminated, of the clergyman. With equal distinctness, under the great law of heredity, he showed himself a genuine American.

Wherever the interests of his country were at stake, he spoke and acted his part well. The spirit of the Revolution was born and bred in him through his ancestry. On the father's side, his grandfather, William Emerson, after being pastor of the church in Concord about ten years, resigned his office, August 16, 1776, and joined the American army at Ticonderoga as chaplain. Attacked by disease, he was led by advice of his physician, to relinquish that office, and, while attempting to return home, he died on the way at Rutland, Vermont, at the age of thirty-three years, and was buried with military honors.

No one who knew them both could fail to remark the indebtedness of Ralph Waldo Emerson to his mother. Frederika Bremer, after her visit at his house, writes of him: "He is a born nobleman." An acquaintance with the mother makes us feel the truth and force of these words. I can never quite separate the two in memory. What intelligence, what sweetness, what wisdom, what strength of character, met in that fortunate woman. The figure and the face of the parent foreshadowed what was developed in the child. Of commanding aspect, and yet most modest, she claimed very little, but received ready attention. The dark, liquid eye and benevolent smile once seen could never be forgotten. The queen of her household, and fitted to grace larger positions, self-possessed and dignified, she moved forward with equal step, sensitive, placid, serene,—toward man sincere and kind, and toward her Father on high (none could doubt it) loyal, loving and devout.

Mr. Emerson's mother married, as her second husband, Rev. Ezra Ripley, minister of Concord, who was filled with the fire of the Revolution, and by deeds, if not arms, took a most able part in sustaining the cause of his country at that trying crisis. Mary Emerson, one of this family in its direct line, married William Cogswell of Concord, who was in the American army at Cambridge in 1776, and also in 1778 at Rhode Island.

With such a lineage Ralph Waldo Emerson could not but be inspired with an undying interest in the history of the War of the Revolution. Read his hymn for the celebration of the inauguration of the Concord monument, April 19, 1836. These immortal lines have stirred patriotic hearts down to this hour: —

> By the rude bridge that arched the flood,
> Their flag to April breeze unfurled,
> Here once the embattled farmers stood,
> And fired the shot heard round the world.
>
> . . . .
>
> Spirit that made these heroes dare
> To die, and leave their children free,
> Bid time and nature gently spare
> The shaft we raise to them and thee.

And his patriotic effusions were not limited to his own immediate locality. They embraced with equal ardor his State — as testified by the verse that follows — and his whole country : —

> As in the day of sacrifice,
> When heroes piled the pyre,
> The dismal Massachusetts ice
> Burned more than others' fire.

We cannot doubt that the father of Mr. Emerson, born in 1769, as a boy in his first fourteen years to the close of the war in 1783, must have been aroused to a sympathy in the Revolutionary zeal all around him, and transmitted it in after life to young Waldo. And living, too, in his childhood in Boston, he must often have gone to hear sermons and orations on liberty in the renowned Old South Church. William Emerson, when minister at Harvard, preached the Artillery Election sermon in Boston, and without doubt it was its eloquent and patriotic strains which so stirred members of the First Church, that it led to his call as pastor to that society. This was "the first instance," said his aggrieved Harvard people, "in which one society stole a minister from another."

My recollection of Emerson extends back to his seventeenth year, when I entered Harvard College, he being then in the senior class. His fine face and figure attracted the attention of us Freshmen; his poem on Class Day gave indication of his future success in verse, no less than prose; and his eloquent words in his "conference part" at commencement, on the "Character of John Knox" indicated in simple, terse, and forcible periods the claims of the great Scottish reformer. In 1826 Mr. Emerson began to preach; and it was while he occupied a room in Divinity Hall, that, as his neighbor in the same building, I became personally acquainted with him. He had then, as ever, great faith in the promptings of nature, which gave him a strong individuality. I saw clearly, from that time, that Mr. Emerson was to be a marked man, in private as in public. His language was keen and piquant in conversation, no less than in his writings. Speaking of one in the building, he said, "S—— is queer: he talks in scraps."

He was sought as a candidate for many pulpits. A new society had been formed in Boston, and four preachers were asked to fill the desk for successive Sundays, that one of them might be selected as a candidate for settlement. Mr. Emerson was invited to preach on one of these Sundays. Referring to this circumstance, I asked him which day he should accept: "I shall decline to go at all," was his prompt reply; "this competition is rather too close." His conceptions of personal dignity and self-respect were here, as everywhere, very delicate; and his manner, though modest, could be pronounced and decided. He was sometimes thought by strangers to be proud. Nothing was more unjust. I have heard him speak to a domestic in his house with as much kindness and consideration as he would manifest to a near member of his own family.

He was settled as colleague pastor with Rev. Henry Ware, in the Second Church of Boston. During his ministry, after Mr. Ware had resigned and become a professor in the Cambridge Divinity School, Mr. Emerson married me to a member of his society. I can never forget the impressive manner in which that service was performed; and the remembrance of that hour, to which he often referred with his genial smile when we met, has been to me no ordinary privilege and pleasure.

When Mr. Emerson resigned his office as pastor, many hearts were grieved at the cause of it, while every one accorded him praise for his sincerity and conscientiousness. He had come to the conclusion that the communion service was not intended to be a perpetual rite, and not believing in its value and efficacy, he made known to his church that he could no longer conscientiously administer this ordinance. They differed from him so decidedly in regard to its authority and value that he felt constrained, on this account, finally to resign his office, and with a tender farewell, in the tone of which with one heart they united, he left his society.

Soon he became noticed for his suspected heresies, and I recollect witnessing the effect of his standing which showed itself on one particular occasion. At the annual Unitarian festival, among those invited to give addresses was Father Taylor, of the Methodist Bethel Church in Boston. " You Unitarians," he said in his speech, " are awfully honest..... What is to become of your heretic Emerson? I don't know where he will go when he dies. He is hardly good enough to be accepted in Heaven, and yet (the dear creature) Satan would n't know what to do with him."

Waldo Emerson might have drawn something of his moral bravery from his renowned ancestor, Peter Waldo, the founder, in the twelfth century, of the noble old Waldenses. That Christian hero exhibited his moral independence by so far departing from the faith of the Romish Church that in 1184 he and his followers were formally excommunicated by Pope Lucius III.

Mr. Emerson felt a deep interest in all that pertains to the life and health of our nation. One of our best critics says of him: "He is the most republican of republicans." Lowell the poet, in an admirable notice of Emerson, affirms that "to him, more than to all other causes, did the young martyrs of our Civil War owe the sustaining strength and thoughtful heroism that is so touching in every record of their lives." In a letter written during that sad yet needful struggle Emerson gives this decided testimony of a custom of nations, which, although as yet almost universal, is abhorrent to some of the best instincts of our higher nature: "I shall always respect war hereafter. The cost of life, the dreary havoc of comfort and time, are overpaid by the vistas it opens of eternal life, eternal law, reconstructing and uplifting society, — breaks up the old horizon, and we see through the rifts a wider."

All his essays, notably those on Character, Politics, and New England Reforms, one in the "Atlantic," entitled, "American Civilization," and that read in the Old South, February, 1878, entitled "Fortune of the Republic," abundantly show his public spirit. He aided every measure designed to educate the community in liberal principles, broad views, and a thorough personal culture. "We should cling," said he, "to the common school. . . . . Let us educate every soul." He thought highly of the system of public lectures, and gave at least three for the purchase of the Old South Church, as a memorial of the Revolution. To the lyceum in his own town, Concord, he gave, during his life, one hundred lectures. I recall an occasion, when, after my reading in that lyceum a lecture on the importance of training and securing good teachers for our public schools, he, in his earnest manner, said to me, "A good teacher is as rare as a good poet."

It was a treat to attend the lectures of Mr. Emerson. He gave, in successive winter seasons, in Boston and other cities, beginning in 1834, for many years, some forty or fifty different lectures, and often whole courses. It was a special pleasure to listen to him year by year. At first, by his quaint, terse, and richly laden sentences, he seemed to perplex some of our wisest men. I sat, one evening, quite near the Hon. Jeremiah Mason, — a man who could penetrate into the deepest depths of the law so long as the speaker or writer kept to the "dry light." But Emerson, I saw, sorely tried him. Two ladies by his side evidently enjoyed every word they heard. The next day Mr. Mason, it is said, being asked how he liked Emerson, replied: "Oh, I could n't understand him at all. You must ask my daughters about him; they took it all in."

Meeting him one day, after one of his lectures, at the store of Little & Brown, where Rev. Dr. Francis and others were present, we were expressing our satisfaction at what we had heard from him, when Dr. Francis remarked: "You must have spent a long time in preparing your lectures, they are so full of thought and of historical material." "Oh, no," said Mr. Emerson; "I never write until I am driven to it by the time each week." And sometimes, while listening to his lectures, they seemed almost extemporaneous. They struck one as full of thoughts entirely fresh and original, and in some passages as if the inspiration of the hour. There was sometimes, in the beginning of a sentence, a little hesitancy, as if he was waiting for a word or words to be given him for utterance at the moment. Still they must have been, we know, the result of long premeditation as well as extensive reading. If there was ever an appearance of disregard of manner in his utterances, this was not true of him. I recollect hearing him, while he was a student in Divinity Hall, reading aloud, evidently for the benefit of his voice; and he would occasionally take up a volume from his table in which he had the speeches of Webster and Everett bound together. "Everett," he once said to me, "is a great word-catcher."

Mr. Emerson's interest in antislavery was profound and unremitting. I remember only one instance in which his sweet serenity seemed for an instant to leave him. After the execution of John Brown, a meeting was called in Boston for indignant denunciation of that act. Mr. Emerson was one of the speakers. Sitting quite near the platform and in front of him, I saw his face wore a passing shade and a slight frown, as if the terror of the deed we had met to consider and comment upon was too great for human endurance.

Mr. Emerson always took the broadest view of every subject before him. At a meeting of the Sunday-school Society in Concord, a few years since, the people opened their houses liberally, and invited those at the church to dine with them. The invitation to his table was most cordial. It gives one no ordinary pleasure to be told, under such a roof, that his name is "familiar as household words." And the country was not forgotten, for I noticed under each plate was a slip on which was written "National Unitarian Sunday-school Convention."

In a book on the families of men of the Revolution it would be unjust to pass by another name, associated with his own, — that of his brother, Edward Bliss Emerson, a college classmate of mine. He bore a name honored in American history, and especially so in his brother, since then of world-wide fame. Had his life been prolonged, he would have given to that name an enhanced and imperishable lustre. I see him to-day as then, more than half a century ago, gifted with rare personal beauty, an eye large and beaming with genius, and a face radiant not more with a surpassing intellect than a fascinating sweetness. He had a mind uniting strength and fertile resources, and even then stored with ample reading, a character manly and influential, and a reverence for divine things seldom equalled at his age. I recall an oration of his at one of our "exhibitions," mature in thought, sparkling with illustration, full of Scriptural allusions, and delivered with a grace and power which showed him destined to stand in the front rank, as of scholarship, so of oratory. Alas that, within the brief space of ten years, the frail body overmastered by a peerless although at last clouded intellect, he passed on, and left an irremovable shadow over the class of 1824!

Meeting Mr. Emerson occasionally toward his last days, and finally at the funeral of a kindred poetic genius, the lamented Longfellow, — children's friend, and a friend honored and cherished wherever our language is spoken, — I saw no change, save that the smile of his youth and manhood had become sweeter with his approaching end, and the grasp of his hand had become warmer. And when, at his own so soon following obsequies, I looked on that noble form, fitly robed in his angel apparel of white, the placid face spoke of the upper serenities in which he had trusted, and on which he had now entered.

JAMES RUSSELL LOWELL.

CHAPTER XXI.

THE SOLDIER OF THE REVOLUTION.

THESE pages have been devoted largely to the officers of the Revolutionary army. I think, in a work of this description, we ought not to lose sight of the men who constituted the rank and file of our military forces. The common soldier, who did his work well in a subordinate position, deserves a distinct notice in the annals of that period. What could the ablest general have accomplished without the support of the men in each separate command below him, as they stood shoulder to shoulder in the ranks?

We are hardly aware of the disadvantages under which our officers were placed, at many points of the contest, in regard to the forces under their command. The British army was made up, not only of good officers, but of men who had been thoroughly drilled and fitted for the service; while our army was composed largely of raw troops, coming from the farm or the workshop, with no military discipline or experience. They were destitute even of common clothing in many cases, provided with no proper arms, and in no sense fitted for the stern tasks before them. They were placed at once in the front, obliged to meet a foe accustomed to war and at home on the battle-field. They enlisted usually for short terms, and frequently they had hardly time to learn the alphabet of military tactics before their term of service expired. Taken sometimes into a new country, and scenes quite new to them, they could not adapt themselves readily to their position, and experienced all the hardships of war without any of its palliating circumstances. In some cases, while their officers had comforts in their tents and on their table, the privates were compelled to sleep without even a shelter from the elements, and to subsist on the poorest rations and a scanty supply perhaps even of these.

In September, 1777, Washington writes: "At least one thousand men were barefooted, and performed the marches in that condition." At one time they were three days without bread; on another two days without a particle of meat; they had no soap or vinegar. Of still a third day we read: "Few men had more than one shirt, many only the moiety of one, and more none at all." During the dreary winter at Valley Forge their commander writes, February 16, 1778, "For some days past there has been little less than a famine in the camp; a part of the army has been a week without any kind of flesh, and the rest three or four days. Naked and starving as they are, we cannot enough admire the incomparable patience and fidelity of the soldiery, that they have not been ere this excited by their sufferings to a general mutiny and dispersion." Congress was sometimes unable, from inability to supply their wants, to grant them relief; or its commissaries, by their negligence, selfishness, or inefficiency, left the army to suffer on without help or hope.

And this was not all; they were surrounded and beset by Loyalists, who were working against them every way in their power; and those who refused to join the English army were sometimes taken by force and delivered up to its officers. Lafayette complained that there were great " numbers who, without actually taking up arms, made it their main object to injure the friends of liberty and to give useful intelligence to those of despotism ; " and Washington, at one crisis, describes himself as " in an enemy's country."

Another source of difficulty was the depreciated state of the currency. The Jersey line of the army, in a memorial to their State legislature, state that " four months' pay of a private would not procure for his family a single bushel of wheat." The Connecticut line at one time refused to accept the depreciated paper money, and a committee of Congress, after examining the state of Washington's army, reported that it had been unpaid for five months, " that every department of the army was without money, and had not even the shadow of credit left."

And, furthermore, the trial of the patience and

loyalty of the army was tested where dependence could no longer be placed upon volunteer troops, but the colonists were compelled to fill up the ranks of the army by a compulsory draft from the local militia. This measure increased the dangers of discontent, desertions, and disloyalty to the American cause.

But still the great body of the army remained faithful and true ; and the record of our men, amid such surroundings, is often worthy of the highest commendation. There were indeed those who complained of their lot, and were restless, and at times insubordinate. But the rank and file of the armies were habitually obedient to their officers and showed a soldierly deportment; and before we condemn any instance of a contrary appearance and reputation, we are bound to look fully and fairly into all the evidence of the case. See what they actually endured, and you will, in a vast majority of cases, find the bearing of our soldiers was calm, dignified and patient, and worthy of high praise.

The progress of the war, the success of our arms, on the whole, from day to day, and the energy with which our men rose above defeat and discouragement, justify the position I take on their behalf. The result shows that not only were the officers firm in their adhesion to the cause of liberty and independence, but that this noble spirit extended through the ranks, down to those who enlisted as privates, and remained in the ranks and received an honorable discharge at the close of their services. Their names should go down to the latest posterity as having borne the burden and heat of the war, as being unambitious of fame, and content with the name and reward of the patient, persistent, good and true common soldier.

I wish to speak of an individual remarkable as a representative of the good soldier remaining in the ranks, and still further for the extraordinary age which he reached, being for some time the sole survivor of those who witnessed the battle of Bunker Hill. I had an opportunity to see him at a Whig celebration in Boston, in the year 1850, when he was ninety-five years old. He had a large and well-shaped head; his eyes were blue, and their expression mild; and his whole countenance beamed with benevolence. Being asked at that time if he had no children then living, he replied, " Yes, I have two sons." " Why did you not bring them with you?" He answered, "I did n't want to be plagued with the boys." " What are their ages?" "Oh, one is seventy, the other seventy-two."

Fortunately we have a letter from one who visited him in 1860, which furnishes us a minute description of his personal appearance, and an account of a conversation with him, the substance of which I give. Ralph Farnham was born in Lebanon, Maine, on the 7th of July, 1756; his residence was in Acton, Maine, and he was, at this interview, in the one hundred and fifth year of his age. His sight was not materially dimmed; his memory, especially for things of former years, still good; his mental powers in general seemed unimpaired and his health excellent.

He was quite ready to converse, and repeated many Revolutionary anecdotes with spirit and great enjoyment. Within six weeks of the time when he was nineteen years old he enlisted in the Continental army. His name was first enrolled on the 26th of May, 1775, and on the 31st of the same month, with his fellow-soldiers from Maine, he reached Cambridge, Massachusetts. The company to which he belonged was detailed to guard the artillery at Cambridge Common, where General Ward expected an attack from the British as well as at Charlestown. Before the battle of Bunker Hill was finished Farnham went to an eminence near that place to aid the Americans in bringing away their wounded. This led him to a point where he had a better view of the engagement than those who were actively employed behind the ramparts. His first campaign was for eight months, after which he returned home; but the letter says that in 1777 he served two short campaigns. He was, at one time, stationed at Providence, in Rhode Island; and was afterward in the battle of Saratoga. He gave the correspondent I quote many interesting reminiscences of Washington, Putnam, Gates, Burgoyne, and Benedict Arnold. Upon this traitor his comments were very severe.

Another case — that of Moses Hale — shows us a soldier who was disinterested, unambitious, and a pattern of fidelity in the ranks. He enlisted as a private, and seemed pleased and content with that position. He was one of the leading men in Winchendon, Massachusetts, for the nearly sixty years of his residence in that town. Only three years after his removal thither, in 1773, we find him made chairman of a meeting " to take into consideration the distressing and dangerous circumstances of our public affairs." He is chosen " chairman of a committee to consider of grievances." A vote is passed to choose " a committee of correspondence," of which he is one, to unite with a similar committee in Boston, and a resolution is adopted " at all times to join heartily with our brethren of this Province for the redress of our grievances and the establishment of our character, rights, privileges, and liberties."

When the news came of the battle of Lexington, the alarm was spread in Winchendon by the firing of guns and the beating of drums. The people sprang to arms, and under the lead of Deacon Moses Hale, *without a commission*, a party of the people started for the scene of action. After a short respite, Abel Wilder, a born hero, was commissioned captain of a company which marched to Cambridge, of which we have subsequent evidence that Moses Hale was a member. This company was in the battle of Bunker Hill. " The Winchendon men," says the record, " engaged in the thick of the fight." Captain Wilder, brave soul, writes to his wife the day after the battle, — we have his own spelling, — " Friday night I was poorly." His doctor urged him to take medicine; " but I told him," writes the Captain, " as there was a battle expected Satterday I would not take it, lest I should be charged of taking it on purpose. And according as was expected, a very hot battle insued Satterday afternoon. I fired nineteen times, and had fair chances, and then they was too hard for us, and we retreated. The bals flew very thick, but through the Divine protection, my company was all preserved but one." We learn from another source that " he had a long, slender gun, and fired it till it was so stopped up that he could not fire it any longer."

In 1776 Moses Hale, who had been a common soldier, was placed by his town on their committee of correspondence. March 13, 1777, the town voted " to hire men to serve in the war for this town in the future." Deacon Moses Hale was on a committee authorized to hire money for that purpose. Throughout the war he was earnest in the cause and foremost in labors for its advancement. The record he has left is most gratifying. " Next to Deacon Wilder," is its testimony, " he filled the largest place in public estimation; and after the death of Mr. Wilder, he was in the first rank. He filled many offices, and was, several years, delegate to the General Court, besides being delegate to the State Convention for adopting the

National Constitution. He was deacon of the Congregational Church for a long term of years preceding his decease in 1828."

Our government rightly opposes a direct union of Church and State. But such a union as this, a patriotism based on the highest principle, and carried out in unambitious service to one's country, bears the mark of a character which does as high honor to religion as it does to the noble institutions of our republic.

Moses Hale belonged to a family remarkable for their longevity. He was born in Boxford, June 5, 1742; he married Ruth Foster, July 2, 1769. They removed to Winchendon, Massachusetts, May 8, 1770. Their children were : (1) Eunice ; (2) Ruth ; (3) Lucy, who was living in 1866, at the age of eighty-nine ; (4) Moses; (5) Achsa ; (6) Artemas, who married Deborah Lincoln of Hingham in 1815. This couple have since lived in Bridgewater, where he died August 3, 1882, at the age of ninety-eight years, five months, and two days. The great-grandfather of Artemas Hale, Joseph Hale of Boxford, Massachusetts, lived to the age of ninety years. His great-uncles, Joseph and Thomas Hale of Boxford, lived to the ages severally of eighty-one and eighty-four years. His father, Moses Hale, died at eighty-six, and his mother, Ruth (Foster) Hale, at ninety-five years and four months. Of his uncles and aunts on his father's side, Nathaniel died at seventy-one ; Amos at seventy-six ; Ruth (Mrs. Curtis) at eighty ; David at eighty-one; Jacob at eighty-seven; Lucy (Mrs. Keyes) at ninety-three years and seven months; while Judith (Mrs. Towne) attained the remarkable age of one hundred and six years, five months, and two days, having been born on October 14, 1747, and died at Paris, New York, March 16, 1854. Of his own brothers and sisters, Moses died at sixty-four; Eunice at seventy-four; Ruth (Mrs. Payson) at eighty-eight; Achsa (Mrs. Coolidge) at ninety-six years, nine months, and twenty-six days; and Lucy at ninety-eight years, five months, and eight days.

Although Artemas Hale was a modest man and retiring in his habits, he was a true patriot and filled various political offices with great success. From 1827 to 1832 he was in the Massachusetts House of Representatives, and from 1833 to 1834 was a member of the Senate. In a heated and prolonged contest of his district, he was chosen on the same day to the Twenty-Ninth Congress and the Thirtieth. In 1853 he was a delegate to the Massachusetts Constitutional Convention; and in 1864 he was a presidential elector on the Lincoln and Johnson ticket.

I speak of him with pleasure and confidence from having known him personally, in the prime of his life, when his rare intelligence and interest in all good works of a public, national, and philanthropic description were apparent from his conversation and character.

He was very regular and temperate in his habits,

abstaining totally from intoxicating drinks and tobacco, and, with the exception of his hearing, he retained the full possession of his faculties, bodily and mental, until near the close of his life; and on his ninety-fifth birthday he gave an address to his Masonic lodge, which was said to be one of the best ever delivered before a body of that order.

Such men as Moses Hale and his son Artemas Hale not only elevate themselves and their families, but present evidence that—however some men may bring and have brought reproach on our country by their sordid aims and selfish course in their public relations — there were those in the infancy of our Union, and have been down to this day, in whose sincere, unpretentious temper and self-devoted services the country may take a just pride.

CHAPTER XXII.

THE BATTLE OF LEXINGTON:

WITH PERSONAL RECOLLECTIONS OF MEN ENGAGED IN IT.

HAVING from my earliest childhood, and in my native place, heard the story of the opening scenes of the Revolution from the lips of several who took part in it, and known, more or less, many others of them, I am unwilling that their share in it should be lost to the annals of that day. To Lexington and Concord belongs the honor of these opening scenes. In all contemporaneous history Lexington stands as the place where the first resistance was made to the King's troops, and Concord as the place where they met their first repulse and began their retreat. Lexington, by her band of protomartyrs, led the determined train that finally threw off the British yoke. "Too few to resist, too brave to flee," their blood was the seed of that great freedom-harvest gathered by those who came after them. Their service was little, of necessity, in a military point of view, but in a national and political aspect its importance was inestimable.

AMOS MUZZEY, IN PARKER'S COMPANY, APRIL 19, 1775.

The motives of the Colonists from the beginning, were high and pure. Their pacific spirit was seen up to the last critical and decisive hour, and the sight of an invading force. Nothing was done at that moment except on the defensive. In view of the threatening condition of the country a military company had been formed in Lexington under Capt. John Parker. It had one hundred and thirty names on its roll. My grandfather, Amos Muzzey, who was a member of this company, and whose name stands also on the roll of five-months' men at Ticonderoga in 1776, and that of the three-months' campaign at Cambridge in 1778, was apprehensive of an approaching conflict. He had seen a few men riding on horseback past his house at dusk on the evening of the 18th, and as, looking beyond the waving grass of that premature season, he saw the wind blow their overcoats open, he noticed their uniforms and swords underneath. This aroused the suspicions of the people, and he, with another man, was sent early the next morning to get intelligence of any movement below by the British troops. He stopped in Arlington, then Menotomy, at a tavern called the Black Horse, kept by a Mr. Wetherby, where the two Provincial committees, of Safety and Supplies, usually met. While there, the enemy arrived, and my grandfather narrowly escaped being made a prisoner. He found his horse let loose and injured, though not disabled. At a later hour in the day Mr. Samuel Whittemore of Menotomy, then eighty years of age, who married, as his second wife, my great-grandmother, was shot, bayoneted, and left for dead; but he was afterward taken to the above tavern, and finally recovered and lived to the age of ninety-six.

My grandmother, when the British troops — eight hundred grenadiers and light-infantry, under Lieutenant-Colonel Francis Smith of the Tenth British Regiment, and Major John Pitcairn of the marines — had passed her house, in the centre of Lexington, on their way to Concord, left the house, taking her two children (my father, who was nine years old that day, and his brother, a boy of four) to spend the dread day with a neighbor and friend. A foot-weary soldier had fallen behind the column, and as the sun was rising he met and saluted my grandmother: "Good-morning, madam; the King's troops are paying you an early visit this morning." Her reply, in the custom of those days, was from Scripture, — in the language of the elders of the town of Bethlehem, who met Samuel, and "trembled at his coming." She said, "Come ye peaceably?" The soldier could not reply as the Prophet did, "Peaceably!" but said with little of her reverence, "Ah, madam! you have carried the joke rather too far with his Majesty."

When the troops returned from Concord they entered my grandfather's house, broke a large mirror, — a part of the frame of which was long kept in the family, and is now in Lexington Memorial Hall, — and demolished the *beaufet*, with its contents of valuable crockery, some of which

I remember seeing in my boyhood. My grandfather said: "They must have dressed their wounded there, for the floor had stripes of blood all over it, as if a pig had been stuck and dragged around the room." The old gentleman's life was prolonged until December 10, 1822, when he died at the age of eighty-two, being already past man's threescore years and ten when the "mere skirmish," as he called the War of 1812, involved the country in new hostilities. In the latter contest our State government located a depot of military stores at Lexington, within sight of our own door; and, as the veteran had so often rehearsed the story of the famous British march to Concord thirty-seven years before, it is no marvel that the narrative made the grandson share his grandsire's anxiety for the safety of these new deposits. The Regulars, not content with other damage, fired at his house, either before or after leaving it, several bullets, one of which passed through a partition on which I often gazed from the bed in my childhood, and two others I took from the brick lining to our wall, when the house was repaired, forty years after the battle. The British, on their retreat, and when reinforced, burned three houses, beside a barn and two workshops within a mile of my grandfather's. They also set fire to several other houses, and pillaged many as they passed on, breaking doors and windows, destroying furniture, and carrying away clothing; and they took the lives of several persons, and in modes hardly less savage than those of our own Indians. It is to the honor of our Provincials that they committed no acts of barbarity, although charged in foreign accounts with all manner of cruelties, even to cold-blooded murder, and mutilating and scalping their victims.

The forbearance of our people was illustrated in the cool and prudent conduct of Captain Parker. Fearing lest some of his men, in their excitement, would fire prematurely, and so begin the contest, he ordered them not to fire unless they were fired upon,—adding, "but if they want a war, let it begin here." As the little band of sixty stood before tenfold their number of disciplined troops, a few of them naturally for a moment faltered. Parker ordered every man to "stand his ground till he should order him to leave it," and added that he would "order the first man to be shot down who should attempt to leave his post."

I often heard individuals, who witnessed the scenes of that morning, describe them in detail. About half-past four o'clock Major Pitcairn, with six companies of grenadiers and light-infantry, rode up on the right side of the meeting-house, saw Captain Parker's company, which was just forming in two ranks, and ordered them to disperse. This command was repeated; and, it not being obeyed, he fired his pistol and brandished his sword. Colonel Smith's force was then about twelve rods distant in front of the meeting-house, and on the left side of it. Pitcairn passed up the

BATTLE OF LEXINGTON.

Bedford road, on the right hand, and around to the back of the meeting-house, where, by his command, after firing over the heads of our men, his troops fired a second volley, and killed Jonas Parker, Robert Munroe, Isaac Muzzey, — a kinsman of mine, — and Jonathan Harrington. Two men, Samuel Hadley and John Brown, fell near the Common. Two others were also killed — Caleb Harrington, as he was leaving the meeting-house, and Asahel Porter, an escaped prisoner, near the Common. The British wounded nine others, and rushed forward to bayonet Parker's men. Jonathan Harrington fell in front of his own house on the Common. His wife saw him fall and then start up, the blood gushing from his breast; he stretched out his hands toward her, and fell again. Rising a little he crept across the road; she ran to meet him at the door, but he died at her feet. Four of the company went into the meeting-house for ammunition. Hearing the discharge of guns, one of them, Joshua Simonds, cocked his piece, and laid down by an open cask of powder, resolved never to be taken alive. Jonas Parker was a true Roman hero. He had often said, "Let others do as they please; I will never run from the British." Having loaded his musket he placed his hat, and in it his ammunition, on the ground between his feet. He was soon wounded, and sunk upon his knees; and in this state discharged his gun. While loading it again, and striving to fire once more, he was pierced by a bayonet, and died as he had said he would.

From the little one-storied New England schoolhouse, which stood a few yards from the monument erected in 1799 on the battle-field, and in which I attended school until I left home to prepare for college, I saw, day after day, the old Jonathan Harrington house, and felt many a thrill at the sad tale of the hero and martyr who once occupied that venerated building.

After the bloody scene just described, Major Pitcairn galloped round to the Concord road, on the left of the meeting-house, and joined Colonel Smith. The engagement lasted about half an hour, when, after giving three huzzas, the column marched toward Concord. About the middle of the forenoon Captain Parker collected a part of his company, and they moved bravely toward Concord in pursuit of the British.

It is said that not less than forty unarmed persons witnessed the engagement. I knew individuals, too young to bear arms, who were on the Common that day, and who, at a greater or less distance of time, gave their accounts of the battle. Levi Harrington, then in his fifteenth year, was quite near, and testified that the British fired first. Abijah Harrington, who was in the fourteenth year of his age at that time, — when, at a later period, it was doubted whether our men returned the British fire at all, — was accustomed to say, " I was on the spot where the Red-coats stood, after the battle that day, and saw in one place a large pool of blood." He himself lived to the advanced age of ninety-one. His testimony was confirmed by the depositions of Elijah Sanderson, who saw blood where the column stood when Solomon Brown[1] fired at them. Rufus Merriam, who lived until May 7, 1847, was in his thirteenth year at the time of the battle. His family were in my boyhood near neighbors to us, and he spoke of standing on the doorsteps of the old Buckman house, afterward his own home, and seeing the British column coming up the road. Some of our men were firing from the house, when Mr. Buckman asked them to stop, as it led the British to fire back. Certain Loyalists then in the house had said: "Oh, they won't fire on us, for we are their friends." Mr. Buckman's house shows to-day that this was no protection; several bullet-holes are still to be seen there.

A British officer, who shared in the expedition that day, testified that "a man of the Tenth Light-infantry was wounded by a Yankee." Another testified that "Major Pitcairn's horse was grazed by a bullet, and a soldier wounded in the leg." Some British prisoners, taken that day, said, "One of our soldiers was wounded in the thigh, and another received a shot through his hand."

It will be recollected that through the night of April 18, John Hancock, who was a grandson of the minister of Lexington by that name, and Samuel Adams, were at the house of Rev. Mr. Clarke, who married a cousin of John Hancock. These

---

[1] An interesting sketch of Solomon Brown, by Rev. Horace E. Hayden, reached me too late, I regret to say, for use in this work.

two Patriots had been marked, and were finally proscribed by King George, whose first order was that " they be sent over to England for trial." The second order was to " hang them in Boston." No wonder they sought shelter at such a moment among kindred and friends. While here they were waked about midnight by the renowned Paul Revere. Mr. Clarke's house, not far north of the Common, was familiar to me in early life. Of Mr. Clarke's twelve children there were two of whom I have a vivid recollection: Sarah, who died unmarried, January 28, 1843, aged sixty-nine; and Elizabeth, who died December 5, 1843, also unmarried, aged eighty. They preserved every object in their house — the old room which Hancock and Adams had occupied, with the table, chairs, and cushions, the high wainscoting, hard pine floors, and even the dilapidated paper—with the utmost reverence. They were very kind to us children, and even to the feline species, nine of which I once saw together around their good old wide fireplace.

While the two Patriots were here they were protected by a guard of eight minute-men, under the command of Sergeant William Munroe. They were advised, after the attack on the Common and when the British had started toward Concord, to flee for safety. At first they retired to a hill southeast of Mr. Clarke's, then, and still partly covered with wood. While waiting there for the British column to pass on toward Concord, the almost inspired Adams—standing on a rock which has been pointed out to me by my brother-in-law, General Chandler, who in recent days owned the premises— uttered, as the sun was a little way up, that immortal sentence : "What a glorious morning for America is this!"

I often heard from my grandfather — one of whose cousins married Ebenezer Fiske, from whom Fiske Hill received its name — the story of the encounter at that place, between James Hayward of Acton and a British soldier. Hayward left his father's house with one pound of powder and forty balls, followed the British from Concord to the foot of Fiske Hill, and, being thirsty, stopped at the well, front of the house. A British soldier, who was in the house for plunder, saw him, stepped to the door and aimed his piece at him. "You are a dead man," said one. "And so are you," was the reply. Both fired and both fell, — the British soldier dead, Hayward mortally wounded. The ball which hit him passed through his powder-horn, and drove the splinters into his body. He lingered eight hours, during which he repeatedly expressed his willingness to die in defending the rights of his country. He was a young man of high character, and died at the age of twenty-five. I recalled the memorable well with new interest, April 19, 1835. It was then, when the remains of the martyr soldiers were removed from the old burying-ground in Lexington, and placed under the monument, that Edward

Everett, the orator of the day, exhibited the powder-horn worn by Hayward in that deadly encounter. I saw the hole made in it by the bullet which killed him, and was glad to learn that this venerated relic was bequeathed by Mr. Everett to the town of Acton, the home of Hayward, and is now deposited in that place.

It will be remembered that a reinforcement of British troops, — a brigade consisting of three regiments of infantry and a detachment of marines, to the number of about twelve hundred, with two fieldpieces, under Lord Percy — came out to Lexington in the after part of the day, and met the force of Colonel Smith about half a mile below the village. One cannon was placed on an eminence near the Munroe tavern, the other on a high point near the fork of the main and Woburn roads. On this latter spot, it is probable, the shot was fired which struck the meeting-house, that stood about twenty feet north of that which was erected afterward, in 1794. It passed through or near the pulpit, and fell at the door of the house belonging to one of Captain Parker's company, back of the green where the enemy were met. This act of desecration shocked all who ever saw its effects. The Rev. Mr. Morrill of Wilmington, who preached the annual sermon, April 19, 1780, says of it: "Let the mark of British tyranny, made in the house of God, remain till time itself shall consume the fabric, and it moulders into dust." I recollect seeing this cannon-ball in my boyhood, and shared in the feeling of horror at its tale of impiety.

I have spoken of Captain Parker's pursuit of the British on their march to Concord. One of his company, Jedediah Munroe, had been wounded in the morning, but the heroic man was not stopped by the loss of blood; he pushed forward with the company, but died in the afternoon. Another, Francis Brown, sergeant of the company, encountered the enemy in the morning, joined his comrades on the march to Concord, and — meeting the British in their flight, at Lincoln — received a very severe wound. A ball entered his cheek, passed under his ear, and lodged in the back part of his neck, where it remained until the next year. But still the brave man commanded the company in 1776, and survived nearly twenty-five years. He died April 21, 1800, aged sixty-two years.

The Provincials were charged with firing only behind houses, trees, and stone fences. This may have been true; it would have been a mark of wisdom and proper self-protection. When results were summed up it appeared that while the British had lost, in killed and wounded, two hundred and seventy-three men, the American loss was only ninety-three.

Of those who bore arms on that eventful morning a number survived to my boyhood, and a few to my early manhood. I recall several of those honored men. There was the venerated Dr. Joseph Fiske, who told in my hearing many a tear-drawing story of his sufferings in the old Continental army. He was in the sixth campaign, in 1776, at Dorchester, at the capture of Burgoyne, the surrender of Yorktown, and in many other battles, and was surgeon during almost the whole Revolution. He was one of the original members of the Society of Cincinnati, and had a certificate, preserved by the family, signed by Washington as president, and General Knox as secretary. He, like the others, carried with him something of the moral power that pervaded the great cause they so nobly defended. He died September 25, 1837, aged eighty-five years.

I remember well the large form of the veteran Colonel William Munroe, the orderly-sergeant of Captain Parker's company, a man of grave and determined aspect. His oldest daughter married my uncle, the boy I have spoken of, less than four years old on the day of the battle. Often, as I sat by the side of Colonel Munroe, I imagined his feelings when he drew up that little band on the Common. He was a man of few words, but they were wise and weighty. Well educated for his time, he was a thorough master as well as reader of Shakespeare. And his moral character stood equally high. No profane sentence ever sullied his lips, any more than those of his commander, Captain Parker, sorely tempted though he was in the peril and excitement of that hour. What a contrast did the language of those men present to that of Major Pitcairn in that scene, "Disperse, ye rebels!" repeated, and with an oath each time. We are impressed with the purity of the men in general on our side, compared with the rank vices tending always to cluster round the camp, and grown to fearful proportions at that period among the hireling army of General Gage. Colonel Munroe — he was a colonel in the militia — was honored in town, being nine years one of its selectmen, and two years representative in the legislature. He was a lieutenant in the army at the capture of Burgoyne in 1777, and took part in suppressing the Shays rebellion. He kept the public house known as the Munroe tavern. Here the British stopped on their retreat, and murdered John Raymond, an inoffensive man, as he was leaving the house; here Washington dined in 1789, when he visited the battle-ground. Colonel Munroe died October 30, 1827, aged eighty-five years.

Next in my memory is Daniel Harrington, who was clerk of Captain Parker's company. His manly form and long white locks impressed me deeply. He was a blacksmith in former days, and in the shop which his son occupied in my boyhood was kept the six-pound cannon-ball fired through the meeting-house. Here also was found the tongue of the bell which sounded the alarm on the morning of the battle. This valuable relic was obtained from Mr. Harrington by a nephew of mine, Colonel John L. Chandler, about forty-five years ago. It was exhibited at the centennial celebration in 1875, and afterward presented by

Colonel Chandler to the town of Lexington, to be preserved as a sacred deposit in their Memorial Hall.

Daniel Harrington was a prominent citizen, and called to many posts of honor and trust; he was a selectman in 1779, 1785, 1786. He married Anna Munroe, daughter of Ensign Robert Munroe, who stood bravely at his post on the battle-field, April 19, 1775, and fell, one of the first martyrs of the Revolution; and who had previously been a soldier in the French War, and bore the standard at the taking of Louisburg, in 1758; he served also in 1762. A wife — the inheritor, we cannot doubt, of such valor and patriotism as his — must have inspired with heroism the husband, and subject of our notice. He died September 27, 1818, aged seventy-nine years.

I pass next to William Tidd. He was a lieutenant in Captain Parker's company, and gave, in an affidavit, 1824, a graphic account of the firing of the Regulars. He adds: "I then retreated up the north road, and was pursued by a British officer on horseback, calling out to me with an oath, 'Stop, or you are a dead man.' I feared I could not escape him unless I left the road. I therefore sprang over a pair of bars and made a stand, and discharged my gun at him; upon which he immediately retreated to the main body."

When a boy I for one season day by day, on my way to school, passed his house,— a venerable mansion of the ancient, rectangular style. He was short of stature, had a compact frame and an erect gait, and was active even in old age. In addition to his services, April 19, 1775, he was in the seventh campaign, September, 1776, to White Plains, contributed to the eleventh campaign, 1777, to Bennington, and enlisted and served some time in the Continental line. He died October 25, 1826, at ninety-one, having filled various offices in town; he was four years an assessor—then a very high and responsible position—and was one of the selectmen in the Revolution. Mr. Tidd belonged to the Old School, who kept their seats in their pews after the service, and bowed to the minister as he passed out first. Instances have been heard of since in which the boys rushed by the preacher, and showed the power of the elbow. Our respected friend, I think on account of his bald head, wore a red cap, which attracted us youths sometimes more than the minister in the pulpit. He varied this practice, I was told, by wearing a white cap when at home. His wife was a daughter of the heroic Ensign Robert Munroe. Her strongly marked character made her a fit companion of her husband, sympathizing alike in his distinguished military and civil services. She lived to May 14, 1839, dying at the advanced age of ninety-seven years.

We come now to Isaac Hastings, who was in Captain Parker's command. He came of a military family; a brother, and their father were with him in the engagement. He was a man of great energy of character, remarkably gifted and fluent in conversation. His life was, at some of its stages, one of great perils, hardships and thrilling adventures, which he would relate with graphic spirit and power. He once gave in my hearing the details of a shipwreck and approaching starvation, when a tallow candle was "one of the sweetest morsels he ever tasted." We find him at Cambridge as a soldier, May 6-10, and at Bunker Hill, June 17, 1775. He was a prominent man in town affairs, and in 1808 was chosen deacon of the church. Throughout my boyhood I remember well his position in the meeting-house, sitting under the pulpit, with his associate, as was the custom, on the opposite sides of the deacon's seat. He lived on the ancient homestead, afterward in the possession of his most respected daughter, Mrs. Cary. His death, at the ripe age of seventy-six, occurred July 2, 1831.

His father and brother were both men of mark, but neither of military age at the time of the battle. The father, Samuel Hastings, was past the military age, but so patriotic and brave that he stood in the ranks that day. He was with the army July 3, the same year, when Washington took command of it. He was distinguished in town affairs, and often called to places of honor and trust. He died February 8, 1820, at the great age of ninety-nine. The brother, Samuel Hastings Jr., was less than eighteen on the day of the battle, but the young hero appeared with the company on the Common. Soon after, he

MINUTE MAN, 1775.

volunteered in the service, and was one of General Lee's life-guard; he was taken prisoner with him at Long Island. At the time of his capture a British officer struck him on the neck with a sword. He used to say: "My cue saved my life, as it broke the force of the blow, though my wound was severe." He was afterward paroled, but never exchanged. He was at one time major of the Lexington artillery. Although he resided on the borders of Lincoln, I was familiar with his house, partly from the circumstance that his eldest daughter was at one time a tenant of my father and lived across the road from our home. I saw him often: he was a man with strongly marked features and a stout vigorous frame; he died January 8, 1834, having nearly reached the age of seventy-seven. His family testified their honor and love for him by erecting, in Lexington Cemetery, a beautiful monument to his memory, with the honorable inscription, "A Revolutionary Soldier."

It should be noticed that while, owing partly to the scarcity of muskets, only some sixty men stood at any one moment in the ranks of Captain Parker's company,— about one third of whom were either killed or wounded on or near the spot, or elsewhere, during the day,— of two published rolls of the company one contains one hundred and thirteen names, the other one hundred and twenty. And there is evidence that there were not less than one hundred and thirty in all, including the "alarm men," the youth and the superannuated, most of whom were in arms that morning. We have in print depositions dated April 25, 1775, taken by order of the Provincial Congress, of fourteen persons, who say: "We were ordered by Captain John Parker (who commanded us)" &c. &c. Of these fourteen, a part must have been under military age. The names of five are not on the printed rolls, but should be preserved in history. They are Samuel Hastings, Nathaniel Parkhurst (whom I cannot identify, but think he was a brother of John Parkhurst, who was in the battle) John Munroe 3d, Jonas Parker 2d, and Micah Hagar, who appears in the list of the "first campaign of eight months, 1775," and again with the "Men who enlisted in Lexington for three years or during the war, and served in the Continental line." Still another roll of one hundred and eighteen names is found in the "Boston News-letter," June 3, 1826, which varies from the two others, containing five names more than one of them, two less than the other, and that of Stephen Munroe, not found on either.

We have also the depositions of several spectators of the battle. Benjamin Tidd of Lexington and Joseph Abbot of Lincoln were upon the Common that morning on horseback. William Draper of Colrain stood within three or four rods of the Regulars, and saw them fire. Thomas Fessenden saw Parker's men eighteen or twenty rods from the meeting-house. A British officer rode up within six rods of the company, and cried out

"Disperse!" A second officer then fired his pistol. John Bateman of the Fifty-second Regiment, a British soldier, probably a prisoner, testified at Lincoln, April 23, 1775. "There was," to use his words, "a small party of men gathered. When our troops marched by I heard the word of command given to the troops to fire, and some of said troops did fire, and I saw one of said small party lie dead on the ground nigh said meeting-house." This may well offset the account given of the battle by his Excellency Governor Gage, in a letter to Governor Trumbull of Connecticut, — which makes one almost despair of the veracity of history: —

I ordered six companies of light-infantry to take two bridges in Concord. When two miles from Lexington they heard five hundred men were in arms to oppose the King's troops. . . . Major Pitcairn saw about two hundred armed men. . . . He ordered his troops not to fire, but surround and disarm them. . . . The people fired behind a wall, wounded a man of the Tenth Infantry, and hit the Major's horse in two places. . . . They also fired from a meeting-house. . . . Then the light-infantry, without order or regularity, killed several of the country-people, but were silenced as soon as the authority of the officers could make them!

I knew well Jonathan Loring, as a neighbor, his dwelling-house being some third of a mile only from my father's. When it was known that several British officers had gone up toward Concord on the evening of the 18th, Loring, with two others, volunteered to follow them and watch their movements. He was taken prisoner and detained several hours, until, on the return of the British officers, he was set at liberty on or near Lexington Common. He bore arms in the battle, and he was a brave man, as his face indicated, although quite lame and bowed, as I recall him. His courage and patriotism were tested by his marching to Cambridge with a detachment, May 6, and also taking part in the battle of Bunker Hill. He was in Cambridge again in the campaign of 1776.

His family took a prominent part on the 19th of April. The church plate was kept at the house of his father, Deacon Joseph Loring; Lydia, a sister of Jonathan, took this plate on that day and concealed it under some brush near the house, to prevent its being carried off by the British soldiers. The house was pillaged and burnt by the British on their return from Concord. Deacon Loring made out a full statement of his loss at that time: —

A large mansion-house, and a barn 70 ft. long, and a corn-house, all burnt £350-0-0
Household goods and furniture, viz: eight good feather beds and bedding; a large quantity of pewter and brass ware; three cases of drawers; two mahogany tables, with the furniture of eight rooms 230-0-0
All the wearing apparel of my family, consisting of nine persons 60-0-0
All my husbandry tools and utensils, with

a cider mill and press, with five tons of hay,
and two calves 72–0–0
About two hundred rods of stone wall
thrown down 5–0–0
Specie 3–0–0

£720–0–0

N. B.—The above mentioned buildings were the first that were destroyed in the town, and near the ground where the brigade commanded by Lord Percy met the detachment retreating under Lieutenant-Colonel Smith. It does not appear that any of our militia were in or near these buildings; neither could they in any way oppose or retard the British troops in their operations; therefore the destruction must be considered as brutal, barbarous, and wanton.

JOSEPH LORING.

I have spoken of Lydia Loring, the energetic sister of our subject. His daughter Polly was a frequent visitor at my father's. She dispelled my belief, as a boy, in the perfect honesty of everybody living, by saying one day in my hearing, "O Mrs. M., there is so much deception in the world." Mr. Loring died in Mason, New Hampshire, September 20, 1830, aged eighty-one years.

The committee appointed by the Provincial Congress, May 12, 1775, to estimate the losses by the British destruction of property, April 19, at Concord, Lexington, and Cambridge, report the whole loss at Concord, £274. 16s. 7d., less than one half of Mr. Loring's at Lexington; at Cambridge, £1,202. 8s. 7d.; while that of Lexington was £1,761.

1s. 15d. The details of the losses at Lexington, embracing no less than twenty-four names of those whose houses were invaded and ravaged, are, in some cases, quite touching. Lydia Winship, believed to have been a widow, testified that her household furniture and wearing apparel were destroyed, with her loss in money, to the amount of £66. 13s. 4d. — over $330, a large sum in that day; while Lydia Mulliken, a widow, with her son, lost house and shop by fire, with furniture, wearing apparel, and clocks and tools of her son, $2,155, in real and personal property. Joshua Bond lost his house, shop, and other property, to the amount of $946. The loss of William Munroe was very heavy, being in household furniture, clothing, and goods in a retail shop, over $1000.

Benjamin Wellington comes before my memory when he was at an advanced age, being thirty-two at the time of the battle. I remember his vigorous and well-knit frame; and that, though of moderate stature, he bore a commanding presence. He had the distinction of being the first prisoner taken within the town that day. He was captured early in the morning, at the foot of what is now called Mount Independence, in East Lexington. The British officer who took him asked: "What are you going to do with that firelock? Where are you going now?" He replied, "I am going home." "I thought within myself," he used to say, "'but not until I have been upon the Common.'" The officer took his firelock from him, and soon released him and passed on. Mr. Wellington then left the main road, waded through swamps, and reached the Common in time to join Captain Parker's company before the engagement, having secured a gun which he doubtless used to good purpose that day. He was with a detachment of the company at Cambridge the ensuing May 6th; in the seventh campaign, 1776, at White Plains; and was a sergeant, having with him eight men from Lexington, at the taking of Burgoyne in 1777. He was honored in town, holding the office of selectman in 1785 and 1792. He died September 14, 1812, in the seventieth year of his age.

Let us next notice Daniel Mason. I premise his record by saying he had a brother Joseph in the battle, of whom I have a slight remembrance. He had a fine form, a gentlemanly appearance, and was a distinguished teacher in the town. He died October 3, 1814, aged seventy-eight years. His estate gave the name to a place still called Mason's Hollow. The house, nearly opposite the old Munroe Tavern, is still standing and occupied. Daniel Mason had little of the soldier in his bearing, as I recollect him, although he did his duty in the little band under Captain Parker. He wore long white locks, and had a grave and apostolic countenance, reminding me of pictures of John Wesley. But he could sometimes make a shrewd remark with a very sober face. One day, speaking to my father of generosity, in my hearing, he said, "I never feel so generous as when I have n't a single cent in my pocket." Hapless man! he was very destitute himself at the last. I was once the bearer of a little gift to him, I think the day before Thanksgiving, and the old man's face lighted up as if he had received a fortune.

Then there was Joseph Estabrook, one of the youngest on the immortal roll of that company; for he was then but a month beyond the age of seventeen. He was of a military family, his father being afterward, in 1776, in the campaign of Ticonderoga. Mr. Estabrook graduated at Harvard College in 1782, and was ordained at Athol, November 21, 1787. He was a fine looking man, and very agreeable in manners and conversation. In my youth I heard him preach, which he did most acceptably. He lived long, active to the last, dying April 30, 1831, in the forty-third year of his ministry, and at the age of seventy-four.

I recall here Joseph Underwood. March 7, 1825, Mr. Underwood testified on oath before my father, who was a justice of the peace, as follows: —

On the evening of April 18, 1775, about forty of the militia company assembled at Buckman's tavern, near the meeting-house, for the purpose of consulting what measures should be adopted. . . . The first certain information we had of the approach of the British troops was given by Thaddeus Bowman, between four and five o'clock on the morning of the 19th, when Captain Parker's company were summoned by the beat of the drum, and the line formed. When the Regulars had arrived within about one hundred rods of our line, they charged their pieces and then moved toward us at a quick step. Some of our men, on seeing them, proposed to quit the field. [And no marvel, fifty or sixty undisciplined men in presence of six hundred regular troops.] Captain Parker gave orders for every man to stand his ground, and said he would order the first man shot that offered to leave his post. I stood very near Captain Parker when the Regulars came up, and am confident he did not order his men to disperse till the British troops had fired upon us the second time.

Mr. Underwood was a man of modest mien, quiet in manner and movement, yet of that firm air and bearing which was needed at the perilous hour of battle. He was a true Independent. I see him in the old meeting-house. He walks to his pew in the broad aisle, with an old Roman air. When, in a midsummer Sabbath afternoon, the preacher is lengthening his discourse on and on, Mr. Underwood takes his coat off, and stands up for a change and relief of posture; and here and there some good old farmer is seen to do likewise. He joined a voluntary detachment to Cambridge, May 10, 1775; and again, June 17, we find him at Bunker Hill. He lived until February 27, 1829, dying at the age of eighty. We may not forget that he married a woman who doubtless sustained and animated his courage. His wife, named Deliverance, was a sister of the patriot hero, Captain John Parker. In commending the bravery of our own sex I think we sometimes overlook and fail to do justice to the noble wives, mothers, and sisters who more than seconded, who often prompted, the heroic deeds of those days. Some wise and true man should seek out and give their due to the as yet unrecognized and unrewarded women of the Revolution.

Something should be said of Amos Locke, who resided in the north part of Lexington, and whose house was familiar to me in boyhood. He was a man of large frame, and above the ordinary height. He was of a martial air and spirit, and had been braced up to the day of blood in our town by having served during the French War in 1762. Like his kinsman Benjamin Locke — who reached the age of eighty-five, and who was also in the battle of April 19 — he had extraordinary vitality; he lived until July 27, 1828, dying at the age of eighty-seven years.

On the list of Captain Parker's company, and as a corporal, stands the name of Joel Viles. In my early days he was quite lame and infirm; but still his florid countenance and commanding figure gave assurance of the energy of his character. His patriotism, generosity, and personal self-sacrifice were attested by the fact that at three several times after the battle — first on May 10 at Cambridge, then on June 17, and finally for two months in 1776 — he bore arms for his country.

A word should be said of John Parkhurst, who married Elizabeth Bowers of Billerica, a sister, I think, of my paternal grandmother. My grand-

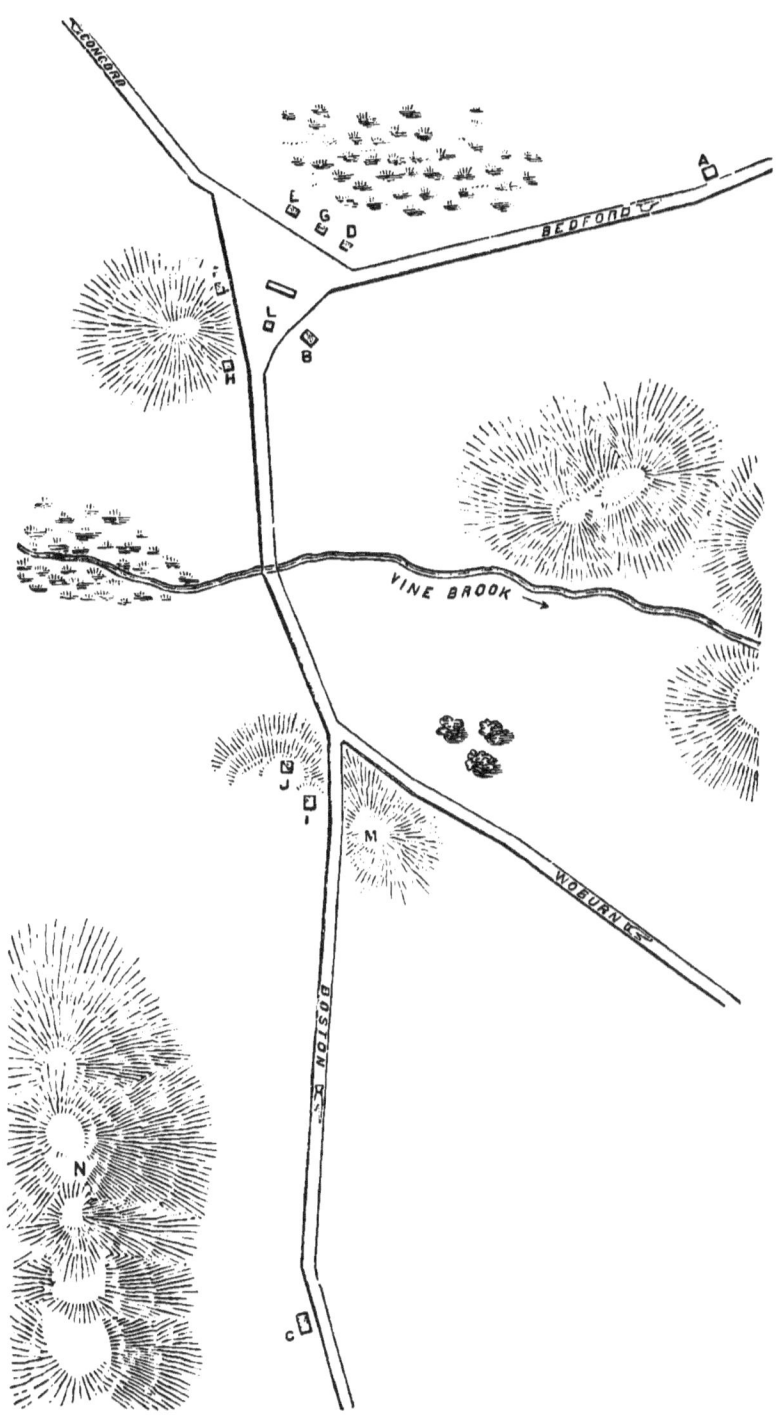

DIAGRAM OF LEXINGTON ROADS.

father and he, both of them in Captain Parker's company, were bound together alike by the ties of home and country, and their remains rest in the same tomb in Lexington churchyard. "They were lovely in their lives and were not divided" in their burial-place. Although Mr. Parkhurst died in my early days, his face was quite familiar. Among other things the red cap of the veteran at church made a strong impression. His house was on the line of march of the British troops toward Concord, a charming location, solid, simple, and firm, like its master. He was in the campaign at White Plains, and was honored as a selectman of the town of Lexington. He died July 2, 1812, aged seventy-seven years.

Joshua Reed I knew well, as his son Charles married one of my sisters. He was a man of portly bearing, tall, well developed, and muscular. His face indicated intelligence; his conversation was wise, accompanied by a manner gentle no less than dignified. His whole character gave assurance of a man of mark. His lineage was rather remarkable. The father, named also Joshua, was a member with him of Captain Parker's company, and a sister of the latter, Betsey Reed, married Ebenezer Muzzey, a brother of the martyr Isaac Muzzey. Mr. Reed died September 8, 1826, aged eighty years.

Ebenezer Simonds, one of Captain Parker's company, and in the battle when but little over seventeen years old, was of a family distinguished as large landholders in Lexington, and who held many public offices in town. They were of remarkable longevity. His father died at eighty-three; Joseph, ensign of Parker's company, died at seventy-three; Joshua, so brave in the battle, died in his seventieth year; his son of the same name, at eighty-eight; and the subject of this notice died August 23, 1845, at eighty-seven. He lived, up to my early manhood, on the old homestead occupied by his grandfather. His clear eye, compressed mouth, firmly set chin, indeed his whole face and his every movement, expressed great force of character. I think of him as erect and stalwart, as belonging to that grand old race of which it was said, " Five of you shall chase an hundred, and an hundred of you shall put ten thousand to flight." To the last his eye was not dimmed, nor his natural force abated. He was sorely afflicted by losing nine of his ten children, and several under trying circumstances. I was impressed, in attending the funeral of one of them in my boyhood, by his fortitude, mingled with a father's tenderness.

It is fitting to close this record of personal recollections with a tribute to him who was the last survivor of those engaged in the battle of Lexington, Jonathan Harrington. For many years a cotemporary with him, I knew him well. He was tall, with a full eye, a firm mouth, and—in general—a marked and strong face. He was a cabinet-maker by trade, and curiosity for such workman-

LEXINGTON MONUMENT

ship made his shop a favorite resort to us boys. Though only sixteen years of age at the time of the battle, he was a fifer in Captain Parker's company. No marvel he began life a Patriot, and continued one to the last, for his own father was in the engagement, beside another of his name, also a kinsman. On the roll of Captain Parker's company we find no less than eleven by the name of Harrington, a noble testimony to the gallant spirit of the family. This number was exceeded only by that of the Munroes, of whom there are fourteen. Then come the Smiths, who sustained the family reputation by a list of ten. We have seven of the Reeds, and four of the Tidds. A proud heredity, all this, of patriotism, self-sacrifice, and bravery. It is due, without disparagement of others, to speak of the noble service of the Munroes in the old French War. Sergeant William Munroe served in 1754–55, Lieutenant Edmund Munroe in 1757, 1758, and 1761, Jonas Munroe in 1755 and 1757, James Munroe in 1757, 1758, and 1759, Ensign Robert Munroe in 1758 and 1762, David Munroe in 1757 and 1759. To these we must add Thaddeus, John, Abraham, Stephen, and Josiah. Eleven of one name and family in the French War, and fourteen in that of the Revolution, from a little town (at the opening of the latter) of only seven hundred inhabitants! Greece and Rome have not outshone this as a military record.

Preparatory to the Centennial celebration in 1875, when the descendants of Ensign Robert

Munroe joined in presenting a standard to the company of Lexington Minute Men, the name of a little boy, six months old, Robert Munroe Harrington, born September 10, 1874, was placed at the close of the list. What a roll to enter, and what a lineage for that unconscious child, the heir of two names, both illustrious, — one in two great wars, and the other in the opening of that Revolution which did so much in laying the foundations of civil and religious liberty on this continent and eventually through the wide world!

Jonathan Harrington died March 27, 1854, having lived to the great age of ninety-five years, eight months, and eighteen days. He would relate the leading incidents of the day of blood with the deepest interest. His mother, a pattern mother, roused him early that day with the cry: "Jonathan, get up; the Regulars are coming, and something must be done." He did get up, hastened to the Common, and was with the company when the British drew near. And "something was done." At the age of ninety-one he attended the seventy-fifth anniversary of April 19 at Concord. Being asked for a sentiment, he gave, out of his full patriotic heart, the following, written with his own hand: "The 19th of April, 1775: all who remember that day will support the Constitution of the United States."

His funeral — of which the Hon. Charles Hudson, in his History of Lexington, gives so graphic an account — was attended by a large concourse;

and it was an imposing spectacle, — thousands of all ages and conditions gathered by one common sentiment of respect and affection. It is worthy of note that, of sixteen survivors of the Lexington battle spoken of above, the average age at their deaths was eighty-two years and six months. A remarkable coincidence at one point — showing that brave men often outlive their great sufferings in war — is that, of the sixteen survivors of the War of 1812, who met in the year 1877, at the end of sixty-five years, the average age was precisely the same, eighty-two years and six months.

One thing should be here said in regard to the motives of the Patriots of the Revolution. From their first to their last act they were, as a whole, free from the temper of malice and revenge. Stirred at some moments to indignation, they were still calm and forbearing. Rev. Mr. Adams of Lunenburg, in the annual sermon at Lexington, April 19, 1783, after the close of the war, says with magnanimity, although he and others could not forget the transactions of the past: "The laws of Christianity oblige us to forgive."

In speaking of the character of the men before us, we should bear in mind that they were, to a large extent, cultivators of the soil which they protected. The occupation of the Patriots at Lexington is indicated by the circumstance that their home was originally called Cambridge Farms. As I look over the roll of Captain Parker's company I find a large proportion of them were farmers. Several family estates of to-day have descended from men of that corps. My grandfather was one of the third generation who had owned and occupied the same estate; and it gives me pleasure to add that it is now occupied by a representative of the sixth generation of the family. It was the taunt of the British aristocracy that they could easily put down "the peasantry of America." "Five regiments of Regulars could," it was boasted, "easily march across the continent."[1] To us it may be a just source of pride that our country gained its independence largely through the toils and sacrifices of the owners and tillers of the soil. "In defiance," says Edward Everett, "of the whole exerted powers of the British Empire, the yeomanry of the country rose as a man, and set their lives on this dear stake of liberty." Without detracting in the least from the noble services, in those trying days, of men

---

[1] Lord Percy, after his return from Lexington, seems to have changed his mind in regard to the intelligence and ability of the Americans. In a letter written the next day, April 20, 1775, he says, in connection with the history of the repulse the day before of the force of Major Pitcairn, and the reinforcement of "grenadiers and light infantry" under Colonel Smith: "the insurrection turns out not so despicable as it is perhaps imagined at home. . . . I never believed they [the rebels] would have had the perseverance I found in them yesterday. . . . They have men among them who know very well what they are about."

The "Columbian Centinel" of Boston, under date September 3, 1817, gives the following obituary: "In England, Prince Hugh Percy, Duke and Earl of Northumberland, Baron Percy &c. and eight other titles, aged seventy-six. He was general of the army. . . . The deceased Duke, at the commencement of the American Revolution, commanded the Fifth British regiment, and the reinforcements sent out to the troops under Colonel Smith, on the 19th of April, 1775."

in other vocations, we may never forget that it
was by the strong arm and wise counsels of the
great agriculturist of Mount Vernon, and the
united labors of men who fought under him for
the soil they owned, that the foundations of our
civil and religious liberties were laid. The Roman Empire fell mainly because her citizens for-
sook the culture of the land by their own hands.
That occupation is the great rock of a nation's virtue and stability. If we wish to uphold this country through all ages we must, like our fathers,
secure homes for the people. So long as our
citizens are living largely on their own acres, able
and ready to defend them against every aggressive
or disorganizing power and influence, the Union
will be safe. We need commerce, the mechanic
arts, manufactures, and every branch of honest
industry for our complete outward prosperity; but
all honor to agriculture, honor to those brave
farmers who " poured out their generous blood
before they knew whether it would fertilize the
land of freedom or of bondage." From that blood-
offering comes a voice : —

> Stern and awful are its tones,
> As the patriot-martyr groans;
> But, the death-pulse beating high,
> Rapture blends with agony.

And let us, looking at the glorious results of
the storm and struggle of that dawn hour of the
Revolution, dwell on the mid-day sun, which, shining out from these our skies, lights up the wide

world of aspirants for liberty. Joy for April 19, 1775, when began forming that patriot procession led by the immortal Parker and his brave associates. Heart to heart and hand to hand, let us pledge ourselves — and may we be followed by our latest posterity — to honor with our lips and our lives the memory of those star-bright names.

THE ENGLISH RIGHT OF SEARCH.

CHAPTER XXIII.

MEN OF THE SOUTHERN AND MIDDLE STATES IN THE REVOLUTION.

THE chapter immediately preceding this gives a narrative of the opening scenes of the Revolutionary War. The events it describes are confined to Lexington, Concord, Boston, and its vicinity. The first act of the great drama was performed by New England. It is fitting that this book should close by a distinct reference to that portion of the country by which the war was more especially conducted to its completion. We ought in justice to speak of the great debt due for these services to the States lying out of New England. We may never forget the noble work which they did in carrying the contest forward to its success. While Massachusetts and her associate States of the North initiated the labors and perils of the war, it was left largely to the Southern and Middle States to consummate their task.

Who was the man chosen to take command of the American army? Not one born and bred under our Northern skies: not a Prescott or a Ward of Massachusetts, not a Putnam of Connecticut, not a Greene of Rhode Island, a Stark of New Hampshire, or an Ethan Allen of Vermont. It was to Virginia the wide-spread colonies turned their asking eyes for this momentous service. It was her soil that gave us our Washington, without whom — so far as human judgment can conceive — this incoherent mass of colonies would never have come together, and clung hand to hand, as they did, — would never have resolved at last to break the yoke of British domination, and never have achieved, declared, and established their freedom and independence.

The New England delegates in Congress were prompt in discerning the military merits of Washington, as seen when he commanded the Virginian forces against the French, — a man marked, as he was, by his skill, bravery and persistence as an officer. Prominent also by the good judgment and sound sense he had exhibited on the committees of the Provincial Legislature and the Continental Congress, he was preferred even by the New England army above General Ward, a commander of their own. It is to be noticed also that, while the chief was taken from Virginia, and the second in command from Massachusetts, the third was Charles Lee, then a citizen of Virginia. To that State the whole country looked for leading spirits.

And, looking back through the whole struggle, we see this choice justified. At every stage of the war, Washington — amid all rivalries, jealousies, envy among officers, distrust of some called servants of the people — steadily rose, and demonstrated his forecast and his rare gifts for military adjustments, combinations, and a comprehensive administration. He manifested, too, an unflinching courage. Systematic, punctual, careful in the details needful for success in active operations, he had also a persistence in waiting for the right moment of advance and a power to endure suspense, which are capital qualities in a good general. He could bear the weightiest responsibilities, and meet the charges that spring from popular impatience and misrepresentation. With an ever-changing army, without discipline and proper respect for his authority, amid local prejudices, with troops miserably clad and armed, and sometimes destitute of food for the day, for eight long years he held his position; and out of clouds and thick darkness a bright sun at last rose, and he reached the end of his anxieties, toils, and sufferings in a glorious victory.

Often we see the South earnest and adroit in movements that sustain the feeble cause. At one moment a few bold men sail from Charleston, S. C., to East Florida, and surprise and capture, near St. Augustine, a vessel containing fifteen thousand pounds of British powder. At another, a like valuable cargo is seized by the inhabitants of Georgia on its arrival from England; and several ships, taking military stores to aid the foe at Boston, are intercepted upon the ocean. Lord

Dunmore orders and effects the burning of Norfolk in Virginia, — so flagitious an act that Washington can restrain his indignation no longer, but hopes this act will "unite the whole country in one indissoluble bond against a nation which seems to be lost to every sense of virtue and those feelings which distinguish a civilized people from the most barbarous savages."

The course of Virginia in the war shows its broad spirit, a patriotism which rose above sectional interests and prejudices, and made common cause with the North in resisting British aggressions, and by word and deed asserting and maintaining the right of the American colonies to freedom and independence. The oldest of the chartered colonies, she played her part firmly and bravely to the end. What Washington did quietly and by his actions, too modest for speech, others of his State seconded and supported by their voices and their pens.

It is interesting to observe the occasions and influences which led the colonies into ultimate harmony. Virginia stands shoulder to shoulder with Massachusetts, and step by step several States join hands on the same side. The opposition in some colonies is strong; but by degrees New Jersey, Maryland, South Carolina, and North Carolina unite their votes for independence. Led by Southern sway, the States of the North are united, and the Middle States give in their adhesion at periods more or less late, until finally thirteen colonies resolve that " these united colonies are, and of right ought to be, free and independent States, that they are absolved from all allegiance to the British Crown, and that all political connection between them and the State of Great Britain is, and ought to be, totally dissolved."

Although the military operations of the war began in New England, it was in effect closed beyond her precinct by the union of troops from the Southern and Middle States with those of the North. In the decisive battle of the storming of Yorktown were seen men from the strong line of Pennsylvania; New Jersey was there with one of her tried brigades; Maryland with the same complement; New York added a battalion; and brave little Delaware sent her two companies.

So early as 1768, William Livingston, editor of the " American Whig " of New York and the subsequent governor of New Jersey, wrote: " The day dawns in which the foundation of this mighty empire is to be laid, by the establishment of a regular American constitution." With a wise and generous outlook to the future, he adds: " As we conduct, so will it fare with us and our children." New Jersey stood firmly by the side of Virginia; and her provincial Congress directed, by a vote passed Aug. 5, 1775, that fifty-four companies, of sixty-four men each, amounting to three thousand four hundred and fifty-six men in all, should be organized.

While we of the North reverence the Old State

House in Boston, — and she has just reinstated it as it was in its pristine day, when John Adams spoke in tones of thrilling patriotism from its old-time portico, — and while we are straining every nerve to save the Old South, where Warren bearded the British lion in his den, we should also venerate Carpenter's Hall in Philadelphia, and bring to memory young Washington, with his noble offer, made within its walls, to march to Boston with a thousand men for its relief; and Independence Hall in the same honored city, from which the brave Declaration of July 4, 1776, was issued.

I am anxious, in all fairness, to do ample justice, in this connection, to individual men of the Southern and Middle States. It was Virginia that produced Patrick Henry, — that man who scented the outbreak with Great Britain afar off, and so early as the month of March, 1775, uttered in Richmond — his tall person "rising erect and his head held proudly aloft" as he spoke — the stirring words: "Our chains are forged! their clanking is heard on the plains of Boston;" and closed his thrilling appeal with the immortal words: "I know not what course others may take; but as for me, give me liberty, or give me death!" It was Virginia that raised up Thomas Jefferson, author of the Declaration of Independence, who was first Secretary of State in Washington's cabinet, founder of the old Republican as opposed to the Federalist party; to whom many of our present most popular and truly democratic principles must be traced; and who was for eight years President of the United States. From Virginia came Richard Henry Lee, who was born January 20, 1732, and died June 19, 1794. It was he who, on June 7, 1776, made the first bold proposition in Congress, seconded by John Adams of Massachusetts, "That the united colonies are, and of right ought to be, free and independent States, and that all political connection between them and the State of Great Britain is, and ought to be, totally dissolved." In this body his labors were incessant; while a member of it he served on nearly a hundred committees. In his own State and in Congress he showed himself a devoted patriot and an eloquent orator. He was a personal friend of Washington, and in private life manifested unbounded kindness and charity. He shed lustre on the name of a family who did much — both in the field and in civil, political, and social circles — to originate and establish American institutions. Of the same lineage was the brave Colonel Henry Lee, who was born January 29, 1756, and died March 25, 1818. He was honored by the commander-in-chief and by a vote of Congress for his brilliant military career in the war. And here was born Thomas Nelson, the heroic commander of Virginia's militia at the siege of Yorktown, and afterward made governor by his own State.

We should advert next to South Carolina, so fruitful in her military gifts to the cause of the Revolution. To her we owe John Laurens, aide to Washington, engaged in the attack on the British lines at Savannah, in the defence of Charleston, and afterward conspicuous at the siege of Yorktown, where he led the forlorn hope, and captured one of the two redoubts which were stormed. He was killed in a skirmish by a party of British, and when the news of his death reached his father — who had been President of the Continental Congress, and for that offence was imprisoned in the Tower of London, and but just released — he said magnanimously, "I thank God I had a son who dared to die for his country." We record here the name of John Rutledge, — a delegate to the Continental Congress, governor of South Carolina, and for two years in the Southern army of the Revolution. This man, so brave in military service, was equally conspicuous in civil affairs. He was a member of the convention which framed the Federal Constitution, and afterward an associate judge of the United States Supreme Court.

Francis Marion, born in Georgetown, S. C., in 1732, died near Eutaw, February, 28, 1795. He was one of the purest patriots of the Revolution. Made a captain in the service so early as June 21, 1775, he continued in the army until the near prospect of peace. He was one of the most adroit and successful of generals. He disbanded his brigade December 14, 1782, with a tender farewell to his faithful followers; and like so many others, South as well as North, he retired to his farm almost in poverty.

It would be unjust to Thomas Sumter not to place his name in the catalogue of those who upheld the war in South Carolina. True, he was born (1734) in Virginia; but he removed early to South Carolina, and lived there until his death, which occurred June 1, 1832, when he was ninety-eight years of age, and the last surviving general of the Revolution. A volunteer soldier in the French and Indian War, he was present at the memorable defeat of Braddock. In March, 1776, we find him lieutenant-colonel of the Second Regiment of South Carolina riflemen. After the capture of Charleston by the British, in 1780, he takes refuge in the swamp of the Santee. Rising to the rank of brigadier-general, he becomes foremost among the active and influential leaders of the South. Follow him in his gallant career. This same year he defeats a British detachment on the Catawba; and, although surprised and routed at Fishing Creek, August 18, he collects another corps, and, November 12, defeats the bold Colonel Wemyss, who had attacked his camp near Broad River. After a few days General Tarleton, a British officer, attempts to surprise him while encamped on the Tiger River, but is driven back with a severe loss of men. We find Sumter, though wounded in this attack, soon again in the field. In March of the next year, 1781, he raises three new regiments, and, co-operating with the brave Marion, Pickens, and others, he harasses the enemy along their posts scattered amid valleys and swamps. For his heroic services Congress, in January, 1781, passed a vote of thanks to him and his men. When the American government was established, General Sumter, from 1789 to 1793, was chosen a representative in Congress; from 1801 to 1809 he was United States senator; and in 1809 he was appointed minister to Brazil, where he continued for two years. In 1811, at the advanced age of seventy-seven years, he closed his long term of honorable and eventful services.

We cannot fail to notice, among the heroes of South Carolina, Isaac Huger. He was of a family illustrious for their services in the Revolution, being one of five brothers active in the war. Of wealthy parentage, the sons all completed their education in Europe. Isaac, at the age of eighteen, joins Colonel Middleton in his bold expedition against the Cherokee Indians in 1760. He is made lieutenant-colonel of the First South Carolina Regiment, June 17, 1775, and soon colonel of the Fifth Regiment; he takes a prominent part in the operations connected with the siege of Savannah in 1778; is made brigadier-general, January 19, 1779; commands a force of cavalry at the siege of Charleston in 1780; and closes his gallant services at the two points of Guilford Court-house, March 15, 1781, and Hobkirk's Hill, April 25, of the same year, commanding on the right wing of a brigade from brave old Virginia. From this family came a nephew of the preceding, Francis

WASHINGTON CROSSING THE DELAWARE.

Kinlock Huger, who was born in 1764, and died at Charleston, S. C., February, 1855, at the great age of ninety-one years. It was he who, with the generous Bollman, made the attempt to rescue Lafayette from the dungeon of Olmutz. Huger, for this offence, was placed eight months in close confinement in an Austrian prison. He came home to serve his country in the War of 1812, and was honored with a seat in both branches of the legislature of his own State.

We ought never to lose sight of our obligations for the Revolutionary services of the Middle States. New Jersey in 1776 became a great battle-ground on which the fortunes of the Revolution were once at stake. Washington was there with his army, and, amid perils and obstacles of fearful proportions, held his position with an almost superhuman firmness, wisdom, skill, and persistency. His own army was disunited, — many threatening to quit the ranks, some tempted by Loyalists to desert his command and join the forces of an enemy proud, strong, and defiant. Forced at length to cross the Delaware and pass from New Jersey into Pennsylvania, it was only a timely reinforcement of troops from that State, of which Philadelphia generously furnished fifteen hundred, that saved him from a disastrous defeat. This reinforcement enabled him to cross the Delaware, and on the field of Princeton win a victory which breathed hope into a desponding people, and gave a new lustre to the name of our immortal chief. For this result the country was largely indebted to one of the Pennsylvanian commanders by whose determined energy those troops had been raised in an adjoining State.

It is not easy to estimate our obligations to New Jersey for military leaders in the Revolution. Give their due weight, in this regard, to her noble services on the fields of Princeton, Monmouth, and elsewhere. Consider the strength of her patriotism, her resistance to the disloyal within her own borders, who constantly opposed her spirit, and — by enticing men to desert our American army, or by enlisting or tempting others to enlist in the British army — would baffle her best efforts in the cause of freedom and independence. Compute also her direct contributions to the Patriot army in the form both of money and men. In that day of small things, out of a population of about one hundred thousand, she raised for the war nearly twenty thousand men, including almost every male capable of bearing arms. Add to all this the wise and steadfast counsels of New Jersey in her Provincial Congress, her early and ready co-operation with the Continental Congress, and the blending of her voice and her vote in the great united resolve for the Declaration of Independence, and you will accord to her a larger part of her sometimes unappreciated dues.

What shall we say of the claims of Pennsylvania? To omit all special notice of them would be gross injustice. In Chester County, Pennsylvania, was born, January 1, 1745, Anthony Wayne. He had martial blood in his veins; his grandfather was in the famous battle of the Boyne, and his father was in several engagements with the Indians. As a young man he was in the Pennsylvania convention and in its legislature. When but thirty years old, in September, 1775, he raised a regiment of volunteers, was commissioned as colonel, and joined General Sullivan in Canada early in 1776. Prominent in the battle of Three Rivers, he was in command of the fortresses of Ticonderoga and Mount Independence. A brigadier-general in May 1777, he was in the army of Washington in New Jersey. Fearless and persistent, at the battle of Brandywine we see him all day opposing the right wing of Howe, and only at sunset does he retreat. At Germantown he leads the attack on the enemy. During the winter he, lion-like, makes a raid within the British lines and captures cattle, horses, and forage. His skilful movements at Monmouth are commended by Washington in his account of that battle. The next year he surprises and captures the strong garrison of Stony Point on the Hudson, and is wounded in the engagement, for which services he receives the thanks of Congress and a gold medal. He is ordered to join the army at the South, and at Jamestown, Virginia, by a gallant, dauntless, and prompt attack he saves the forces of Lafayette from defeat. He closes his brilliant career by aiding in the capture of Cornwallis, soon after which he is assigned to a command in Georgia, puts to flight large bodies of Indians on their way to reinforce the British, and at length drives the whole enemy from that State. After a respite on his farm, he is appointed major-general and commander-in-chief in the war against the Indians at the West, and gains a victory over the determined Miamis in August, 1794. Appointed sole commissioner to treat with the Indians of the Northwest, he takes possession of all the British forts in that region, and while on his way home from that victorious movement, he dies in armor.

Among the men distinguished, not only in the Revolution, but both in his previous and subsequent career in our civil history, is Thomas Mifflin. Born in Philadelphia, 1744, he died in Lancaster, Pennsylvania, January 20, 1800. Of a family marked by their culture, wealth, and social position, he was called into public life in 1772 as a representative from Philadelphia in the Colonial Assembly, and in 1774 was a delegate to the first Continental Congress. The all-observing eye of Washington saw his military capacities and attractive qualities, and selected him to accompany himself, as his first aide-de-camp, to Cambridge, in June 1775, with the rank of colonel. He was soon promoted to the office of adjutant-general, and in the spring of 1776 he was commissioned as a brigadier-general. In the battle of Long Island he distinguished himself, and was active during the latter part of 1776 in raising large reinforcements in Pennsylvania for the army of Washington. For his zeal and efficiency in the service he was raised to the rank of major-general in 1777.

In 1783 General Mifflin had the honor of receiving the resignation of Washington as commander-in-chief of the army. The same year he was elected to Congress, and at the close of that year became its president. A great favorite in his own State, in 1785 he was chosen speaker of the Pennsylvania legislature. In 1787 he was elected a member of the convention which formed the Federal Constitution. While Washington was president of the Society of the Cincinnati, Thomas Mifflin had the honor of being its vice-president. He succeeded Franklin as president of the supreme executive council of Pennsylvania in October, 1788. He was chosen governor of Pennsylvania in 1790, and by successive re-elections held that office until a short time before his death,

We cannot sum up our military obligations to Pennsylvania better than by a sketch of the career of the undaunted and resolute Peter John Gabriel Muhlenberg. Born October 1, 1746, he died near Philadelphia, October 1, 1807. He was ordained to the ministry in England, and preached at Woodstock, Virginia. While in the church, and after delivering the last sermon he ever preached, — which closed with these patriotic and brave words, "There is a time for all things, a time to preach and a time to fight, and now is the time to fight,"— he stripped off his gown, put on a uniform, read his commission as colonel, and began the formation of a regiment among his parishioners. He was made a brigadier-general in 1777, and a major-general at the close of the Revolution.

General Muhlenberg crowned these services by filling several important civil offices. He was vice-president of the Commonwealth of Pennsylvania in 1785, a member of Congress from 1789 to 1791, from 1793 to 1795, and from 1799 to 1801. That year he was elected United States Senator, but resigned the next, and was appointed supervisor of the revenue for the district of Pennsylvania; from 1803 until his death he was collector of the port of Philadelphia.

We do not forget all we owe to Maryland, for the services of her men at Yorktown,—to the commanders of her regiments and battalions, the brave General Mordecai Gist, and, foremost of all, to Tench Tilghman, the brave colonel, favorite aide of Washington, selected by him to bear tidings of the surrender of Cornwallis to Congress.

Let us give due credit to Georgia, if for none other of her many offerings, yet for the gallant deeds and sacrifices of her General James H. Screvner, who fell at the hard-fought battle of Sunbury. From this same Sunbury it was that the patriot and philanthropist, Lyman Hall, was sent in the beginning of the Revolution, May 13, 1775, to represent St. John's Parish — of which Sunbury was a part — in the colony of Georgia in the General Congress of the colonies gathered at that early day. He went from a district which had in it the blood of the venerated Puritans. This grand patriot carried from little Sunbury the precious gift to the suffering republicans of the Massachusetts colony, of one hundred and sixty barrels of rice and £50 sterling! And out of the same St. John's Parish, and from that illustrious little town of Sunbury, went two men, Lyman Hall and Button Guinnett, to place their names on the immortal Declaration of Independence.

And when we reflect that all the while Georgia was not only beset by a foreign enemy, but by disloyal men from her own ranks, and by " predatory incursions of men out of other disaffected regions, — to the great loss and disquietude of portions of our Province," as the sufferers modestly record,—we must say: Well done brave, patient, persistent Georgia; great should be your commendation now and forever.

How shall we represent the debt of the Revolution to that pivotal colony and original Middle State, New York? It is a sketch only of her claims and merits that we can here give. From this mother of heroes and statesmen came the Livingstons. Philip Livingston, a signer of the Declaration of Independence, was born in Albany, New York, January 15, 1716, and died June 12, 1778. He was a member of the first Continental Congress and the second, was in the New York Provincial Congress, and at the time of his death a delegate to the Continental Congress, then sitting in New York. Brockholst Livingston, a soldier and jurist, son of the preceding, was born November 25, 1757, and died March 18, 1823. He was aide-de-camp of General Schuyler in 1776, and attended him in the army of the North; was in the suite of General Arnold with the rank of major; was at the surrender of Burgoyne, and promoted to the rank of colonel. In 1802 he was appointed judge of the Supreme Court of New York; and in November, 1828, was raised to the bench of the United States Supreme Court. Robert R. Livingston, born in New York City, November 27, 1746, died February 26, 1813. A member of the Second Continental Congress, he was on the committee of five who drafted the Declaration of Independence. He was a member of Congress in 1780; was the first Chancellor of State, and in that office until 1801. He had the honor of administering the oath of office to Washington on his first assuming the duties of President of the United States, April 30, 1789.

From New York went forth James Clinton, brother of Vice-president George Clinton, who, at the battle of Yorktown, as major-general, commanded the New York, New Jersey, and Rhode Island troops. New York gave to the Revolution Alexander Hamilton, whose illustrious and patriotic virtues shone forth from the nineteenth year of his age, in 1776, when he sought and obtained a commission as captain of an artillery company in the

State of New York. He soon attracted the notice of Washington by his labors in the construction of earthworks at New York, by his impulsive energy at the battle of White Plains, and by his valiant services during the battles of Trenton and Princeton. For these he was placed as aide-de-camp on the staff of the commander-in-chief. He took an active part in the battles of Brandywine and Germantown. He was with the army at the dreary camp of Valley Forge, and united with Lafayette, Greene, and Wayne at the battle of Monmouth, June 28, 1778; and after other valuable services, he commanded a New York battalion at the battle of Yorktown, and under Lafayette led in the attack and capture of a British outwork at that siege. To these early military exploits we should add his immortal work (together with that of Jay — a New York man — and Madison) on "The Federalist;" his being selected by President Washington in 1789 as the first secretary of the treasury; and his rare ability in founding a wise and judicious system for managing the financial affairs of our infant republic. All honor to Hamilton that he immediately succeeded Washington as president of the Society of the Cincinnati, and retained that position until — a victim to misguided views — he met his death by a duel July 11, 1804, at the prime age of forty-seven years.

In New York, Washington spent large portions of his military life during the Revolution. It was to her borders that he took the little American army, after expelling the British foe from Boston, March 17, 1776. It was on her soil that Ethan Allen — when asked at Ticonderoga, May 10, 1775, by a British officer, by whose authority he demanded the surrender of that fort — uttered the startling announcement: " In the name of Jehovah and the Continental Congress." It was there the treason of Arnold was consummated; there, at Newburgh, April 19, 1783, that Washington issued a proclamation of the cessation of hostilities between the American and British armies; there, May 13, 1783, — as the officers of our army were contemplating their near and final separation, in order to keep alive perpetually, in themselves and through their posterity, their long-cemented and tender friendships. — that they instituted the order of the Society of the Cincinnati. On that spot they received the exhilarating news that a treaty of peace and amity between Great Britain and the United States of America had been signed in Paris; and New York has the honor of being the one of all the original States destined for that event, — the act of sundering the bonds which bound the great heart of the commander-in-chief to every officer and every soldier, down to the humblest in the ranks. personally to himself. It was at Newburgh, November 2, 1783, that he promulgated his Farewell Address to that brave band of comrades, some of whom for eight long years had stood side by side with him in what to others had been their death struggle. And " on that sad day," wrote a witness of the scene, "how many hearts were wrung."

From the capital of this State, November 25, 1783, the once proud British army finally, after years of dominant possession, went forth forever; and Washington entered its limits, master of his ground, with none to molest or disturb him.

It is proposed to celebrate, on the 19th of April of the coming year, the centenary of Washington's proclamation of the cessation of hostilities between Great Britain and this country. The people, one and all, may well feel the pertinence and the urgency of the patriotic call. If, as we know, on that day, guns were fired by the little remnant of the army at headquarters, aroused by cannon from Fort Putnam at West Point, and " the hills were lighted by fires kindled by the rejoicing people," we ought, in this day of fifty millions of a prospering population, to repair to the old house, once the home of Washington, and still standing, and recall the sacrifices of that nature's nobleman, and think of that hour when the dissatisfied army around him, in their poverty, were threatening to march to the capital and demand justice of Congress. See the worn and wearied hero as he rises to read his patriotic appeal to those men. He pauses before he proceeds, to adjust his glasses. and utters the touching words: " These eyes, my friends, have grown dim, and these locks white in the service, yet I never doubted the justice of my country." Happy for us if, in our brighter days, we can catch something of his noble unselfishness, his unwavering sense of duty. Happy for us, whether present or absent on that closing day of these centennial observances, if we try to do something that shall quicken in our generation, — and leave, as our best legacy to those who come after us—a love of country, sincere and deep, nourished in their childhood, pure and active in their manliest years, and steadfast to the end.

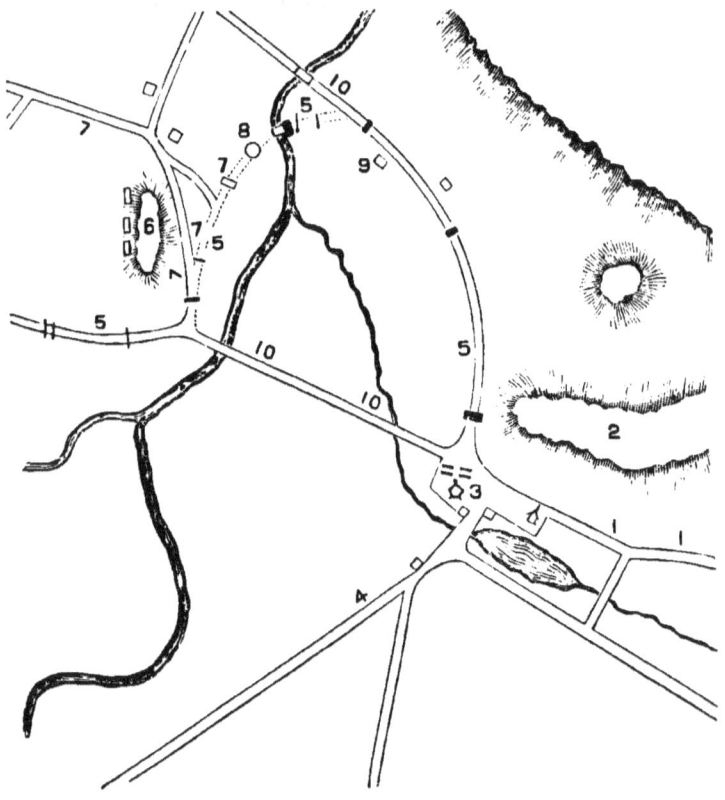

DIAGRAM OF CONCORD VILLAGE.

INDEX OF NAMES.

A.

Abbot, John, 317.
   Joseph, 378.
Adams family, 8, 9, 54, 140, 173.
   Abigail, 64.
   Charles Francis, 52, 66.
   Elizabeth, 72.
   Henry, 65, 70.
   John, 13, 45-52, 54, 59-64, 66-70, 75, 76, 80, 93, 162, 180, 237, 282, 286, 400, 401.
   John Quincy, 9, 48, 52-55, 57, 58, 62, 64, 66, 67, 80, 93, 94, 216, 283.
   Mrs. John, 62, 85.
   Rev. Mr., 391.
   Samuel, 13, 30, 68-72, 75, 76, 162, 189, 282, 310, 367, 368.
Aikin, Miss, 175, 177.
Aldrich, Jonathan, 296, 298.
Alexander, Sarah, 260.
Alfred the Great, 3.
Allen, Ethan, 396, 414.
Allston, Washington, 305.
Allyne, Mary, 25.
   Samuel, 26.
Ames, Fisher, 30, 93.
Andre, 199.
Andros, Gov. Edmund, 284.
Armstead, Col. George, 248.
Arnold, Benedict, 193, 211, 244, 354, 412, 414.
Aubury, a British writer, 198.

B.

Bacon, Mercy, 23.
Bailey, Ebenezer, 96.
Bainbridge, Commodore, 256.
Balcom, Joseph, 207.
Bancroft, Captain, 195.
   George, 266.
Barbour, John N., 296.
Barclay, Commodore, 262, 264, 265, 267.
Burrow, Isaac, 163.

Batchelder, Samuel, 191.
Bateman, John, 379.
Baury family, 218.
   Francis, 218.
   Frederic, 218.
   Louis, 218.
   Rev. Dr. A. L., 219.
Baylies, Hodijah, 34.
Beal, Israel, 108, 112, 113.
Beattie, Amelia L., 242.
Belcher, Governor, 24.
Bemis's Heights, 108.
Benton, Thomas H., 281, 290.
Bernard, Governor, 135.
Bigelow, Abijah, 305.
   Colorel, 136.
Billings, William, 23.
Bingham, Jerusha, 146.
Blaxton, William, 77.
Bliss, George, 34.
Bollman, 405.
Bond, 222.
   Joshua, 382.
Bourbon family, 10.
Boutelle, Caleb, 307.
   Charles Otis, 307.
   Enoch, 306.
   James Thacher, 307.
   Lydia, 305.
   Rachel, 305.
   Timothy, 105, 106, 300-302, 305.
   Timothy, Jr., 305.
Bowditch, Dr. Nathaniel, 311.
Bowdoin, Governor, 109, 301.
Bowers, Elizabeth, 386.
   Hannah, 292.
   Josiah, 292.
Bowman, Samuel, 207.
   Thaddeus, 384.
Braddock, General, 403.
Bremer, Frederika, 338.
Brewster, 9, 75.
Brooks, Abby, 66.
   Charles T., 296.
   John, 206-208, 220, 277, 282, 313, 320.

INDEX OF NAMES.

Brooks, Peter C., 66.
  Preston S., 224.
Brown family, 138, 141.
  Captain, 44.
  Dorothy, 138.
  Edward, Jr., 296.
  Elizabeth, 115.
  Francis, 138, 139, 141, 371.
  James, 140.
  John, 138, 365.
  John (martyr), 346.
  Sergeant, 140.
  Solomon, 367.
Brownell, Thomas, 266.
Buckman, Mary, 140.
  John, 140, 367, 384.
Buckminster, Rev. Joseph Stevens, 305.
Burgoyne, Gen., 112, 133, 136, 191, 192, 198, 209, 244, 257, 354, 372, 373, 412.
Burke, Edmund, 63.
Burn, Thaddeus, 78.
Burr, Aaron, 31.
Buss, Ensign John, 301.

C.

Cabot, George, 34, 93.
  John, 119.
  Lydia D., 119.
  Lydia (Dodge), 119.
Cæsar, Julius, 3.
Calhoun, John C., 281, 290.
Calvin, John, 163.
Carver, John, 9.
Cary, Mrs., 376.
Chamberlain, Henry M., 296, 298.
Chandler, Col. John L., 373, 374.
  Gen. Samuel, 369.
Channing, William, 171.
  William Ellery, 156, 157, 163, 169-177, 179-185, 229.
  William H., 236.
Charlemagne, 3.
Chastellux, Marquis de, 326.
Chatham, Earl of, 63, 163.
Chauncey, Commodore, 261, 262.
Cheverus, Bishop, 30.
Church, Benjamin, 190 191, 284.
Cicero, 238.
Cincinnati, Society of the, 15, 16, 186-242.
Cincinnatus, 187.
Clark family, 78, 140, 141, 368.
  Rev. Mr., 128, 367, 368.
Clay, Henry, 281, 283, 290.
Clinton, George, 412.
  Gen. James, 412.
Cobb, Gen. David, 240, 241.
  Lois, 231.
  Mayor S. C., 96, 241, 242.
Cockburn, Admiral, 246.
Cogswell, William, 339.

Coggswell, Joseph Green, 367.
Colby, Lot, 292.
Conway, 193.
Corbine, Margaret, 197.
Cornwallis, General, 109, 111, 196, 209, 210, 241, 328, 330, 331, 334, 410.
Cranch family, 60, 61.
  Judge, 60.
Crane's Artillery, 229, 231, 278.
Cromwell, Oliver, 20.
Croswell, Doctor, 204.
  Susan C., 203.
Cunningham, Ruth, 44.
Custis, G. W. P., 321.

D.

Dana, Chief Justice Francis, 220.
  Francis, 58.
  Lydia, 220.
  Lydia (Trowbridge), 220.
  Richard, 220.
Dandridge, Martha, 195.
Dane, Nathan, 34, 223.
Danforth, Samuel, 74.
Davis, Admiral Charles Henry, 231, 232.
  Daniel, 231.
  Mrs. C. H., 231.
Day, John Q., 296.
Dearborn, Gen. Henry, 243-245, 256, 283.
  Henry A. S , 255.
Decatur, Commodore, 268.
Degrand, P. P. F., 54, 55.
De Grasse, Count, 283, 334.
De Kalb, Baron, 331.
Demosthenes, 238.
Dennie, Joseph, 93.
Dexter, Samuel, 31, 93.
Dickinson, John, 46.
Dennison, William, 70, 74.
Downes, Harriet, 134.
  Lydia, 134.
Drake, 46.
Draper, Moses, 222.
  William, 378.
Dryden, John, 43.
Dudley, Governor, 102.
Dudley Observatory, 213.
Dunham, Daniel, 24.
Dunmore, Lord, 397.
Dummer, Shubael, 125.
Dupont, Admiral, 232.
D'Ynigo, Chevalier, 274.

E.

Eliot, Apostle, 256.
Eliot professorship, 229.
Ellery, Lucy, 171.

INDEX OF NAMES. 419

Ellery, William, 156-160, 162-165, 171, 172, 177.
Elliot, Rev. Andrew, 78.
Emerson, Edward Bliss, 346.
  Mary, 339.
  Ralph Waldo, 337-347.
  William, 338, 340.
Estabrook, Rev. Joseph, 384.
Eustis, Benjamin, 226.
  Gov. William, 35, 225-227, 277, 282, 313.
Everett, Edward, 17, 37, 91, 128, 238, 281, 312, 313, 334, 346, 370, 392.

F.

Fairbanks, 31.
Fairfield, 79.
Farnham, Ralph, 353, 354.
Farwell, Levi, 296.
  William, 296.
Fenwick, Bishop, 36.
Fessenden, E. S., 136.
  Thomas, 378.
Fichte, 56.
Fish, Hamilton, 239, 240.
  Nicholas, 239.
Fiske, Ebenezer, 369.
  Dr. Joseph, 209, 211, 371.
Flint, Mrs., 81.
  Rev. James, D.D., 317.
Follen, Rev. Charles, LL.D, 175, 296-298.
Foster, Daniel, 211.
  Ruth, 357.
Fowlis, barony of, 130.
Fox, Charles James, 63.
Francis, Rev. Dr., 345.
Franklin, Benjamin, 92, 282, 310, 332, 409.
Frederick the Great, 204.
Freeman, Constant, 231.
  Edward, 25.
  Lois, 231.
  Rev. James, D.D., 231.
French, Rev. Jonathan, 82.
Frost, Rev. Barzillai, 296.

G.

Gage, General, 70, 195, 373, 379, 413.
Gardner's Regiment, 222.
Garfield, President James A., 18, 106.
Garrison, Wm. Lloyd, 175, 297, 299.
Gates, General, 108, 136, 193, 204, 354.
George III., 63, 368.
Gerry, Elbridge, 31.
Gibbs, Major, 326.
Gist, Gen. Mordecai, 410.
Goodwin, Anne, 307.
  General, 307.
Gore, Christopher, 92.
Gould, Benj. Apthorp, 212.
  Capt. Benjamin, 211.
  Hannah F., 212.
  Prof. B.A., 212.
Grant, President U. S., 240.
Graves, Hon. J. W., 237.
Gray, 116.
  Edward, 28.
  Edwin, 305.
  Harrison, 28.
  John, 26.
Greaton's Regiment, 222, 229.
Greene, General, 162, 261, 312, 332.
Gridley, 225, 229.
  Jeremiah, 43.
Griffith, Master, 29.
Grinnell, Susan B., 133.
Guinnett, Button, 411.

H.

Hadley, Samuel, 365.
Hagar, Micah, 378.
Hale family, 357.
  Amos, 357.
  Artemas, 357-359.
  Jacob, 358.
  Joseph, 357.
  Moses, 355, 356.
  Nathaniel, 357.
  Thomas, 357.
Hamilton, Alexander, 31, 32, 262, 312, 326, 330, 412.
Hamlin family, 221.
  Africa, 221.
  Asia, 222.
  Cyrus, 221.
  Hannibal, 221.
Hampden, 19.
Hall, Lyman, 411.
Hancock, John, 70, 71, 78, 92, 140, 161, 173, 282, 367, 368.
Hannibal, 78.
Harper, 30
Harrington family, 389.
  Abigail (Dunster), 135.
  Abijah, 366.
  Caleb, 365.
  Daniel, 373, 374.
  Jonathan, 135, 365, 366, 388, 390.
  Levi, 366.
  Robert Munroe, 390.
Harrison, Gen. Wm. H., 261, 262.
Hastings, Edmund Trowbridge, 220.
  Edmund T., Jr., 221.
  Elizabeth (Cotton), 220.
  Isaac, 375.
  John, 220.
  Jonathan, 220.
  Samuel, 376.
  Samuel, Jr., 376, 378.

INDEX OF NAMES.

Hatch, John B., 221.
Hayden, Horace E., 367.
Hayward, James, 369, 370.
Heath, General, 116.
Hedge, Professor, 24.
  Rev. Frederick H., D.D., 296.
  Susan, 24.
Henry, Patrick, 400.
Higginson, Francis J., 296, 298.
Hill, Elizabeth, 226.
Hoar, Colonel, 135.
  Leonard, 80.
Hobart, Rev. Peter, 104.
Holmes, 268.
Hopkins, Edward, 83.
  Rev. Samuel, D.D., 165.
  Stephen, 159.
Horace, the Latin poet, 212.
Horton, Rev. Edward A., 106.
Houdin, Captain, 210.
Howe, General, 407.
Hudson, Hon. Charles, 125, 254, 390.
Huger, Francis Kinlock, 404.
  Gen. Isaac, 404.
Hull, Commodore, 249.
  Gen. William, 256-258.
Hunt, Nathaniel P., 296.
  Thomas, 297.
Hutchinson, Thomas, 194.

J.

Jackson, 207.
  Col. Henry, 220, 241.
  Francis, 100.
  Joseph, 111.
  President Andrew, 283, 285-291.
James, St., court of, 67.
Jarvis, Charles, 71.
Jay, John, 413.
Jefferson, President Thomas, 51, 52, 63, 237, 258, 274, 282, 286, 400.
Johnson, Abram, 253.
  Andrew, 358.
  Joshua, 66.
  Louisa Catharine, 66.

K.

Key, Francis Scott, 248, 249.
Keyes, Lucy, 358.
King, Rufus, 32.
Kirkland family, 143.
  Daniel, 143.
  George Whitefield, 146.
  Mrs. C. M., 271.
  Mrs. Samuel, 146.
  Rev. John Thornton, D.D., 86, 143, 146, 151, 152, 154.
  Samuel, 143-146, 148, 150, 151, 155.
Knox, John, 340.
  General, 112, 113, 201-204, 210, 229, 231, 275, 278, 282, 283, 312, 326, 372.

L.

Lafayette, 11, 12, 15, 82, 109, 113, 186-188, 203, 204, 211, 275, 279, 308, 310-336, 405, 407, 413.
  Edmond, 187.
  Madame de, 333.
Lane, Henry, 72.
Langdon, Caroline, 227.
Laurens, John, 401.
Lee, Charles, 116, 193 377, 396.
  Col. Wm. Raymond, 256.
  Henry, 279, 280, 400.
  Richard Henry, 401.
Levaseur, Monsieur, 330.
Lillie, John, 278.
Lincoln family, 101-113.
  Abner, 105.
  Benjamin, Jr., 44.
  Caleb, 104.
  Countess of, 102.
  David, 105.
  Deborah, 357.
  Ebenezer, 104.
  Gen. Benjamin, 44, 106-113, 218, 229, 282, 301, 312.
  Hosea H., 101.
  Isaac, 105.
  Jacob, 103.
  James, 105.
  James Otis, 44.
  Joshua, 104.
  Loring, 105.
  Lydia, 105.
  Lydia (Loring), 104.
  Luke, 104, 106, 302.
  Luther B., 101.
  Mary, 105, 112.
  Mordecai, 103.
  Percy, 106.
  President Abraham, 103, 286, 299, 358.
  Rachel, 101, 105, 106, 302.
  Rev. Calvin, 101, 106.
  Samuel, 103.
  Solomon, 103.
  Stephen, 105.
  Thomas, 104.
  Thomas the Cooper, 103, 107.
  Thomas the Husbandman, 101-105.
  Thomas the Miller, 103.
  Thomas the Weaver, 103.
  William, 104.
Little, 211.
Little & Brown, 345.
Livermore, John, 296.
Livingston family, 411.
  Colonel Brockholst, 412.
  Philip, 411.
  Robert R., 412.
  William, 399.
Locke, Amos, 386.
  Benjamin, 386.

INDEX OF NAMES. 421

Longfellow, Henry Wadsworth, 347.
   Stephen, Jr., 34.
Loring, Deacon Joseph, 380, 381.
   Jonathan, 379.
   Lydia, 380, 381.
   Polly, 381.
Lothrop, Jerusha (Kirkland), 155.
   John H., 155.
   Rev. S. K., D.D., 155.
Louis XIV., 105.
Lovell, Master, 28.
   Stephen, 296.
Lovejoy, Rev. Elijah, 172.
Lowell family, 93.
   James Russell, 348.
   Judge John, 30.
Lucius III., Pope, 343.
Lyman, Joseph, 34.

M.

Macomb, General, 253.
Madison, President, 63, 226, 245, 258,
Makepeace, Hester, 138.
Malcolm II., King, 130.
Marion, Gen. Francis, 277, 402, 403.
Marshall, Chief Justice, 310.
   Emily, 40.
   Josiah, 39.
Mason, Daniel, 383.
   Jeremiah, 344, 345.
   Joseph, 383.
Mather, Cotton, 102.
Mauduit, political agent, 45.
May, Samuel, 112.
Meriam, Asa, 105.
Merriam, Rufus, 367.
Middleton, Colonel, 404.
Mifflin, Gen. Thomas, 408, 409.
Monro, 130.
Moore, Dorothy, 105.
   Lydia, 116
Morrill, Rev. Mr., 370.
Moseley, Ebenezer, 213.
   Edward Strong, 213, 214.
   Hon. Ebenezer, 213, 319.
   Samuel, 23, 24.
Motier family, 308.
Moultrie, General, 309.
Muhlenburg, General, 409, 410.
Mulliken, Lydia, 382.
Munroe family, 9, 130–137, 370, 389.
   Abraham, 389.
   Anna, 374.
   Anna (Smith), 133.
   Captain, 136, 137.
   Capt. Edmund, 142.
   Capt. George, 131.
   Col. William, 131–133, 368, 372, 373, 382, 389.
   David, 132, 389.
   Doctor, 131.

Munroe, Dorcas, 129.
   Edward, 117.
   Ensign Robert, 132, 374, 375, 389.
   George, Baron of Fowlis, 131.
   James, 64, 132, 142, 389.
   Jedediah, 370.
   John, 389.
   John, 3d, 378.
   Jonas, 132, 389.
   Joseph, 68.
   Josiah, 389.
   Lieut. Edmund, 117, 132, 135, 389.
   Pamelia, 142.
   Robert, 117, 131, 365.
   Sir Robert, 131.
   Stephen, 378, 389.
   Thaddeus, 389.
   "Uncle Jonas," 134.
   William, 130, 133.
   William, the immigrant, 134, 135.
Muzzey, Amos, 361.
   Amos, Jr., 305.
   Ebenezer, 387.
   Rev. A. B., 296.
   Rev. William, 133

N.

Napoleon I., 3, 164, 165, 218, 246, 249.
Nash, N. C. 126.
Nelson, Thomas, 401.
Nixon, Thomas, 207.
Noailles, 308.
Norris, Thomas F., 296, 298.
Norton, Jacob, 58, 59.
   Rev. Andrews, 51.

O.

O'Hara, General, 330.
Oliver, Chief Justice, 49, 193.
Oneida Indians, 253.
Onondaga, Indian Chief, 149.
Orne, the Patriot, 116.
Otis family, 8, 9, 21–47, 173.
   Bethiah, 24.
   Elizabeth, 44.
   Harrison Gray, 21, 28, 31, 32, 34, 36, 37, 88, 90, 93.
   James, 13, 26, 37, 41–46, 68, 283.
   Mrs Harrison Gray, Jr., 39.
   Nathaniel, 25.
   Samuel Allyne, 28, 110.
   Wm. F., 39.
Ovid, 212.
Owen, John, 296.

P.

Paddock's Artillery, 229.
Paddy, William, 35.
Palfrey, Rev. Cazneau, D.D., 53.
Palmer, Ann, 77.

Pares, Judith, 77.
Parker family, 114-129.
　Amy, 114.
　Andrew, 127.
　Capt. John, 114, 118, 129, 209, 226, 283, 361, 364, 366, 370-378, 383-389, 391, 394.
　Daniel, 228.
　Ebenezer, 114, 129.
　Isaac, 226, 228.
　John, 116, 117, 119, 125, 127, 128, 130, 139.
　Jonas, 114, 127, 128, 365.
　Jonas, 2d, 378.
　Jonathan, 125.
　Josiah, 115.
　Lydia (Moore), 119.
　Margaret (Jarvis), 228.
　Mrs. Theodore, 123.
　Thaddeus, 114, 128
　Theodore, 114, 118-127.
　Thomas, 114, 125.
Parkhurst, John, 378, 386, 387.
　Nathaniel, 378.
Parsons, Judge Theophilus, 31, 93, 216.
　Surgeon Usher, 266, 267.
Payson, Ruth, 358.
Peabody, Augustus, 39.
Percy, Lord, 28, 370, 381, 392.
Perkins, Thomas II., 34.
Perry, Christopher Raymond, 260.
Perry, Commodore O. H., 163, 249, 260-267.
　Commodore Matthew Calbraith, 268.
　Oliver H., Jr., 265, 267.
Peter the Great, 3.
Phillips, Jonathan, 97.
　Samuel, Jr., 110.
　Wendell, 173.
Phinney, Maj. Elias, 314.
Pickens, General, 403.
Pickering, John, 217.
　John, Jr., 217, 218.
　Octavius, 218.
　Timothy, 216, 218.
Pierce, Henry L., 279.
　Mrs., 55.
Pierpont, Rev. John, 90, 155, 317.
Pinckney, Charles, 323.
Pitcairn, Maj. John, 362, 364, 366, 367, 372, 379, 392.
Pitt, William, 9.
Plantagenet family, 10.
Pope, Alexander, 43.
Popkin, John, 228.
　John S., 229.
Porter, Asahel, 365.
Porter's Hall, 237.
Prescott, William, 29, 34, 284, 316, 395.
Prince, James, 318.
Prince's Chronology, 23.
Proctor, 264.

Putnam, Gen. Israel, 283, 353, 396.
Putnam's Regiment, 213.
Pym, 19.

Q.

Quincy family, 8, 9, 22, 36, 38, 65, 77-100, 173.
　Col. Josiah, 79.
　Dorothy, 78.
　Edmund, 77-80, 99, 100.
　Eliza S., 98.
　Gen. Samuel M., 99.
　John, 80.
　Josiah, 13, 21, 35, 37, 77, 80-98, 153, 283, 313.
　Josiah, Jr., 77, 81, 91, 96-98.
　Josiah, 3d, 90.
　Mrs. Edmund, 81.
　Mrs. Josiah, 85.

R.

Raymond, John, 133, 373.
Reed, Abigail (Stone), 128.
　Betsey, 387.
　Charles, 387.
　Colonel, 136.
　Joshua, 387.
　Mary, 128.
　William, 128.
Renau, Ernest, 124.
Revere, Paul, 68, 368.
Ripley, Rev. Ezra, D.D., 339.
Ro family, 130.
Roe family, 130.
　Ocon, 130.
Rochambeau, Count de, 187, 188, 283, 330, 334.
　General, 218.
Rodgers, Commodore, 268.
Rogers, Helen, 305.
　Judge, 305.
　Major, 135.
　Polly, 132.
　Secretary, 262.
Royall Professorship, 227.
Russell, Jonathan, 25, 42.
　Abigail, 25.
Rutledge, John, 402.

S.

Salem (negro), 292.
Sanderson, Col. Henry S., 248, 249.
　Elijah, 367.
　Mrs., 134.
　Mrs. Margaret, 248.
Sargent, Hosea, 266.
Schuyler, General, 257, 412.
Screvener, Gen. J. H., 410.
Sewall, Sophia, 134.
Shakespeare, 43.

INDEX OF NAMES. 423

Shaw, Chief Justice, 36, 305.
  Samuel, 96.
Shays Rebellion, 30, 109, 133, 151, 218, 226, 300, 373.
Shepard, Rev. Thomas, 303.
Sheridan, Richard Brinsley, 63.
Shirley, Governor, 226.
Simonds, Ebenezer, 387.
  Joseph, 387.
  Joshua, 365, 387.
Skeneando, the Indian Chief, 147.
Smith family, 58–62, 389.
  Abigail, 66.
  Abigail C., 134.
  Anna, 132.
  Anna (Parker), 132.
  Benjamin, 132.
  Col. Francis, 362, 364, 366, 370, 381, 392.
  Isaac, 28.
  John M., 296.
  Lucy, 296.
Sparks, Rev. Jared D.D., LL.D., 155.
Spencer, General, 213.
Sprague, Charles, 90, 333.
Stanley, Dean, 124.
Standish, Miles, 9.
Stark, Gen. John, 244, 284, 396.
Stearns, Hannah, 119.
Stebbins, Rev. Rufus P., D.D., 84.
Steuben, Baron Von, 15, 109, 204–208, 276, 283, 332.
Stone, Anna, 115.
  Elizabeth, 211.
  John, 115.
  Rachel (Shepard), 115.
  Susanna, 222.
Story, Judge Joseph, 31, 223, 255, 313.
Streame, Elizabeth, 22.
Strong, Rev. Mr., 162.
  Governor, 202.
Stuart family, 10.
  F. T., 278.
  Gilbert, 89, 265, 277, 283, 334.
Stuyvesant, Governor, 240.
Sullivan, Gen. John, 244, 407.
  William, 34, 90.
Sumner, Benjamin, 73.
  Charles, 223.
  Charles Pinckney, 222.
  James, 73.
  Job, 222.
Sumter, Gen. Thomas, 403, 404.
Sydney, Algernon, 20.
Syms, Rev. Mr., 303.

T.

Tappan, Professor, 152.
Tarleton, General, 403.
Taylor, Father, 36, 342.
Thacher, Surgeon, 197.

Thatcher, Henry Knox, 203.
Thaxter, Rev. Joseph, 316, 318.
Thomas, Joshua, 34.
Thomson, Charles, 159.
Tidd family, 389.
  Benjamin, 378.
  William, 374, 375.
Tighlman, Colonel, 326, 410.
Towne, Judith, 358.
Trumbull, Col. John, the artist, 271, 324.
  Gov. Jonathan, 379.
Tuckerman, Rev. Joseph, D.D., 179.
Tudor family, 10.
  William, author, 30.
  Judge, 228.

U.

Underwood, Deliverance, 385.
  Joseph, 384, 385.

V.

Van Buren, President Martin, 67, 290.
Vassall, Colonel, 191, 194.
Viles, Joel, 386.
Vinton, Rev. Dr. Francis, 266.
Virgil, 212.
Vose's Regiment, 209.

W.

Walcott, Robert F., 100.
Walcutt, William, 266.
Waldo, Da iel, 34.
  Peter, 343.
Walker, Rev. James, D.D. LL.D., 92, 318.
  Joseph, 292.
Ward, Gen. Artemas, 29, 354, 395, 396.
Ware, Rev. Henry, D.D., 44, 293–296.
  Rev. Henry, Jr., D.D., 296, 343.
Warren, Abigail (Collins), 233.
  Dr. John, 233.
  Dr. John Collins, 233, 234.
  Dr. Joseph, 117, 225, 233, 400.
  Gen. James, 26.
Washington, 17, 24, 27, 63, 108–113, 133, 136, 186, 210, 215, 216, 239, 241, 244, 257, 259, 269–282, 309, 310, 313, 317, 323–335, 350, 351, 354, 372, 373, 396, 398, 400–415.
  Martha, 85, 194.
  Mary, 85.
Waterhouse, Dr. Benjamin, 112.
Wayne, General, 326, 328, 407, 413.
Webb, Colonel, 257.
Webster, Daniel, 8, 52, 66, 69, 235–239, 283, 290, 317, 318, 346.
  Hon. Ebenezer, 235.

Wellington, Benjamin, 382, 383.
Wemyss, Colonel, 403.
Wesley, John, 383.
West, Rev. Dr., 152.
Wetherby's Tavern, 70, 361.
Wheelock, Jona'han, 133.
   Rev. Dr., 144, 146.
Whitcomb, Col. Asa, 300.
White, Hatfield, 207.
Whitney, Sarah, 127.
   George, 48, 51, 53.
Whittemore, Samuel, 361.
Whittier, John G., 201.
Wigglesworth, Rev. Dr., 149.
Wilde, Samuel S., 34.
Wilder, Abel, 355, 356.
   David, 106.

Willard, President, 149.
   Sidney, 296.
Winship, Lydia, 382.
Winthrop family, 9, 238.
   Robert C., 238.
Wirt, William, 238, 255.
Woodbridge, Rev. John, 125.
Wright, John, 115.
   Mary, 115.
Wyer, Edward, 135.
   Elizabeth, 135.

Y.

York family, 10.
Young, Rev. Alexander, D.D., 102.

www.ingramcontent.com/pod-product-compliance
Lightning Source LLC
Chambersburg PA
CBHW051900300426
44117CB00006B/477